Y0-BGE-341

THE SECRETS OF GREAT MYSTERY AND SUSPENSE FICTION

David Schmid, Ph.D.

THE
GREAT
COURSES®

PUBLISHED BY:

THE GREAT COURSES
Corporate Headquarters
4840 Westfields Boulevard, Suite 500
Chantilly, Virginia 20151-2299
Phone: 1-800-832-2412
Fax: 703-378-3819
www.thegreatcourses.com

Copyright © The Teaching Company, 2016

Printed in the United States of America

This book is in copyright. All rights reserved.

Without limiting the rights under copyright reserved above,
no part of this publication may be reproduced, stored in
or introduced into a retrieval system, or transmitted,
in any form, or by any means
(electronic, mechanical, photocopying, recording, or otherwise),
without the prior written permission of
The Teaching Company.

DAVID SCHMID, PH.D.

ASSOCIATE PROFESSOR OF ENGLISH
UNIVERSITY AT BUFFALO, THE STATE UNIVERSITY OF
NEW YORK

D avid Schmid is an Associate Professor in the Department of English at the University at Buffalo, The State University of New York (SUNY). The recipient of the Milton Plesur Excellence in Teaching Award and the SUNY Chancellor's Award for Excellence in Teaching, he teaches courses in British and American fiction, cultural studies, and popular culture.

Born and raised in England, Dr. Schmid received his B.A. from Oxford University, his M.A. from the University of Sussex, and his Ph.D. in Modern Thought and Literature from Stanford University.

Dr. Schmid has published on a variety of subjects, including the nonfiction novel, celebrity, film adaptation, *Dracula*, and crime fiction. He is the author of *Natural Born Celebrities: Serial Killers in American*

Culture; coauthor of *Zombie Talk: Culture, History, Politics*; editor of *Violence in American Popular Culture*; and coeditor of *Globalization and the State in Contemporary Crime Fiction: A World of Crime.* ∎

TABLE OF CONTENTS

The Secrets of Great Mystery and Suspense Fiction

Scope

This course does justice to the complexity and diversity of the perennially popular genre of mystery and suspense fiction by exploring the subject from multiple angles and providing a multifaceted picture of this fascinating subject.

Although not organized chronologically, the course encompasses mystery and suspense fiction from its very beginnings to the present day. Represented in the lectures is the genre-founding work of Edgar Allan Poe; the creations of giants of the genre such as Sir Arthur Conan Doyle, Agatha Christie, Dashiell Hammett, and Raymond Chandler; and the recent best-selling and influential writing of authors such as Thomas Harris, Stieg Larsson, Megan Abbott, and Walter Mosley.

Throughout the lectures, you will encounter some of the same writers in multiple contexts—sometimes through a direct examination of their work and sometimes through a discussion of their influence on others. In this way, the course offers a multilayered examination of mystery and suspense fiction that will allow you to appreciate the writers' achievements from many different points of view.

This course includes clusters of lectures on different aspects of the genre that together form a comprehensive survey of mystery and suspense fiction. One group of lectures, for example, examines the key figures of the genre: the detective, the criminal, the sidekick, the private eye, the police, and the femme fatale. In the same vein, another group of lectures examines some of the defining features and concepts of mystery and suspense fiction, including the way the genre uses clues, solutions, poetic justice, and violence.

Because one of the defining features of the genre is the manner in which it utilizes a variety of settings, another group of lectures explores the locked room, the cozy spaces of country houses and small villages, and the expanses of large, anonymous cities. With this emphasis on spaces and settings in mind, the course also surveys the global spread of mystery and suspense fiction that has defined the genre in recent years, including lectures on the work of Japanese, African, Latin American, Scandinavian, French, German, Italian, and Spanish writers.

The lectures in this course demonstrate that the key to the success of the genre is its ability to respond to societal changes by innovating while still remaining true to its foundational features. With this in mind, the course examines the many different varieties of the genre, including classic mystery fiction, hard-boiled crime fiction, historical mysteries, courtroom dramas, police procedurals, female-centered suspense narratives, true-crime narratives, espionage and thriller fiction, and crime narratives featuring psychopaths. By examining the genre's almost-infinite variety, the course showcases and underlines the diversity and inventiveness of mystery and suspense fiction.

Because mystery and suspense fiction is such a sensitive barometer of social change, the course also presents a group of lectures that examine how examples of the genre have represented the experiences of various minority groups, including gays and lesbians, African Americans, the Latino population, and Native Americans.

Although the majority of the course focuses on novels, the lectures also acknowledge the impact that mystery and suspense fiction has had on artists working in a variety of other media; accordingly, the course addresses the ways in which the genre has inspired films, television, graphic novels, comic books, and even the work of writers of fan fiction.

By the end of this course, you will have learned a tremendous amount about the history, structure, and impact of mystery and suspense fiction. By examining both familiar and lesser-known writers of mystery and suspense fiction, you will come to appreciate both how and why the genre continues to entertain and enlighten millions of readers. ∎

VIOLENCE TAKES CENTER STAGE

There is little doubt that both the amount and the intensity of violence in mystery and suspense fiction has steadily increased over time. In this lecture, we'll focus on examples of and reasons for this rise, concentrating in particular on the period between World War II and the present. Then, we'll explore the types of violence that mystery and suspense writers do *not* focus on. Sometimes, what is not there can tell us just as much about a genre as what is there.

MICKEY SPILLANE

- One of the most controversial figures in mystery and suspense fiction is author Mickey Spillane. Spillane was born in Brooklyn, New York, in 1918. After serving in the Army Air Corps in World War II, where he was a fighter pilot and flight instructor, Spillane started writing, first of all for comic books. To earn additional money, Spillane wrote the novel *I, the Jury*—reportedly in 19 days. Published in 1947, the novel introduced private eye Mike Hammer, Spillane's most famous series character.

- To say that *I, the Jury* was successful would be a colossal understatement. It sold millions of copies in the United States alone, and by the end of his career, Spillane was estimated to have sold more than 225 million books. Hammer went on to appear in a number of other novels published in rapid succession.

- The Mike Hammer novels became a lightning rod for criticism because of what reviewers regarded as their excessive amounts of sex and violence. In fact, the more successful the novels, the sharper the criticism. For example, Anthony Boucher, the noted mystery critic for *The New York Times*, criticized what he described as "the usual Spillane sex cum sadism."

- But what critics tended to ignore and leave unexamined is exactly why Spillane's work, and especially its sex and violence, were so phenomenally popular with American audiences in the post-World War II period.

- Critics Max Allan Collins and James Traylor explain Spillane's success by noting that he had an intuitive understanding of his audience, "a reading public that consisted largely of ex-servicemen, who had fought a tough, brutal war; who would expect the violence (and the sex) of even their fantasy to reflect the loss of innocence of that war.... The seven novels Spillane produced between 1947 and 1953 have a level of sex and particularly violence that seems to come out of nowhere; but it did come from somewhere: It came from World War II."

MIKE HAMMER'S VIGILANTE VIOLENCE

- Despite the critics, there's no denying the appeal of what Spillane wrote. The Mike Hammer novels are a landmark in the representation of violence in mystery and suspense fiction: They contained more graphic violence than anything seen before.

- In *One Lonely Night*, Hammer remarks about his commitment to the use of violence: "I lived to kill so others could live... I was the evil that opposed other evil, leaving the good and the meek in the middle to inherit the earth!" In this regard, it's important to emphasize another landmark feature of the violence that Hammer uses: It's extralegal, vigilante violence.

- This kind of vigilante violence speaks to the way in which much of Hammer's audience—against the context of their World War

II experiences and the developing Cold War—had lost confidence in the system. Specifically, Spillane's readers were unconvinced that the police and government could protect them. Hammer's audience, in short, not only tolerated but also celebrated his violence because they believed it was both necessary and effective.

> The Mike Hammer novels became a lightning rod for criticism because of what reviewers regarded as their excessive amounts of sex and violence.

PSYCHOPATHS

- A novel that was just as influential in its portrayal of violence as *I, the Jury* was Robert Bloch's 1959 novel, *Psycho*.

- Bloch was born in 1917 in Chicago and began his writing career at the suggestion of celebrated horror writer H. P. Lovecraft. For the first part of his career, Bloch focused on publishing short stories in magazines such as *Weird Tales* and *Fantastic Adventures*. But in 1947, he published his first novel, *The Scarf*, in which he takes on the persona of his protagonist, a psychopathic strangler.

- By far, the most famous of Bloch's psychopath novels was *Psycho*. Of course, much of that fame can be attributed to Alfred Hitchcock's iconic film adaptation of Bloch's novel, but the novel also deserves to be read on its own terms. A primary reason is Bloch's memorable fictional creation Norman Bates. At the center of *Psycho* is the character of Norman Bates himself. And this is where we arrive at the true significance of this novel in terms of its representation of violence in mystery and suspense fiction.

- As in many of his other novels, Bloch's focus in *Psycho* is to reconstruct, in as dramatic and frightening a manner as possible, the way a psychopath thinks and acts. This means that although there's no denying that Bates's violence is there, at least in part, to shock and appall the audience, it's also there to show us exactly what psychopaths are capable of doing, the motives and causes behind their acts, and what those acts mean to the people that commit them.

SERIAL KILLERS

- Robert Bloch's *Psycho* is the direct ancestor and inspiration for the explosion of fiction that centered on psychopathic—especially serial—killers that began in the 1970s and peaked in the 1980s and 1990s. Consider Thomas Harris's novel *The Silence*

of the Lambs as an example. Like Bloch, Harris draws on real-life cases in creating his serial killer characters. But the differences between Bloch and novelists such as Harris are pronounced and significant.

- For one thing, because Harris is writing novels about serial killers, not one lonely psychopath, there is necessarily more violence in Harris's work. What's more, between 1959 and 1981 (when Harris's most famous character, Dr. Hannibal Lecter, first appeared in print), readers had become accustomed to extreme violence in fiction.

RISE OF THE PAPERBACK ORIGINAL

- Aside from post–World War II anxieties and the advent of psychopath fiction, there is another reason why the market for more extreme examples of violence in mystery and suspense fiction began to flourish in the 1950s.

- According to critic Lee Horsley, "Post-World War II American publishing was transformed by the introduction of the paperback." Again, we can thank the massive success of Mickey Spillane's work for inaugurating the boom in paperback publishing. Although the hardback version of *I, the Jury* sold relatively modestly, the paperback version went through the roof. In this way, the era of what became known as the paperback original, which refers to a book that was never published in hardcover, was born.

- Some of the most exciting and innovative mystery and suspense fiction of the 1950s appeared in the form of paperback originals. And because these paperbacks were beneath the critical notice of most reviewers, they gave writers an unparalleled degree of freedom to develop and express their own personal views, no matter how violent those views were.

DAVID GOODIS

■ Authors David Goodis and Jim Thompson found the genre of paperback crime to be surprisingly congenial. In Goodis's case, over the course of a series of novels, beginning with *Dark Passage* in 1946 and ending with *Somebody's Done For* in 1967, he develops a relentlessly paranoid, dark, and fearful fictional universe filled with losers whose hope that things will get better is inevitably and brutally punished.

■ As one might expect, violence plays a large role in Goodis's universe—but there's nothing gratuitous about it. Instead, in Goodis's work, violence serves as what the poet and critic T. S. Eliot once described as an "objective correlative"—that is, something that gives a reader access to traditionally inexplicable concepts.

■ In other words, Goodis uses violence as a way to communicate with almost unbearable vividness the emotional texture of his fictional world. Far from being gratuitous, in Goodis's work, the intense and brutal violence suffered by his characters plays a foundational role.

JIM THOMPSON

■ Although Jim Thompson's vision of the world is just as dark and depressing as that of David Goodis (if not more so), there's surprisingly little violence in many of his crime novels, which stretch from *Nothing More Than Murder* in 1949 to *King Blood* in 1973. But what violence there is usually makes a devastating impression—because we're never allowed to look away from it and because Thompson has a rare gift for conveying its full horror to us.

■ In Thompson's *The Killer Inside Me*, the protagonist Lou Ford beats prostitute Joyce Lakeland nearly to death, and the description of the beating is very graphic. However, perhaps the most horrifying detail comes when Joyce tries to speak to Lou before she loses consciousness, and we realize that she's trying to say "Goodbye kiss."

■ Later in the same novel Lou is beating his fiancée, Amy, in a similar manner. Again, the description is very graphic. But once more, it's Thompson's eye for detail that makes this incident stick in the reader's mind. As Amy is dying, she reaches her hand out very slowly and grasps Lou's boot. Lou's so terrified that he can't shake it off—and we can't forget Amy's hand.

■ The violence in Thompson's work is anything but gratuitous. Through his uncanny eye for the uncomfortable detail, Thompson is able to convey the true horror of violence.

MEANING TO VIOLENCE

■ Despite the fact that mystery and suspense fiction is incredibly diverse when it comes to depicting violence, the genre does have one very noticeable blind spot: The violence is almost always interpersonal, not collective, as in a violent labor dispute, a riot, a revolution, or a war.

■ Even if forms of collective violence do appear in the genre, they're usually in the background rather than the foreground of the narrative; what's more, they certainly are not the focus of any investigation by the detective.

■ The reason may be that mystery and suspense fiction attempts to give meaning to violence. No matter what form it takes, who commits it, and why, the genre seems committed to the principle that violence must not grow beyond a certain scale. Only in this way, it seems, can violence remain something that the genre can use, rather than something that risks overwhelming it.

QUESTIONS TO CONSIDER

1. What factors led to the gradual increase of violence in mystery and suspense fiction?

2. Can there ever be too much violence in the genre? If so, how do we know when we've reached that point?

SUGGESTED READING

Åström, Gregersdotter, and Horeck, eds., *Rape in Stieg Larsson's Millennium Trilogy and Beyond.*

Forter, *Murdering Masculinities.*

VIOLENCE TAKES CENTER STAGE

I n another lecture in this series, we looked at the various roles that violence has played in early examples of mystery and suspense fiction. We saw that not only are there many forms of violence in the genre, but also that some mystery and suspense narratives contain no violence at all, and instead center on such crimes as theft, fraud, and mistaken identity.

With that said, there is little doubt that both the amount and the intensity of violence in the genre has steadily increased over time. So in the first part of this lecture, we'll focus on both examples of and reasons for this rise, concentrating in particular on the period between World War II and the present.

In the final part of this lecture, our focus will shift somewhat, as we'll discuss what types of violence mystery and suspense fiction tends not to focus on. Why? Because sometimes what is not in a genre can tell you just as much about it as what it actually contains.

We'll start our investigation into how violence moved center stage in mystery and suspense fiction by looking at the work of a figure who, by any measure, is one of the most controversial figures in the genre. Mickey Spillane.

Spillane was born in Brooklyn, New York, in 1918. After serving in the Army Air Corps in World War II, where he was a fighter pilot and flight instructor, Spillane started writing, first of all for comic books. When he and his wife wanted to buy a house in Newburgh, New York, Spillane decided to raise the money by writing a novel. The result was *I, the Jury*, which Spillane reportedly wrote in 19 days. It was published in 1947. The novel introduced private eye Mike Hammer, Spillane's most famous series character.

To say that *I, the Jury* was successful would be a huge understatement; it sold millions of copies in the United States alone, and by the end of his career Spillane was estimated to have sold over 225 million books. Hammer went on to appear in a number other novels published in rapid succession, including *My Gun Is Quick*, *Vengeance Is Mine*, *One Lonely Night*, *The Big Kill*, and *Kiss Me, Deadly*.

As soon as the Mike Hammer novels began to appear, they became a lightning-rod for criticism because of what reviewers regarded as the excessive amounts of sex and violence they contained. In fact, the more successful the novels became, the sharper the criticism became.

Anthony Boucher, the famous mystery critic for the New York Times, criticized what he described as the usual Spillane sex cum sadism. And in "Mickey Spillane and his Bloody Hammer," a 1954 article that appeared in the Saturday Review, author Christopher La Farge compared Hammer to the notorious anti-Communist Senator Joseph McCarthy. "Mike Hammer is the logical conclusion, almost a sort of brutal apotheosis, of McCarthyism. when things go wrong, let one man cure the wrong by whatever means he, as a privileged savior, chooses."

Critics such as La Farge were on to something, at least in the sense that Hammer was indeed a staunch anti-Communist. A typical Hammer novel sees Spillane's detective being pitted against a much larger organization, such as a crime ring or the Mafia, and Communists obviously fit this bill very well. Hammer's battles with Communists emphasized not only what a danger they represented but also how the single figure of Mike Hammer was capable of defeating that danger.

But what La Farge and others tend to ignore and leave unexamined is exactly why Spillane's work, and especially its sex and violence, were so phenomenally popular with American audiences in the post–World War II period.

Critics Max Allan Collins and James Traylor explain Spillane's success by saying that he had an intuitive understanding of his audience,

> A reading public that consisted largely of ex-servicemen, who had fought a tough, brutal war; who would expect the violence and the sex of even their fantasy to reflect the loss of innocence of that war; who were, to put it less pompously if more crudely, a bunch of horny ex-GIs looking for a hot read. The seven novels Spillane produced between 1947 and 1953 have a level of sex and particularly violence that seems to come out of nowhere, but it did come from somewhere. it came from World War II.

As Spillane's novels continued to be best-sellers, critics could deplore what they disliked about them all they wanted—and they have largely continued to do so—but there's no denying the appeal of what he wrote. In that sense, the Mike Hammer novels are a landmark in the representation of violence in mystery and suspense fiction.

I use the word landmark here in several senses. First, in the obvious sense that Spillane's work contained both more and more graphic violence than anything seen before with the exception of some of the more gruesome 19th-century dime novels that focused on crime. Although Hammer is a fast shot, most of the time he seems to prefer hitting people with his fists, and the books are filled with graphic descriptions of broken bones, hoods getting their teeth knocked out, and people vomiting after Hammer punches them in the gut.

But the Spillane novels are also a landmark in the sense that Hammer's violence is rarely presented as self-evidently good or unproblematic. In other words, Spillane frequently has Hammer justify the necessity of his tactics. It's true that Hammer occasionally doubts the efficacy of the way he always relies on violence, such as when he remarks to himself in *One Lonely Night* that "Maybe I did have a taste for death. Maybe I liked it too much to taste anything else. Maybe I was twisted and rotten inside. Maybe I would be washed down the sewer with the rest of all the rottenness sometime."

Later in the same novel, however, when his beloved secretary and love interest, Velda, is kidnapped by communists, we get a much more representative statement from Hammer about his commitment to the use of violence. "I lived to kill so others could live… I was the evil that opposed other evil, leaving the good and the meek in the middle to inherit the earth." In this regard, it's important to emphasize a final landmark feature of the violence that Hammer uses. it's extra-legal, vigilante violence.

Why is this important? Because it speaks to the way in which much of Hammer's audience, again with the context of their World War II experiences and the developing Cold War in mind, had lost any confidence in the system that they might once have had. Specifically, Spillane's readers were unconvinced that the police and government could protect them adequately from such phenomena as rising urban crime and the threat of Communist conspiracy and nuclear war. Hammer's audience, in short, not only tolerated but also celebrated his violence because they believed it was both necessary and effective.

If Mickey Spillane's work speaks to a geopolitical context in a way that many of his readers and critics may not have expected, I don't think the same can be said of a novel that's very different from *I, the Jury* and its successors but that is just as influential in terms of how mystery and suspense fiction represents violence. I'm referring to Robert Bloch's famous 1959 novel, *Psycho*.

Bloch was born in 1917 in Chicago and began his writing career at the suggestion of famous horror writer H. P. Lovecraft. Bloch was a big fan of the horror stories that Lovecraft published in pulp magazines during the 1930s, and after the two had exchanged a number of letters, Lovecraft suggested that Bloch try his own hand at writing.

For the first part of his career, Bloch focused on publishing short stories in magazines like Weird Tales and Fantastic Adventures. But in 1947 he published his first novel, *The Scarf*, in which he takes on the persona of his protagonist, a psychopathic strangler. Despite the fact that the novel was poorly reviewed, Bloch went on to write a number of other novels with psychopathic protagonists, although not always using a first-person point of view, including a con artist in *The Dead Beat* and a pyromaniac in *Firebug*.

But by far the most famous of Bloch's psychopath novels was *Psycho*. Of course, much of that fame can be attributed to Alfred Hitchcock's iconic film adaptation of Bloch's novel, but the novel also deserves to be read on its own terms. Why? Primarily because Bloch's Norman Bates is a genuinely memorable fictional creation. Although Hitchcock and his screenwriter Joseph Stefano made a number of changes to the character of Bates to make him more appealing to a film viewer, Bloch felt no need to make Bates palatable, and his book is all the better for it.

Bloch's Bates is a thoroughly unpleasant character in every way, most of all because he not only murders Mary Crane but then also beheads her, in a scene that would have been considered very graphic for its time. Spillane can be said to have had a moral reason for depicting violence in a graphic manner in a way that perhaps helped to redeem—or at least contextualize—that violence. Can we say the same about Bloch's *Psycho*? Not really, no, or at least, not in as explicit a manner, but I don't mean that as a criticism of either Bloch or the novel.

First, we need to consider the genre in which Bloch was writing, which owes as much if not more to horror than it does to mystery and suspense fiction. Although a crime is committed in Psycho, and that crime is investigated by both a private detective and by Mary's sister and boyfriend, and the perpetrator is even caught and arrested by novel's end, in my view, the crime and its solution is not really at the center of this narrative.

What is at the center of *Psycho*? The character of Norman Bates himself. And this is where we arrive at the true significance of this novel in terms of its representation of violence in mystery and suspense fiction.

As in many of his other novels, Bloch's focus in Psycho is to reconstruct in as dramatic and frightening a manner as possible the way a psychopath thinks and acts. This means that although there's no denying that Bates's violence is there, at least in part, to shock and appall the audience, it's also there to show us exactly what psychopaths are capable of doing, the motives and causes behind their acts, and what those acts mean to the people that commit them.

The other point to bear in mind here is that *Psycho* was based on, or at least inspired by a real-life case. In 1957, two years before Bloch published *Psycho*, police in Plainfield, Wisconsin, interviewed Ed Gein after Bernice Worden, a local hardware store owner, disappeared. When the police searched Gein's property, they found Worden's decapitated body hanging upside down in a shed but this was just the beginning of what they would find.

When questioned, Gein admitted to making a number of nocturnal visits to the local graveyard between 1947 and 1952, where he would exhume the bodies of recently buried middle-aged women that reminded him of his mother. He would then take the bodies back to his farm, where he tanned their skins to make various objects that the police found at his farm, including a wastepaper basket, a belt, a lampshade, and even a corset made from a female torso.

To put it bluntly, next to real-life horror like that represented by the Ed Gein case, anything in Bloch's novel seems very mild indeed. At the very least, we can say that mystery and suspense narratives that focus on psychopathic characters, especially characters inspired by real-life models, must necessarily include an unusual amount and intensity of violence in order to capture both their reader's attention and the truth of what psychopaths are capable of doing.

It's no exaggeration to say that Robert Bloch's *Psycho* is the direct ancestor and inspiration for the explosion of fiction that centers on psychopathic, and especially serial killers that began in the 1970s and peaked in the 1980s and 1990s. What does this later fiction share with *Psycho* in terms of its representation of violence, and how does it differ?

Let's take Thomas Harris' famous novel *The Silence of the Lambs* as an example. Like Bloch, Harris draws on real-life cases in creating his serial killer characters. Buffalo Bill, for example, pretends to have an injured arm in order to trick his intended victims into helping him, a trick used by actual serial killer, Ted Bundy. Also, Buffalo Bill's ambition to make himself a woman suit from the skins of his victims is an obvious allusion to Ed Gein.

But the differences between Bloch and novelists like Harris are just as pronounced and important. For one thing, because Harris is writing novels about serial killers, rather than a stand-alone novel featuring a single psychopath as in *Psycho*, there is necessarily more violence in Harris' work than there is in Bloch's.

Moreover, because mystery and suspense fiction readers between 1959 and 1981 when Harris' most famous character, Dr. Hannibal Lecter, first appeared in print in *Red Dragon* had perhaps become used to, and perhaps even somewhat blasé about, psychopaths in general and serial killers, in particular, the violence contained in such novels became not only more frequent but also more extreme. We can see examples of this tendency not only in the work of Thomas Harris but also in the work of those writers often grouped with him, such as James Patterson and Patricia Cornwell.

In *Kiss the Girls*, for example, one of his novels featuring African-American forensic psychologist and detective Alex Cross, Patterson gives us not one but two serial killers. "Casanova" abducts and then imprisons young women in underground cells, where he rapes and eventually murders them. "The Gentleman Caller" takes body parts from his victims and then keeps them as trophies. The two killers eventually meet and form a bond defined by mutual admiration, at which point they become a killing team.

As for Patricia Cornwell, two of her novels featuring medical examiner Kay Scarpetta also feature serial killer Temple Gault who, like Hannibal Lecter, is elusive, cunning, brutal, and derives great enjoyment from tormenting and terrifying not only his victims but also the novel's law enforcement protagonist.

The fact that Temple Gault evades capture in *Cruel and Unusual* and then returns in *From Potter's Field* illustrates the way in which later novels featuring psychopathic serial killers and Thomas Harris's work definitely falls into this category often keep bringing these characters back for encore performances. This is because they're the most reliable way of continuing to generate extreme violence in their narratives and because they often share center stage with the law enforcement characters although, in fact, Lecter refuses to share the stage with anybody.

This is a good time to acknowledge an unavoidable problem with these narratives. Their dependence on characters that commit extreme acts of violence repeatedly is both a strength and a weakness. It's a strength in the sense that their violence does a good job of establishing the stakes of the narrative. The more extreme the violence, the more the reader—at least theoretically—wants to see the perpetrator of such violence arrested or killed.

But it's a weakness in the sense that, if you write a series of narratives featuring such characters, you inevitably commit yourself to upping the ante a little more each time by making the violence more grotesque and explicit. The trouble is, you can only up the ante a certain number of times before one of two things happens. You either disgust your reader or—much more likely—you bore them.

There are, after all, only so many things that one human being can do to another. And the more inventive you get in this area, the more you risk becoming over-the-top and ridiculous. Surely I wasn't the only one who laughed in disbelief when we learn in Thomas Harris' *Hannibal* that Mason Verger wants to kill Lecter by having him eaten alive by trained boars? This seems more like something Dick Dastardly would dream up on Wacky Races.

In a moment, I want to turn to the subject of the kinds of violence the genre tends not to be interested in. Before that, however, I want to backtrack a little to explore a final reason, apart from post–World War II anxieties and the advent of psychopath fiction, why the market for more extreme examples of violence in mystery and suspense fiction began to flourish in the 1950s.

The easiest and most automatic criticism that one can make of violence in mystery and suspense fiction is to call it gratuitous. Unfortunately, gratuitous is an inexact term at best because it is so dependent on context. A particular act of violence, such as beating someone to death, may indeed be gratuitous in the context of a middlebrow novel that has been recommended by the Book of the Month Club. But that same act may be read very differently by fans of pulp fiction.

According to critic Lee Horsley, "Post–World War II American publishing was transformed by the introduction of the paperback." Again, we can thank the massive success of Mickey Spillane's work for inaugurating the boom in paperback publishing. Although the hardback version of *I, the Jury* sold relatively modestly, the paperback version went through the roof, and companies like Gold Medal were quick to take notice of this fact. In this way, the era of what became known as the paperback original, which refers to a book that was never published in hardcover, was born.

Some of the most exciting and innovative mystery and suspense fiction of the 1950s appeared in the form of paperback originals. And because these paperbacks were beneath the critical notice of most reviewers, they gave writers an unparalleled degree of freedom to develop and express their own personal views, no matter how violent those views were.

A brief discussion of the work of David Goodis and Jim Thompson will illustrate my point. Neither Goodis nor Thompson began their respective careers with the intent of publishing paperback crime novels, which they would have regarded as the ghetto of the publishing world. However, after their early attempts at publishing straight mainstream literary novels were unsuccessful, at least in terms of generating significant amounts of money, both Goodis and Thompson turned to producing paperback originals in order to make a living.

Once they did so, they both found the genre to be surprisingly congenial. In Goodis's case, over the course of a series of novels, many of which are set in his native Philadelphia, beginning with *Dark Passage* in 1946 and ending with *Somebody's Done For* in 1967, he develops a relentlessly paranoid, dark, and fearful fictional universe filled with losers whose hope that things will get better is inevitably and brutally punished.

As one might expect, violence plays a large role in Goodis' universe, but there's nothing gratuitous about it. Instead, in Goodis' work, violence serves as what the poet and critic T. S. Eliot once described as an objective correlative—that is, something that gives a reader access to traditionally inexplicable concepts. In other words, Goodis uses violence as a way to communicate with almost unbearable vividness the emotional texture of his fictional world. Far from being gratuitous, in Goodis' work, the intense and brutal violence suffered by his characters plays a foundational role.

Although Thompson's vision of the world is just as dark and depressing as that of David Goodis—if not more so—there's surprisingly little violence in many of his crime novels, which stretch from *Nothing More Than Murder* in 1949 to *King Blood* in 1973. But, and this is a major exception, what violence there is usually makes a devastating impression, both because we're never allowed to look away from it and because Thompson has a rare gift for conveying the full horror of violence to us.

Two examples from many others will suffice to make my point. In *The Killer Inside Me*, the protagonist Lou Ford beats prostitute Joyce Lakeland nearly to death, and the description of the beating is very graphic. However, perhaps the most horrifying detail comes when Joyce tries to speak to Lou before she loses consciousness and we realize that she's trying to say "Goodbye kiss."

Later in the same novel Lou is beating his fiancée, Amy, in a similar manner, and again the description is very graphic. But once more, it's Thompson's eye for detail that makes this incident stick in the reader's mind. As Amy is dying, she reaches her hand out very slowly and grasps Lou's boot. Lou's so terrified that he can't shake it off—and we can't forget Amy's hand.

Whenever I teach *The Killer Inside Me*, I always point out these details, not because I like to make my students uncomfortable—well, maybe I do—but because this is the way they can see that the violence in Thompson's work in anything but gratuitous. Through his uncanny eye for the uncomfortable detail, Thompson is able to convey the true horror of violence.

You may have noticed that, no matter how diverse they are in other respects, the examples of violence I've discussed in this lecture have one thing in common. they all deal with forms of interpersonal violence. Usually, that violence takes place between a single perpetrator and a single victim, sometimes with a group of perpetrators and a single victim, and sometimes with a single perpetrator and a group of victims—think of Mike Hammer laying waste to a room filled with Communists. But usually, the numbers involved are pretty small.

Why is this a significant detail? Despite the fact that mystery and suspense fiction is incredibly diverse when it comes to depicting both types and levels of violence, the genre does have one very noticeable blind spot. depicting collective violence in pretty much any form, whether that be a violent labor dispute, a riot, a revolution, or a war.

I'm sure we can all immediately think of exceptions to this rule. Indeed, we discuss some of these exceptions in other lectures, such as when Chester Himes and Walter Mosley write about urban riots or when Mukoma wa Ngugi discusses the Rwandan genocide in his novel *Nairobi Heat*. My point, however, is that even if forms of collective violence do appear in the genre, they're usually in the background rather than the foreground of the narrative, and they certainly are not the focus of any investigation by the detective.

Why is this? To be perfectly honest, I'm not absolutely sure, but my hunch is that it has something to do with how mystery and suspense fiction attempts to give meaning to violence. No matter what form it takes, who commits it, and why, mystery and suspense fiction seems committed to the principle that violence must not grow beyond a certain scale. Only in this way, it seems, can violence remain something that the genre can use, rather than something that risks overwhelming it.

PSYCHOPATHS AND MIND HUNTERS

I n early examples of the genre of mystery and suspense fiction, there was rarely any consideration of the criminal's psychology. But once writers of these narratives became interested in psychology, several new possibilities opened up. For example, an emphasis on the psychology of the criminal often means that the criminal's identity is not a mystery. Instead of a whodunit, we now have a whydunit. What's more, writers now had fresh ways to explore the similarities and differences between the detective and the criminal psychopath, especially when that detective is a "mind hunter," or psychological profiler.

JACK THE RIPPER

- Although a sustained interest in criminal psychopathy among mystery and suspense writers is a relatively recent development, psychopathic characters in the genre have been around for a long time. To take an early example, the series of murders committed by Jack the Ripper in the Whitechapel area of London in 1888 inspired a flurry of dime novels featuring Jack the Ripper as a character.

- These novels included *The Whitechapel Murders: Or, On the Track of the Fiend*; *Jack the Ripper in New York; or, Piping A Terrible Mystery*; and *The Whitechapel Murders; Or, An American Detective in London*. None of these explores Jack the Ripper's psychology in any detail, though. Instead, they use the Ripper for this figure's rich melodramatic, horrific, and gothic overtones.

- In fact, any suggestion of psychological interiority in these texts would risk humanizing this monstrous figure in novels where the authors wanted the emphasis to remain firmly on horror and spectacle rather than motive and psychology.

THE ABC MURDERS

- We wouldn't expect Agatha Christie, who personifies all that is most traditional in mystery fiction, to attempt to integrate psychopaths into her work. But in fact she does exactly that in *The ABC Murders*. Hercule Poirot investigates a series of murders in which the victims seem to be chosen only because of the letters that start their first and last names. The first victim is called Alice Ascher, the second Betty Barnard, and so on.

- Such an unusual situation suggests to Poirot that the murderer is not motivated by any ordinary drive. Consequently, Poirot stresses throughout the book the necessity of understanding the killer's psychology. Ultimately, he turns out to be right in the sense that he realizes that the murders are not being committed by a psychopath at all. Instead, an "ordinary" murderer (with the mundane motives of envy and greed) is pretending to be a psychopath in order to achieve his goals.

Hughes's novel takes place in Los Angeles immediately after World War II. Her protagonist is Dix Steele, a veteran who was a fighter pilot during the war.

- Christie deserves credit for innovating the typical characteristics of the puzzle mystery. But the way she ultimately pulls back from including a psychopathic murderer in *The ABC*

Murders suggests just how difficult it is for traditional mystery fiction to write convincingly about such a figure. Exploring the psychology of a psychopath risks going down paths that might be too uncomfortable for the average reader of a cozy mystery.

IN A LONELY PLACE

■ Hard-boiled mystery and suspense fiction is a friendlier environment for the figure of the psychopath. Consider Dorothy Hughes's groundbreaking 1947 novel *In a Lonely Place*.

■ Hughes's novel takes place in Los Angeles immediately after World War II. Her protagonist is Dix Steele, a veteran who was a fighter pilot during the war. Steele is also a psychopath and a serial murderer of young women. Hughes puts together a fast-paced, suspenseful, and disturbing portrait of a psychopathic personality that is a landmark in the genre.

■ Because Hughes forces her reader to see the world from Steele's point of view, even when Steele is arrested at the end of the novel, this resolution isn't quite as comforting as it should be. Once we've been exposed to what the world and the people in it look like from a psychopath's point of view, that knowledge is hard to shake off.

STRANGERS ON A TRAIN

■ Perhaps more than any other writer in the genre, Patricia Highsmith enjoyed using psychopathic characters in her work. Unlike Hughes's Dix Steele, who's clearly mentally deranged and whose crimes are vicious and cruel, Highsmith's psychopathic characters are likeable. That doesn't necessarily make Highsmith's psychopaths any less disturbing, however. If anything, they unnerve us even more because they seem to be so similar to us.

- For example, in *Strangers on a Train*, her tour de force, Highsmith brings together two characters, Guy Haines and Charles Anthony Bruno. At first glance, it seems that these two men could not be more different from each other. Guy is a successful aspiring architect in the midst of a divorce, while Bruno is the ne'er-do-well son of a wealthy family with no goals in life.

- Bruno eventually reveals himself to be not only a sadistic psychopath but also someone with the ability to bring the seemingly normal Guy around to his point of view. Bruno is eventually able to persuade Guy to murder Bruno's father. The secret to Highsmith's success in this novel, as in so much of her other work featuring psychopathic characters, is that she develops her plot and the interactions between characters very gradually.

- Both Dorothy Hughes and Patricia Highsmith demonstrate that once mystery and suspense fiction begins to explore the psychology of the psychopath in more depth, that figure inevitably becomes the center of the narrative. Although this doesn't necessarily mean the reader will identify with the psychopathic character, it is true that other characters (including members of law enforcement) tend to take a backseat in relation to the psychopathic protagonist.

PSYCHO

- Unlike Highsmith, some mystery and suspense writers make it more difficult for their readers to identify with the psychopathic protagonists.

- For example, although the reputation of Robert Bloch's 1959 novel *Psycho* is largely based on Alfred Hitchcock's famous film adaptation, the novel is important in its own right in the context of how psychopaths are represented in the genre. In fact, one of the best ways to illustrate the distinctive power of Bloch's novel is to explore the changes that Hitchcock and his screenwriter made to Bloch's work.

■ Apart from promoting Marion Crane from a relatively minor into a major character, the other significant change was to transform Bloch's Norman Bates, who was in his 40s, pudgy, balding, and an alcoholic, into the much younger, more attractive, more childlike, and more vulnerable version of Norman Bates portrayed so brilliantly by Anthony Perkins.

■ With these changes, it was easier for the audience to identify with Norman Bates, which was especially important once Marion Crane had been killed. After the shower scene, in other words, the audience is now on Norman's side because Hitchcock has worked so hard to make him sympathetic.

THE KILLER INSIDE ME

■ More than any other writer we have studied, Jim Thompson makes creative and effective use of the first-person point of view to put his reader inside the psychopath's head. Once there, we're trapped. No matter how badly we want to get out, we're forced to experience the character's thoughts and actions firsthand.

■ Thompson is issuing a challenge to the reader. The author knows that our natural inclination is to see the psychopath as an inhuman monster. By putting us inside the psychopath's head, Thompson forces us to think twice, to recognize the humanity of the psychopath, and to consider what it says about us when we find ourselves identifying with this character.

■ In Thompson's *The Killer Inside Me*, Lou Ford, Thompson's protagonist, is a deputy sheriff in a small Texas town. He's also a serial killer. And although there's actually less violence in this novel than in many other mystery and suspense novels, Thompson's violence is shattering because we can't look away from it.

- Moreover, since Lou Ford is a sheriff, *The Killer Inside Me* also enables us to consider the place of law enforcement figures in mystery and suspense narratives that are organized around psychopaths. Thompson's approach to this issue is typically creative and subversive: He makes the cop and the killer the same person.

THE SILENCE OF THE LAMBS

- Thomas Harris's novels are among the most popular and influential examples of suspense fiction featuring psychopaths. Critic Philip Jenkins has discussed the significance of Thomas Harris's work for popularizing the "mind hunters" in the FBI's Behavioral Science Unit. According to Jenkins, novels by Harris such as *The Silence of the Lambs* provided the FBI's violent-crime experts with invaluable publicity and unprecedented visibility.

- A major exception to Harris's generally positive portrayal of the Bureau comes at the point in *Silence* when Jack Crawford, Clarice Starling's boss at the FBI, receives an address for the man they suspect is notorious serial killer Buffalo Bill. The FBI immediately heads off to the address in a plane bristling with high-tech weapons and gadgetry, while Clarice Starling, seemingly left out of the hunt, is out in the field tracking down leads.

- However, it is in fact Starling who eventually finds and kills Buffalo Bill, whereas the others go to the wrong address and only arrive at the right address when it's all over. The Bureau's failure and Starling's success suggest that there's a part of Harris that wants to leave space for the valorization of individual pluck and initiative, for the intuitive hunch that often cannot be accommodated within the bureaucratic structure.

THE PSYCHOPATH IN "HIGH" AND "LOW" LITERATURE

- Some critics have noted that the elements of mystery and suspense fiction centered on the psychopath can easily become a codified formula and that the market may have become oversaturated to the point of exhaustion.

- The genre has shown itself to be flexible and adaptable, however. Although the vast majority of popular fictional appropriations of the psychopath have drawn on the thriller, suspense, and horror genres, there are also examples of psychopaths in classic detective fiction both old and new.

- Another reason for optimism comes from the presence of psychopaths in many examples of "high" as well as "low" literary culture. Although we're used to thinking of serial killers as a staple feature of genre fiction, Bret Easton Ellis notoriously draws on the psychopath as a symptom of the ills of postmodernity in both *American Psycho* and *Glamorama*.

- Most interestingly, in *Zombie*, Joyce Carol Oates uses a technique we saw in the dime novels on Jack the Ripper. She writes a thinly fictionalized version of real-life serial killer Jeffrey Dahmer. In doing so, Oates substantially revises the popular account of what motivates psychopaths, thus also revising conventional explanations of why we're fascinated by them.

QUESTIONS TO CONSIDER
1. What were the factors that led to the introduction of psychopaths and serial killers in the genre?

2. What are the similarities and differences between the figures of the detective and the psychological profiler?

SUGGESTED READING
Schmid, *Natural Born Celebrities*.

Simpson, *Psycho Paths*.

PSYCHOPATHS AND MIND HUNTERS

F or the first part of its long and complex history, the vast majority of mystery and suspense fiction was relatively uninterested in why criminals do the things they do. Instead, examples of the genre usually contented themselves with describing what criminals do, and how they can be stopped.

This doesn't mean that earlier examples of the genre have nothing to say about motive. Indeed, if the genre remained completely silent on this issue, criminal acts would seem random and inexplicable. But most discussions of motive in early examples of the genre are brief and typically involve a limited number of the usual suspects, such as greed, revenge, and lust. Very rarely is there any consideration of the criminal's psychology.

Once mystery and suspense writers start to become interested in psychology in a substantive sense, several new possibilities open up for the genre. First, an emphasis on the psychology of the criminal often means that the criminal's identity is not a mystery. Instead of a whodunit, we now have a whydunit.

Second, the suspense now comes not from uncertainty about whether the criminal will be caught, but under what circumstances he will be caught, and how much damage he will do first. And third, an emphasis on psychology gives the genre new ways of remarking the similarities and differences between the detective and the criminal, especially when that detective is a so-called mind hunter or psychological profiler.

This lecture will be dedicated to exploring the emergence of psychopaths and mind hunters in mystery and suspense fiction and examining the impact of these figures on the genre as a whole.

Although a sustained interest in criminal psychopathy among mystery and suspense writers is a relatively recent development, psychopathic characters in the genre have been around for a long time. To take an early example, the series of murders committed by Jack the Ripper in the Whitechapel area of London in 1888 inspired a flurry of dime novels featuring the Ripper as a character.

These included *The Whitechapel Murders: Or, On the Track of the Fiend*; *Jack the Ripper in New York; or, Piping A Terrible Mystery*; and *The Whitechapel Murders; Or, An American Detective in London*. None of these explore the Ripper's psychology in any detail, though. Instead, they use the Ripper for this figure's rich melodramatic, horrific, and Gothic overtones. In fact, any suggestion of psychological interiority in these texts would risk humanizing this monstrous figure in novels where the authors wanted the emphasis to remain firmly on horror and spectacle rather than motive and psychology.

A later example of Ripper-inspired suspense fiction, Marie Belloc Lowndes' 1913 novel *The Lodger*, uses a very different tactic. Instead of presenting the Ripper as a bloodthirsty monster, Lowndes instead emphasizes his mundane ordinariness. The Buntings are a couple who are having trouble making ends meet, and so they're grateful when Mr. Sleuth rents a room in their house. Their gratitude changes to fear, however, when they begin to suspect that Sleuth is The Avenger, the nickname of a local serial killer.

The majority of the suspense in Lowndes' novel is generated by uncertainty about whether or not the eccentric Mr. Sleuth is indeed a killer. However, *The Lodger* doesn't explore Sleuth's psychology in any detail, mostly because the novel is told from the Buntings' point of view.

We wouldn't expect Agatha Christie, that personification of all that is most traditional in mystery fiction, to attempt to integrate psychopaths into her work. But in fact, she does exactly that in *The ABC Murders*. Hercule Poirot investigates a series of murders in which the victims seem to be chosen only because of the letters that start their first and last names. The first victim is called Alice Ascher, the second Betty Barnard, and so on.

Such an unusual situation suggests to Poirot that the murderer is not motivated by any ordinary motive. Consequently, Poirot stresses throughout the book the necessity of understanding the killer's psychology. Ultimately, he turns out to be right, but only in the sense that he realizes that the murders are not being committed by a psychopath at all. Instead, an ordinary murderer with the mundane motives of envy and greed is pretending to be a psychopath in order to achieve his goals.

Christie deserves credit for innovating the typical characteristics of the puzzle mystery. But the way she ultimately pulls back from including a psychopathic murderer in *The ABC Murders* suggests just how difficult it is for traditional mystery fiction to write convincingly about such a figure. Exploring the psychology of a psychopath risks going down paths that might be too uncomfortable for the average reader of a 'cozy' mystery.

The apparent disconnect between traditional mystery fiction and the psychopath implies that hard-boiled mystery and suspense fiction might be a friendlier environment for this figure. This hunch is confirmed by Dorothy Hughes' groundbreaking 1947 novel *In a Lonely Place*.

Hughes' novel takes place in Los Angeles immediately after World War II, and her protagonist is Dix Steele, a veteran who was a fighter pilot during the war. Steele is also a psychopath and a serial murderer of young women. Hughes puts together a fast-paced, suspenseful, and disturbing portrait of a psychopathic personality that is a landmark in the genre.

Crucially, Hughes is very inventive in her use of point of view in order to achieve this goal. Although the novel is not told from Steele's first-person point of view, he's the character Hughes insists we stay connected to. His limited point of view is the way we experience the world of the novel. Consequently, we have to deal with the uncomfortable feeling of being inside Steele's head, even when he brutally describes one of his victims in the following manner. "The only exciting thing that had ever happened to her was to be raped and murdered."

Because Hughes forces her reader to see the world from Steele's point of view, even when Steele is arrested at the end of the novel, this resolution isn't quite as comforting as it should be. Once we've been exposed to what the world and the people in it look like from a psychopath's point of view, that knowledge is hard to shake off.

The same is true of the writing of Patricia Highsmith, who perhaps more than any other writer in the genre enjoyed using psychopathic characters in her work. Unlike Hughes' Dix Steele, who's clearly mentally deranged and whose crimes are vicious and cruel, Highsmith goes out of her way to make her psychopathic characters likable. It's important to recognize, however, that this doesn't necessarily make Highsmith's psychopaths any less disturbing. If anything, they disturb us even more because they seem to be so similar to us.

In Strangers On a Train, her tour-de-force debut novel, for example, Highsmith brings together two characters, Guy Haines and Charles Anthony Bruno. At first glance, it seems that these two men could not be more different from each other. Guy is a successful aspiring architect in the midst of a divorce, while Bruno is the ne'er-do-well son of a wealthy family with no goals in life.

Bruno eventually reveals himself to be not only a sadistic psychopath but also someone with the ability to bring the seemingly normal Guy around to his point of view. After casually mentioning the possibility to Guy when they first meet on the train, Bruno is eventually able to persuade Guy to murder Bruno's father, even though everything in Guy rebels against the thought of doing so. The secret to Highsmith's success in this novel, as in so much of her other work featuring psychopathic characters, is that she develops the plot and the interactions between characters very gradually.

Consequently, by the time Guy becomes a murderer, we can sympathize with and understand his decision. We may be horrified by the way we've internalized the worldview of the psychopath if we realize it at all, but Highsmith is so masterful at making the extreme seem ordinary, and even inevitable, that we can hardly blame ourselves.

Highsmith goes even further in making her psychopath likable in her series of novels featuring murderous conman Tom Ripley. Rather than being a socially marginal figure, Ripley uses his psychopathic tendencies to achieve goals with which the majority of readers will empathize. financial security, personal happiness, and the good life.

Even though we recognize that Ripley's disturbed, since his victims are frequently less than sympathetic and since Ripley only seems to murder when it's absolutely necessary to either protect himself or achieve his goals, we're inclined to sympathize with him. We celebrate the fact that he's never caught, and over the course of the novels in which he appears, Ripley inevitably becomes the character that we identify with, if only because he's the one constant in the fictional world that Highsmith builds around him.

Both Dorothy Hughes and Patricia Highsmith demonstrate that once mystery and suspense fiction begins to explore the psychology of the psychopath in more depth, that figure inevitably becomes the center of the narrative in which they appear. Although this doesn't necessarily mean the reader will identify with the psychopathic character, it is true that other characters including members of law enforcement tend to take a backseat in relation to the psychopathic protagonist.

As we've seen, Highsmith uses the way in which psychopaths tend to dominate the narratives in which they appear to manipulate her readers into identifying with them. But other writers of mystery and suspense fiction often make it more difficult for their readers to identify with their psychopathic protagonists.

For example, although the reputation of Robert Bloch's 1959 novel *Psycho* is largely based on Alfred Hitchcock's famous film adaptation, the novel is important in its own right in the context of how psychopaths are represented in the genre. In fact, one of the best ways to illustrate the distinctive power of Bloch's novel is to look at the changes that Hitchcock and his screenwriter, Joseph Stefano, made to Bloch's work.

Apart from promoting Marion Crane from a relatively minor into a major character, the other big change that Hitch and Stefano made was to change Bloch's Norman Bates, who was in his 40s, pudgy, balding, and an alcoholic, into the much younger, more attractive, more childlike, and more vulnerable version of Norman Bates portrayed so brilliantly by Anthony Perkins.

Why did they make these changes? Basically, to make it easier for the audience to identify with Norman Bates, which was especially important once Marion Crane had been killed and removed from the film. Part of the reason the death of Hitchcock's Marion was so shocking to contemporary audiences was because the film's main character had been killed before the film's halfway point.

Presenting the psychopathic Norman Bates as a likable and sympathetic character made it much easier for Hitchcock's unsettled audience to make the switch that, in truth, they had no choice but to make. After the shower scene, in other words, the audience is now on Norman's side because Hitchcock has worked so hard to make him sympathetic that we don't suspect him.

By contrast, although he portrays Bates as a sympathetic character, Bloch does not make it easy for the reader to identify with him. Even though he has clearly been traumatized by his nightmarish childhood, the physical repulsiveness of Bloch's Norman, quite apart from the things he does, such as chopping off Marion's head, makes it more difficult for Bloch's reader to connect with him.

So, you could argue that Bloch's version of the psychopath is more honest than Highsmith's in the sense that, if readers are going to identify with him, they'll have to do so by accepting everything about him, even those things that are distinctly unpleasant.

This is also true of Jim Thompson's novels that feature psychopathic characters, such as *Pop. 1280* and *The Killer Inside Me*. More than any other writer we have looked at in this lecture, Jim Thompson makes creative and effective use of the first-person point of view to put his reader inside the psychopath's head. Once there, we're trapped. No matter how badly we want to get out, we're forced to experience the character's thoughts and actions first-hand.

Why does Thompson do this? Basically, because he wants to issue a challenge to the reader. Thompson knows that our natural inclination is to see the psychopath as a monster and to keep him at a safe distance by thinking of him as inhuman. By putting us inside the psychopath's head, Thompson forces us to think twice, to recognize the humanity of the psychopath and to consider what it says about us when we find ourselves identifying with this character, despite his actions.

Let's look a little more closely at how Thompson does this in *The Killer Inside Me*. Lou Ford, Thompson's protagonist, is a deputy sheriff in a small Texas town. He's also a serial killer. And although there's actually less violence in this novel than in many other mystery and suspense novels, Thompson's violence is shattering because we cannot look away from it.

Exposing us to the gruesome reality of Ford's violence is just one of the ways in which Thompson refuses to let us off the hook. He makes it very difficult for us to sympathize with Ford. We receive plenty of information about Ford's traumatic childhood, a childhood that began what Ford calls the sickness, a sickness that continues to plague him as an adult.

This information should make us feel sympathetic toward Ford, but given the fact that Ford proves himself to be a notoriously unreliable narrator again and again over the course of the novel, we can never be sure that he's telling us the truth. Even when he presents us with a medical diagnosis of his condition taken right out of a psychology textbook, we suspect it's is a trick.

Do we accept the diagnosis and thus feel that we can accurately label someone like Lou Ford and file him away neatly? Or, do we accept what I think Thompson sees as the truth that a psychopath like Lou Ford will always evade any attempt to classify him, but that we should attempt to understand and sympathize with him anyway?

As so often in his work, under the cover of seemingly disposable and lightweight pulp fiction, Thompson is raising serious and complex questions that have no easy answers. Moreover, since Lou Ford is a sheriff, *The Killer Inside Me* also enables us to consider the place of law enforcement figures in mystery and suspense narratives that are organized around psychopaths.

Thompson's approach to this issue is typically creative and subversive. he makes the cop and the killer the same person. In most other early psychopath narratives, however, both amateur detectives and police prove to be singularly ill-equipped to respond to the challenge of the psychopath. Why? Because this figure's motives are so different from the run-of-the-mill impulses, such as lust, greed, and anger that populate the vast majority of the genre.

The stage is set, then, for the emergence of a different type of law enforcement officer, with a different skillset that makes him better able to respond to the challenge of the psychopath. But what would become known as the mind hunter did not emerge in the genre until relatively recently.

Although mystery and suspense fiction featuring psychopaths has a venerable history, it would be perverse to deny the fact that the popularity of the genre exploded in the 1970s and beyond. The main reason for this rapid growth is the FBI's success in constructing a full-scale moral panic around serial murder by claiming that hundreds of unidentified serial killers were at large in the U.S., a claim that the media eagerly picked up on and disseminated widely. The Bureau then capitalized on the American public's fear by presenting itself as the solution to the epidemic of marauding serial killers that was supposed to be plaguing the land.

Just as its hunting down of gangsters in the 1930s produced the image of the FBI agent as the G-Man, so the Bureau's profiling of serial killers in the 1970s and 1980s produced an analogous image. the FBI agent as mind hunter, an individual who is supposedly uniquely qualified to deal with the serial murder menace.

Thomas Harris' novels are easily the most popular and influential examples of suspense fiction featuring psychopaths ever written. At first glance, they appear to owe their success to the way they celebrate the FBI mind-hunter image. The reality, however, is more complicated.

Rather than simply reproducing the law enforcement perspective on serial murder and psychopathy, Harris's work avoids the extremes of either attacking the FBI or viewing it completely uncritically. This is one reason why his work has made such a strong impression on readers of the genre.

Critic Philip Jenkins has discussed the significance of Harris's work for popularizing not only the mind-hunter image of the Bureau's Behavioral Science Unit but also the investigative techniques and methods of the FBI more generally. According to Jenkins, novels by Harris such as *Red Dragon* and *The Silence of the Lambs* provided the FBI's violent crime experts with invaluable publicity and unprecedented visibility.

There's a lot of truth to what Jenkins says, but it's also ironic that Harris's work gave such a boost to the FBI's authority over serial murder because Harris' most famous book, *The Silence of the Lambs*, contains a major criticism of both the Bureau and the image of the infallibly effective mind hunter. For much of the novel, the resources and investigative techniques of the FBI are seen in a positive light and are not treated as problematic. The Bureau, after all, was responsible for capturing and imprisoning Hannibal Lecter, possibly mystery and suspense fiction's most famous psychopath character. Moreover, in *Red Dragon*, the first book in the series, FBI agent Will Graham is presented as an effective protagonist to set against the novel's antagonists Lecter and Francis Dolarhyde, the titular Red Dragon around whose crimes the novel turns.

A major exception to Harris' generally positive portrayal of the Bureau comes at the point in Silence when Jack Crawford, Clarice Starling's boss at the FBI, receives an address for Jame Gumb, the man they suspect is notorious serial killer, Buffalo Bill. The FBI immediately heads off to the address in a plane bristling with high-tech weapons and gadgetry, while Clarice Starling, seemingly left out of the hunt, is out in the field tracking down leads.

However, it is, in fact, Clarice who eventually finds and kills Buffalo Bill, whereas the official face of the FBI, despite all its sophisticated resources and technology, goes to the wrong address, and only arrives at the right address when it's all over.

This is a rare exception to the praise and admiration that suspense fiction generally lavishes on the FBI and its ability to capture psychopaths. The Bureau's failure and Clarice's success suggest that there's a part of Harris that wants to leave space for the valorization of individual pluck and initiative, for the intuitive hunch that often cannot be accommodated within the bureaucratic structure of an organization like the FBI.

In this context, I also want to mention Harris' later novel, *Hannibal*. This third entry in Harris' Hannibal Lecter series received a lot of criticism for the way it turns Lecter into a victim by showing us episodes from his traumatic childhood and by making him the target of a plot organized by the wealthy Mason Verger, a vengeful former patient of Lecter's.

In some ways, however, I would argue that this novel represents a distinct advance over Harris' earlier work in that it contains an even more jaundiced picture of a corrupt and ineffective FBI. Clarice Starling's participation in a disastrously botched drug raid gives her enemies in the Bureau the excuse they've been waiting for to destroy her career. Ironically, in doing so, the Bureau also contributes indirectly to driving Clarice into Lecter's arms, the other aspect of this novel that was heavily criticized when it came out.

But the immensity of Harris' success can't be explained solely by his complex relationship to the image of the FBI mind hunter. I think a large part of Harris' success, and the success of those fiction writers who have come after him and have clearly been influenced by him, depends on how skillfully they combine different elements from mystery and suspense fiction into something new and innovative.

In particular, Harris' most fundamental contribution to the genre is the way he's able to combine elements of the police procedural with an emphasis on the psychology of the criminal. He does this in order to both indulge his reader's fascination with serial killers like Hannibal

Lecter and give that reader a way to either disavow that fascination altogether or contain it by identifying with a law enforcement protagonist or organization.

Indeed, it may well be that this dialectic between indulgence and disavowal is the key to the success of psychopath popular culture as a whole. By presenting and then killing off Red Dragon, Buffalo Bill, or Mason Verger, and by encouraging us to identify with the FBI or Clarice Starling, Harris allows us to maintain our uncomfortably and exhilaratingly complex relationship with Hannibal Lecter. Harris is able to maintain the most enduring feature of suspense fiction featuring serial killers—namely, the sequel.

Harris manages the balancing act that both creates and sustains readerly pleasure better than anyone else in the genre. That's why he's so successful. Others working in the field do so with varying degrees of success, but also in a way that inevitably reveals how the elements that make up serial killer fiction can easily become a codified formula.

Beginning in *Cruel and Unusual*, for example, Patricia Cornwell gives us the vicious and demented serial killer Temple Gault to be fascinated by, but then she balances that fascination with the safely technical and heroically plucky medical officer Kay Scarpetta.

Writers such as James Patterson in *Kiss the Girls*, Jeffery Deaver in *The Bone Collector*, Michael Connelly in *The Concrete Blonde*, and many others all have their variations on the formula, but that doesn't make them, in many cases, anything more than formulaic. So, does suspense fiction featuring psychopaths and mind hunters have any future, or has the market become oversaturated that it is exhausted?

When we look to the future, I think there's reason to be cautiously optimistic, partly because the past of the genre indicates how enormously flexible the figure of the psychopath is. As we saw earlier, although the vast majority of popular fictional appropriations of the psychopath have drawn on the thriller, suspense, and horror genres, there are also examples of psychopaths in classical detective fiction both old and new.

Admittedly, the serial killers in such novels as Agatha Christie's *The ABC Murders* and P. D. James' *Devices and Desires* are not very convincing. But their mere presence testifies to the psychopath's adaptability, and this might encourage more writers of traditional varieties of mystery and suspense fiction to incorporate this figure into their work in the future.

Another reason for optimism comes from the presence of psychopaths in many examples of high as well as low literary culture. Although we're used to thinking of serial killers as a staple feature of genre fiction, Bret Easton Ellis notoriously draws on the psychopath as a symptom of the ills of postmodernity in both *American Psycho* and *Glamorama*, while outlaw novelists such as Dennis Cooper in a quintet of novels beginning with *Closer* in 1989 and Poppy Z. Brite, in *Exquisite Corpse*, use psychopathic characters to dramatize the violence that in their opinion is inherent to sexual and interpersonal relations.

Most interestingly, in *Zombie*, the literary novelist Joyce Carol Oates uses a technique we saw in the dime novels on *Jack the Ripper* by writing a thinly-fictionalized version of real-life serial killer Jeffrey Dahmer. In doing so, Oates substantially revises the popular account of what motivates psychopaths, thus also revising conventional explanations of why we're fascinated by them.

In these ways, mystery and suspense fiction may not only show the way for how other writers can use psychopaths in their work but also contribute to the ongoing dissolution of the formerly secure boundaries between popular and literary fiction.

POLICE AS ANTAGONIST

I n mystery and suspense fiction, the police and the detective figure often have an antagonistic, even hostile relationship with each other. This situation may seem contradictory: The police and the detective are ostensibly on the same side—dedicated to fighting crime, capturing the bad guys, and restoring order. This lecture will take a closer look at the complexities of the relationship between police and detective and highlight how the contrast with the police can be one of the main ways in which we come to understand the peculiar personality, methods, and motives of the detective.

THE POLICE: DULL AND UNIMAGINATIVE

- The antagonistic relationship between the detective and the police is introduced in Edgar Allan Poe's first mystery tale, "The Murders in the Rue Morgue." The detective C. Auguste Dupin is particularly critical of the police investigation, saying, "The Parisian police, so much extolled for acumen, are cunning, but no more. There is no method in their proceedings, beyond the method of the moment."

- The picture that emerges of the Parisian police is of a group that is busy and diligent but also dull and unimaginative, ineffective and slow. If the police are often busy and active just for the sake of it, the detective chooses carefully when to be active. If the police are unimaginative and have a tendency to apply the same set of methods to every case, no matter what the circumstances, then the detective's methods will be characterized by imagination, creativity, flexibility, and variety.

- Both Poe and Dupin are at pains to stress that Dupin's success is the product of a method, rather than being a result of intuition, a hunch, or a lucky guess. The police may be methodical, but in this context, that word is almost a criticism. What the detective does is to combine method with imagination; the resulting activity of analysis is the key to the detective's success.

THE DETECTIVE: CREATIVE AND FLEXIBLE

- The competitive relationship between the detective and the police is quite evident in Poe's "The Purloined Letter." The prefect of the Parisian police and Dupin discuss the suspect, Minister D—, at length. In this instance, the detective actually has more in common with the criminal. Dupin and Minister D— are both highly educated, extremely cultured, and consider themselves superior to their peers.

- At one point in their conversation, the prefect describes Minister D—: "But then he's a poet, which I take to be only one remove from a fool." What happens next is a delicious detail that is easily overlooked but is crucial to understanding both Dupin's treatment of the prefect and the relationship between the detective and the police. In response to the prefect's comment, Dupin says, "True... although I have been guilty of certain doggerel myself." We now know that Dupin feels insulted and has a good reason (at least in his own mind) to torment the prefect.

- The prefect of the Parisian police tells Dupin about the ridiculously painstaking and unsuccessful search he has conducted for the missing letter. Frustrated and exhausted, the prefect has come to Dupin for advice, and Dupin advises him to re-search the premises.

- Here is another example of a crucial detail that is easy to overlook. Consider the precise words Dupin uses when he gives the prefect

his advice. He doesn't say, "Search the house again." Instead, he says, "Make a thorough re-search of the premises."

- The prefect, being the unimaginative character he is, assumes that the word "premises" refers to the minister's house. In fact, Dupin is using the word in a more abstract sense, to refer to the principles the prefect is using when conducting his search. In other words, Dupin is ironically giving the prefect very good advice: If you want to find the letter, you need to proceed from a different set of premises, a different set of principles and assumptions (just as Dupin will do).

A COMPLICATED RELATIONSHIP
- Even though Sherlock Holmes and C. Auguste Dupin have many characteristics in common, including their eccentricity, arrogance, and intelligence, Conan Doyle's character is notably

more generous toward the police than Dupin. Part of the reason for this difference undoubtedly has to do with changes that took place between the 1840s, when Poe was writing his mystery tales, and the late 19th century, when Sherlock Holmes appeared.

- When Poe wrote "Rue Morgue" in 1841, the police were a relatively new phenomenon and were still viewed with some degree of skepticism by most Americans. By the time Sherlock Holmes first appeared in *A Study in Scarlet* in 1887, however, the police were not only a well-established presence in Great Britain but also had a reputation for being reliable and effective.

- With this in mind, it becomes easier to understand a character like Inspector Lestrade. Despite the fact that Lestrade is a police detective and therefore, from Holmes' point of view, inherently limited, Holmes frequently comments to Watson that Lestrade is the best detective at Scotland Yard.

- In "The Red-Headed League," Conan Doyle explains Holmes's complicated relationship with the police, as he describes police detective Jones: "He is not a bad fellow, though an absolute imbecile in his profession. He has one positive virtue. He is as brave as a bulldog and as tenacious as a lobster if he gets his claws upon anyone." Holmes acknowledges the mental limitations of Jones, but at the same time, he's careful not to understate the importance of bravery and determination.

"I AM BETTER THAN THE POLICE"

- This same combination of admiration for what the police do well and criticism of their limitations can also be found in Agatha Christie's work. In *The ABC Murders*, for example, Captain Hastings frequently criticizes Hercule Poirot for what he perceives as Poirot's inactivity during their search for what appears to be a serial killer.

- First, Poirot points out that his characteristic activity is mental. Second, Poirot observes that all the physical (that is, more mundane) aspects of the investigation are being handled by the police.

- Like Holmes, Poirot allows that the police do have a role to play, albeit a rather limited one, but there are also clear limits to the police's utility. This is why, at another point in the novel, when a character asks Poirot if he is from the police, he says unambiguously, "I am better than the police."

> The picture that emerges of the Parisian police is of a group that is busy and diligent but also dull and unimaginative, ineffective and slow.

- Poirot insists on a clear difference between the detective and the official police force. The police might be useful, they can even help the detective in a small way, but there's never any doubt about the fact that it's the detective—and only the detective—who will solve the case.

COMPETITIVE BUT COLLABORATIVE

- One element that stands out immediately in hard-boiled crime fiction is that the private eyes tend to have a much closer relationship to law enforcement than detectives such as Dupin, Holmes, and Poirot. Indeed, in some cases, the private eye can actually have a very friendly, even collaborative relationship with the police. We see this very clearly, if somewhat unexpectedly, in *I, the Jury*, Mickey Spillane's first Mike Hammer novel.

- Mike Hammer works closely with the police detective Pat Chambers as they try to solve the murder of Hammer's friend, Jack Williams. Being a firm supporter of law and order, Hammer has more respect for the police than any other private eye. He both admires their resources and has sympathy for the difficulties of their job.

- And yet, the antagonism remains. Mike Hammer, despite his friendship with Pat Chambers, makes no bones about the fact that they're in competition over finding Jack Williams's killer. In Hammer's words: "From now on it's a race. I want the killer for myself. We'll work together as usual, but in the homestretch, I'm going to pull the trigger."

ECCENTRIC LONER VERSUS CALLOUS COLLECTIVE

- The reason that antagonism between the police and the detective remained such a stable part of hard-boiled crime fiction, when that genre eagerly overturned so much of what came before it, is that the classic detective and the private eye—despite all their differences, have much in common with each other: their independence and their individualism.

- Beginning with C. Auguste Dupin, the detective figure has always tended to be something of an outsider. Not only is it difficult for him to form emotional attachments with others, but also it is extremely unlikely that this figure could work easily or comfortably within the limits of a large organization. Whether we're talking about the classic versions of this figure, such as Dupin, Holmes, and Poirot, or their hard-boiled counterparts, such as Spade, Marlowe, and Hammer, the detective figure works best alone.

- Many varieties of mystery and suspense fiction, despite the genre's apparent cynicism about human nature, actually have a quite romantic and idealistic side that expresses itself in the belief that one person can make a difference. Readers of mystery and suspense fiction are attracted to the idea that the eccentric outsider, with an individual moral and ethical code, can take a stand against everything that is wrong in the world.

- The detective has come to personify our emotional attachment to the idea of the uncompromised individual, while the police, for better or worse, have come to personify the collective, the organization, with all its negative attributes of callousness, inefficiency, and bureaucracy.

DETECTIVE AND KILLER AS ONE

- In closing, we will discuss an example of the antagonistic relationship between the detective and the police in mystery and suspense fiction that could be said to cross a line.

- Up to this point, detectives have criticized the police for a number of reasons, but none of the writers has gone so far as to suggest that the police might be antagonistic in a much more basic sense—that is, by being the criminal.

- In *The Killer Inside Me*, Jim Thompson comes up with a particularly creative way to blend the categories of police officer and criminal by making them the same person. Lou Ford is a deputy sheriff in a small town in Texas and as such is supposedly there to either prevent crime or capture and punish the criminal. In fact, Ford himself *is* the criminal, responsible for a series of murders over the course of the book that, at least in some cases, he is involved in investigating.

- Thanks to Thompson's use of first-person narration, the reader gets a vivid sense of what it feels like for Ford to occupy these diametrically opposed identities simultaneously. In Lou Ford, the antagonism between detective and criminal is focused in a single body and expresses a split in Lou's personality. In this way,

Thompson finds a very imaginative way to give new life to a well-established tension in the genre.

QUESTIONS TO CONSIDER
1. What was the relationship between the detective and the police in early examples of the genre?
2. Why did it take so long for the police to become protagonists in mystery and suspense fiction?

SUGGESTED READING
Emsley and Shpayer-Makov, eds., *Police Detectives in History, 1750–1950.*

Miller, *The Novel and the Police.*

POLICE AS ANTAGONIST

I n "The Purloined Letter," the third of Edgar Allan Poe's mystery tales, his detective, Auguste Dupin, does something quite cruel. The Prefect of the Parisian police has just finished telling Dupin about the ridiculously painstaking and unsuccessful search he has conducted for the missing letter.

The Minister D– is suspected of having stolen the letter, and in his efforts to recover it and claim a large reward, the prefect has searched not only every square inch of the Minister's house but also the houses on either side. Frustrated and exhausted, the prefect has come to Dupin for advice, and Dupin advises him to research the premises.

Why is this advice so cruel? Because Dupin already knows the prefect's second search, just like his first, will end in failure. So why does Dupin give the prefect this useless advice?

Partly because, by the time the prefect returns to Dupin even more frustrated and desperate, the reward for the missing letter, which Dupin now has in his possession, will have increased considerably. And so Dupin can enrich himself by returning the letter and claiming the reward.

But the main reason that Dupin has the prefect conduct a second useless search is that he delights in tormenting the prefect, for whom he has no respect whatsoever. This incident, in other words, demonstrates the fact that in mystery and suspense fiction, the police and the detective figure often have an antagonistic, even hostile relationship with each other.

But why is this? Aren't the police and the detective on the same side? Aren't they both dedicated to fighting crime, capturing the bad guys, and restoring order? Technically, yes, but their methods of doing so can be so different that in many examples of the genre, the detective and the police are antagonists rather than collaborators.

This lecture will take a closer look at the complexities of this apparently straightforward relationship in order to show how the contrast with the police can be one of the main ways in which we come to understand the peculiar personality, methods, and motives of the detective.

As I've already indicated, the work of Edgar Allan Poe is a great place to begin this investigation because the antagonistic relationship between Dupin and the police is present in his very first mystery tale, "The Murders in the Rue Morgue." When Dupin asks the narrator for his opinion about the murders, the narrator states that he agrees with all Paris that they are an insoluble mystery.

Dupin, obviously, disagrees and is particularly critical of the police investigation saying, "The Parisian police, so much extolled for acumen, are cunning, but no more. There is no method in their proceedings, beyond the method of the moment."

After criticizing the police for their lack of method, Dupin goes on to admit that the police do occasionally achieve results, but even this faint praise is accompanied by further criticism, "The results attained by them are not unfrequently surprising, but, for the most part, are brought about by simple diligence and activity. When these qualities are unavailing, their schemes fail."

The picture of the police that emerges from Dupin's comments is a group that is busy and diligent, but also dull and unimaginative. Not actively malevolent like the criminal, the police are, instead, ineffective and slow.

But the importance of Dupin's comments goes beyond simply telling us what the detective thinks about the police. They also serve as a kind of guide to understanding what defines the detective and his methods. If the police are often busy and active just for the sake of it, the detective as personified by Dupin chooses carefully when to be active. If the police are unimaginative and have a tendency to apply the same set of methods to every case, no matter what the circumstances, then the detective's methods will be characterized by imagination, creativity, flexibility, and variety.

There can be no better demonstration of Dupin's ability to think outside the box than the fact that he goes on to deduce that the murders were committed by an escaped orangutan. There has been much critical speculation about why Poe chose such an unlikely murderer for his first mystery tale. One major reason is that this bizarre choice allows Poe to show his reader how the work of analysis is more creative and imaginative than the stolid, predictable, and unsuccessful work of the police.

Just as importantly, both Poe and Dupin are at pains to stress that Dupin's success is the product of a method, rather than being a result of intuition, a hunch, or a lucky guess. The police may be methodical, but in this context, that word is almost a criticism. What the detective does is to combine method with imagination, and the resulting activity of analysis is the key to the detective's success.

Poe uses the police in his first mystery tale to provide a point of contrast with his detective figure. Mindful of the novelty of a character like Dupin, Poe uses the police to represent the ordinary in order to underline how extraordinary his detective is. Small wonder, then, that at the end of the Rue Morgue case, apart from having solved what was considered to be an insoluble crime, Dupin derives his main satisfaction from having beaten the prefect or, in his own words, having defeated him in his own castle.

This competitive relationship between the detective and the police comes back in "The Purloined Letter." Only, in this case, the stakes are somewhat higher, in the form of a very large reward. As in the other Dupin tales, the detective's motives for solving the case are a combination of several factors, including the desire for monetary gain, the intellectual challenge, and the desire to help others. But in the Purloined Letter case, Dupin is also motivated by the desire to teach the prefect a lesson.

Where does this desire come from? When the prefect comes to Dupin and tells him about the case, they discuss the suspect, the Minister D–, at length. Generally, we might assume the detective and the police have a lot in common. But in this instance, the detective actually has more in common with the criminal. Dupin and the Minister are both highly educated, extremely cultured, and consider themselves to be superior to their peers.

At one point in their conversation, Dupin comments to the prefect that the Minister is by no means a fool and therefore should not be underestimated. The prefect replies by saying, "But then he's a poet, which I take to be only one remove from a fool."

What happens next is a delicious detail that is easily overlooked but is crucial to understanding both Dupin's treatment of the prefect and the relationship between the detective and the police. In response to the prefect's comment, Dupin says, "True… although I have been guilty of certain doggerel myself."

If the prefect had an ounce of sense, as soon as he finds out that Dupin writes poetry, he would apologize to Dupin for insulting him. But the dim-witted and self-involved prefect doesn't even notice his blunder. Poe's reader does notice it, however, and so we now know that Dupin has a good reason at least in his own mind to torment the prefect.

Now let's go back to the incident we discussed earlier in which Dupin advises the prefect to search the minister's house again. We now realize that Dupin is motivated not only by a desire to increase the reward but also by a desire to torture the prefect, perhaps for insulting him earlier in the story.

And this is another example of a crucial detail that is easy to overlook. We need to consider the meaning of the exact words Dupin uses when he gives the prefect his advice. He doesn't say search the house again. Instead, he says make a thorough research of the premises.

The prefect, being the unimaginative character he is, assumes that the word premises refers to the minister's house. In fact, Dupin is using the word in a more abstract sense, to refer to the principles the prefect is using when conducting his search. In other words, Dupin is ironically giving the prefect very good advice, "If you want to find the letter, you need to proceed from a different set of premises, a different set of principles and assumptions," just as Dupin will do.

Once again, the police are condemned not because they're bad, but because they're stupid and unimaginative. Or as Dupin puts it, when explaining to the narrator why the prefect failed to find the letter, "The measures… were good in their kind, and well executed; their defect lay in their being inapplicable to the case, and to the man." Dupin is stressing the need for creativity and imagination rather the mindless application of the same method to every situation, regardless of the circumstances.

As with so many other aspects of Poe's foundational mystery tales, his characterization of the police, and his description of the relationship between the police and the detective would both have a profound influence on later examples of the genre. However, neither of these aspects of Poe's work were simply adopted uncritically by later writers, and we can see evidence of this if we now turn to the work of Sir Arthur Conan Doyle and Agatha Christie.

Even though Sherlock Holmes and Auguste Dupin have many things in common, including their eccentricity, arrogance, and intelligence, Doyle's character is notably more generous toward the police than Dupin. Part of the reason for this difference undoubtedly has to do with changes that took place between the 1840s, when Poe was writing his mystery tales, and the late 19th century when Sherlock Holmes appeared.

Policing in the modern sense of the word that is, the establishment of a centralized, independent, 24-hour, and preventive police presence dates back to 1829 in London. This same model was later adopted by American cities, such as Philadelphia in 1833, Boston in 1838, and New York City in 1844. So when Poe wrote Rue Morgue in 1841, the police were a relatively new phenomenon and were still viewed with some degree of skepticism by most Americans.

By the time Sherlock Holmes first appeared in *A Study in Scarlet* in 1887, the police force was not only a well-established presence in Great Britain but also had a reputation for being reliable and effective. Even if Doyle, who in practice held rather conservative social and political views, had been inclined to portray the police as bumbling idiots, it's likely that his readers would have rejected such a portrayal as being unrealistic.

With this in mind, it becomes easier to understand a character like Inspector Lestrade. Despite the fact that Lestrade's a police detective and therefore, from Holmes' point of view, inherently limited, Holmes frequently comments to Watson that Lestrade is the best detective at Scotland Yard.

Although this is an example of damning with faint praise, the fact that Doyle kept bringing this character back he makes 13 appearances in total, the first in 1887 and the last in 1924, testifies both to his reliability and to the unavoidable presence of the police as an entity in mystery and suspense fiction written during this period.

Still, I don't want to give the impression that Holmes is a big fan of the police. It would be more accurate to say that, unlike Dupin, Holmes recognizes that the police can be useful on occasion, and he's willing to include them in his cases when he deems it necessary to do so.

For example, in *The Red-Headed League*, Holmes sets a trap for John Clay, a dangerous and skilled bank robber, in the basement of a bank in London. While the preparations are underway, Doyle gives us an amusing glimpse of what the police think of Holmes. Jones, the Scotland Yard detective who appears in this story, says of Holmes,

> He has his own little methods, which are if he won't mind my saying so, just a little too theoretical and fantastic, but he has the makings of a detective in him. It is not too much to say that once or twice… he has been more nearly correct than the official force.

This comment is a wonderful example of grudging praise—can you imagine anything more tortured than the phrase more nearly correct? But Jones's remarks do give the reader a very good sense of how frustrating it must be for the police to constantly be shown up and outdone by someone like Holmes.

And just in case you were wondering how Holmes might react to a policeman saying that he has the makings of a detective in him, there's a wonderful incident in *The Adventure of the Speckled Band* when Dr. Grimesby Roylott, the villain in this particular story, bursts into Holmes' rooms, hurls a string of insults and threats at him, and then storms out.

Readers are likely to laugh out loud when they realize that the insult that stung Holmes the most was when Roylott describes him as Holmes, the Scotland Yard Jack-in-office. As Holmes complains to Watson after Roylott leaves, "Fancy his having the insolence to confound me with the official detective force."

Returning to *The Red-Headed League*—if Holmes has a rather dim view of the police, why does he take Jones with him when they go hunting for John Clay? Doyle makes sure that Holmes explains his reasoning to Watson, He is not a bad fellow, though an absolute imbecile in his profession. He has one positive virtue. He is as brave as a bulldog and as tenacious as a lobster if he gets his claws upon anyone.

This is a perfect example of the extent to which Holmes is willing to praise a member of the police, and it's not something we could imagine Dupin saying about the prefect. Holmes acknowledges the mental limitations of Jones, but at the same time, he's careful not to understate the importance of bravery and determination.

This same combination of admiration for what the police do well and criticism of their limitations can also be found in Agatha Christie's work. In *The ABC Murders*, for example, Captain Hastings frequently criticizes Hercule Poirot for what he perceives as Poirot's inactivity during their search for what appears to be a serial killer.

Poirot defends himself in two ways. First, Poirot points out quite correctly, of course, that his characteristic activity is mental, whereas what Hastings is referring to is busy physical activity that ultimately will do nothing to solve the case.

Second, Poirot points out that all the physical that is, more mundane aspects of the investigation are being taken care of by the police, "But what is it that you would have me do, my friend? The routine inquiries, the police make them better than I do. Always… you want me to run about like the dog."

Like Holmes, Poirot allows that the police do have a role to play, albeit a rather limited one, but there are also clear limits to the police's utility. This is why, at another point in the novel, when a character asks Poirot if he is from the police, he says unambiguously, I am better than the police.

What does Poirot mean? Even if his relationship with the police is not as antagonistic as that of Dupin, Poirot still insists on a clear difference between the detective and the official police force. The police might be useful, they can even help the detective in a small way, but there's never any doubt about the fact that it's the detective, and only the detective, who will solve the case successfully.

In *The ABC Murders*, this point is driven home when the police arrest and charge a suspect who is obviously guilty, he's even confessed. The police are satisfied, but Poirot is not. Why?

Despite all the physical evidence pointing to this man's guilt, Poirot cannot believe that he's psychologically capable of committing the crimes he's been charged with. Working from this basis, which the police conveniently ignore because it doesn't serve their purposes, Poirot is able to discover the identity of the real killer and the innocent man is released. In this way, Christie suggests why the difference between the detective and the police matters. It's not just about competition or antagonism. The detective's superiority to the police, his ability to add another dimension to the mundane investigative abilities of the police, ensures that justice is done and order restored.

If we now move from the classical mystery fiction of Doyle and Christie to the hard-boiled crime fiction of Raymond Chandler, Dashiell Hammett, and Mickey Spillane, we might expect the antagonistic relationship between the detective and the police to be set to one side, just as the hard-boiled revolution in the genre rejected so many of the defining elements of the English mystery. But that is not what happens. Although the nature of and the reasons for the antagonism change somewhat, the antagonism itself persists, for reasons we'll discuss a little later.

First, though, let's look at some of the forms that the antagonism between the detective and the police takes in hard-boiled crime fiction. One thing that stands out immediately is that hard-boiled private eyes tend to have a much closer relationship to law enforcement than detectives like Dupin, Holmes, and Poirot.

Although we know very little about Sam Spade's life before he became a private eye, his friendship with cop Tom Polhaus in *The Maltese Falcon*, along with his familiarity with police procedure, both suggest at least the possibility that Spade worked for law enforcement before becoming self-employed. Similarly, we know from *The Big Sleep* that Raymond Chandler's Philip Marlowe at one time worked for the local D.A.'s office before starting up on his own. Moreover, Marlowe's friendship with Bernie Ohls, his former colleague, like Spade's friendship with Polhaus, suggests that the private eye doesn't always automatically have an antagonistic relationship with the police.

Indeed, in some cases, the private eye can actually have a very friendly, even collaborative relationship with the police. We see this very clearly, if somewhat unexpectedly, in *I, the Jury*, Mickey Spillane's first Mike Hammer novel.

Mike Hammer works hand in hand with the police detective Pat Chambers as they try to solve the murder of Hammer's friend, Jack Williams. Being a firm supporter of law and order, Hammer has more respect for the police than any other private eye. He both admires their resources and has sympathy for the difficulties of their job. In fact, it would be no exaggeration to say that Hammer, as stubborn and bull-headed as he is, realizes that to some extent he needs to rely on the police to get his job done, a realization that would seemingly preclude an antagonistic relationship with the police.

And yet, the antagonism remains. While Spade and Polhaus are friends, Spade and Polhaus' colleague Lt. Dundy absolutely loathe each other, and Polhaus has a full-time job trying to separate them. When he's called into the D.A.'s office to be questioned, the normally tight-lipped Spade devotes one of his longest speeches in the entire novel to explaining why he's not going to cooperate with him.

Similarly, despite his friendship with Ohls, Marlowe is usually uncooperative with the police, ostensibly out of loyalty to his client, but at least partly because he neither respects nor likes law enforcement as an institution.

And even Mike Hammer, despite his friendship with Pat Chambers, makes no bones about the fact that they're in competition over finding Jack Williams' killer. In Hammer's words, "From now on it's a race. I want the killer for myself. We'll work together as usual, but in the homestretch, I'm going to pull the trigger."

Hammer, ever a man of his word, keeps his promise to avenge his friend by killing his murderer. Although getting justice for Jack Williams is undoubtedly Hammer's main motivation, in this case, it's safe to say he also takes some satisfaction from beating Pat Chambers to the punch.

Why has the antagonism between the police and the detective remained such a stable part of hard-boiled crime fiction when that genre eagerly overturned so much of what came before it? The answer, I think, can be found by recognizing what the classical detective and the private eye, despite all their differences, have in common with each other, their independence and their individualism.

Beginning with Auguste Dupin, the detective figure has always tended to be something of an outsider. This means not only that it is difficult for him to form emotional attachments with others, but also that it is extremely unlikely that this figure could work easily or comfortably within the limits of a large organization. Whether we're talking about the classical versions of this figure, such as Dupin, Holmes, and Poirot, or their hard-boiled counterparts, such as Spade, Marlowe, and Hammer, the detective figure works best alone.

Why? Partly because many varieties of mystery and suspense fiction, despite the genre's apparent cynicism about human nature, actually have quite a romantic and idealistic side that expresses itself in the belief that one person can make a difference. Perhaps because, the world around us suggests the opposite, readers of mystery and suspense fiction are attracted to the idea that the eccentric outsider, with their own individual moral and ethical code to which they cling tenaciously, can take a stand against everything that's wrong in the world.

The detective has come to personify our emotional attachment to the idea of the uncompromised individual while the police, for better or worse, have come to personify the collective, the organization, with all its negative attributes of callousness, inefficiency, and bureaucracy. That is why the antagonism between police and detective is so persistent, although, as we will see in another lecture, in some types of mystery and suspense fiction, the collective aspects of law enforcement are viewed positively.

In closing, I would like to discuss an example of the antagonistic relationship between the detective and the police in mystery and suspense fiction that could be said to cross a line. Let me explain.

Up to this point, detective characters have criticized the police for a number of reasons, including their inflexibility, their stupidity, and the limitations imposed on them by the fact that they have to respect the letter of the law, no matter how illogical that law might be. But none of the writers we've looked at have gone so far as to suggest that the police might be antagonistic in a much more basic sense, that is, by being malevolent, by being the criminal.

Given mystery and suspense fiction's endless appetite for innovation and change, it should come as no surprise that the genre can supply us with examples of criminal police officers. In *The Killer Inside Me* Jim Thompson comes up with a particularly creative way to blend the categories of police officer and criminal by making them the same person.

Lou Ford is a deputy sheriff in a small town in Texas and as such is supposedly there to either prevent crime or capture and punish the criminal. In fact, Ford himself is the criminal, responsible for a series of murders over the course of the book that, at least in some cases, he is involved in investigating.

Thanks to Thompson's use of first-person narration, the reader gets a vivid sense of what it feels like for Ford to occupy these diametrically opposed identities simultaneously. Just before Lou kills Johnnie Pappas in order to prevent information about his previous crimes coming out, Lou explains to Johnnie what has happened to him, "I guess I kind of got a foot on both fences, Johnnie. I planted 'em there early, and now they've taken root, and I can't move either way, and I can't jump. All I can do is wait until I split. Right down the middle."

In Lou Ford, the antagonism between detective and criminal is focused in a single body and expresses a split in Lou's personality. In this way, Thompson finds a very imaginative way to give new life to a well-established tension in the genre.

But there is more at stake here for Thompson than diagnosing an individual character with a psychological condition. Inasmuch as Lou Ford is a police officer, for Thompson he also represents authority and power in a world that, in Thompson's eyes, has gone badly wrong. As Ford puts it to Johnnie, "We're living in a funny world, kid, a peculiar civilization. The police are playing crooks in it, and the crooks are doing police duty."

In Thompson's deft hands, what began in Poe's work as a way of distinguishing the novel figure of the detective from the police has now become a tool to dissect and analyze social ills. In this way, mystery and suspense fiction once again demonstrates its variety and depth.

POLICE AS PROTAGONIST

With the emergence of the police procedural, the police become protagonists in their own variety of mystery and suspense fiction. If detectives dominated the early stages of the genre, when the police become protagonists, the official forces of law and order take center stage in a way that innovates and updates the genre as a whole. In this lecture, we'll study the history of the police procedural, examine its many forms, and explain how it differs from other types of the genre.

INSPECTOR MAIGRET

- The precise origins of the police procedural are difficult to pin down, but a compelling candidate emerges in 1931, when Belgian novelist Georges Simenon published *The Strange Case of Peter the Lett*. In this novel, Simenon introduced one of the most famous characters in mystery and suspense fiction: Inspector Jules Maigret of the Parisian police.

- In Maigret, Simenon created the minimalist hero who possesses none of the flamboyant traits we associate with either the gifted amateur detective or the hard-boiled private eye. Instead of relying on abstruse scientific or technical knowledge, Maigret usually investigates his cases by means of intuition, a knowledge of human nature, and vast amounts of patience. The way the Maigret novels are rooted in the mundane details of police procedure is the best reason to describe these novels as police procedurals.

- The noted American mystery critic Anthony Boucher observed that Simenon's work differs from most examples of mystery fiction in that it does not rely on "the well-shaped plot and the devious gimmick (though he could be very good at these when he chose) to lay stress on the ambience and milieu of the crime and on the ambivalent duel… between the murderer and Maigret."

■ Boucher's reference to the "ambivalent duel" is particularly significant because it suggests that, in many ways, Maigret resembles the figure of the classic detective more closely than we might think. While Maigret is definitely not flamboyant or eccentric in the manner of a Dupin or a Holmes, he does share with these figures a very dominant personality.

■ In novel after novel, Maigret remains relatively unchanged as the world around him changes, and this fact suggests that Simenon is reworking the individualism of the detective rather than rejecting it altogether. The focus on police procedure notwithstanding, there are qualities of the Maigret novels that make them not quite fit as police procedurals in the accepted sense of the term.

INSPECTOR WEST

■ John Creasey, while not widely read by fans of mystery and suspense fiction, should be acknowledged as a master of what comes close to being police procedurals. Creasey was born in England in 1908 and went on to have an incredibly prolific career under several pseudonyms.

■ After reportedly being challenged by his neighbor, a retired Scotland Yard detective, to "write about us as we are," Creasey published under his own name a series of realistic crime novels featuring Roger West of the London Metropolitan Police. The first novel in the series, *Inspector West Takes Charge*, appeared in 1942, and the series eventually included more than 40 novels, the last of which was *A Sharp Rise in Crime*, published in 1978.

■ For their time, the Inspector West novels were an unusually detailed and realistic look at the ways in which Scotland Yard detectives actually conducted cases. But their realism was undermined by two factors. First, the plots tended to be rather melodramatic. And second, in order to get around problems in legal procedure, Creasey frequently had West use the services of an amateur detective friend who was able to subvert the law in a way that West, as a police officer, could not.

THE 87TH PRECINCT NOVELS

- Just as the hard-boiled crime fiction that began to appear in American pulp magazines in the 1920s redefined what was meant by realism in mystery and suspense fiction as a whole, so the American version of the police procedural was considered to be grittier and more realistic than its transatlantic cousins. More than any other author, Ed McBain epitomizes the realism of the American police procedural.

- Ed McBain was one of several pen names of Evan Hunter, who was born as Salvatore Albert Lombino in New York City in 1926 before legally adopting the name Evan Hunter in 1952. After serving in the U.S. Navy in World War II, he graduated from Hunter College and began to publish short stories while working at a literary agency.

- Hunter achieved true and lasting success as Ed McBain, however, when he published *Cop Hater* in 1956, the first novel in a series that would eventually feature dozens of titles. These are collectively known as the 87th Precinct series. The 87th Precinct novels were inspired by the television series *Dragnet*, as we can tell from the fact that each novel begins with the same disclaimer: "The city in these pages is imaginary. The people, the places are all fictitious. Only the police routine is based on established investigatory technique."

- Fans of *Dragnet* may recognize the phrasing of McBain's disclaimer because it echoes the statement made at the start of every episode of the television show: "The story you are about to see is true. The names have been changed to protect the innocent."

- But note the differences as well as the similarities. McBain emphasizes the fictional status of his narrative rather than its truth, and in doing so, he both acknowledges his inspiration while also announcing that he's changed the rules of the game.

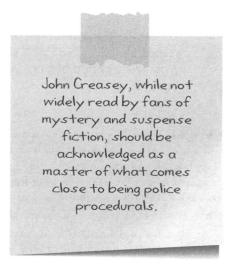

John Creasey, while not widely read by fans of mystery and suspense fiction, should be acknowledged as a master of what comes close to being police procedurals.

HUMANIZING THE POLICE

- The 87th Precinct novels undoubtedly form one of the most significant contributions, if not the most significant, to the police procedural genre in the history of mystery and suspense fiction.

- As its collective title indicates, every novel in the series is based on the work of a group of police detectives in the 87th Precinct in Isola, a district of a large fictional city based on the New York City borough of Manhattan. In fact, the fictive setting of Isola is a big part of the success of the series. The fictionalized setting gives us the freedom to see Isola as any city in the general sense. In other words, fictionalizing the urban setting makes the 87th Precinct series more relatable to a wider range of readers.

- Apart from the setting, the success of the 87th Precinct novels is also a product of its cast of recurring characters. They are, on the whole, a diverse group, which means that the 87th Precinct novels do try to replicate the diversity of an actual city. What's more, because all these characters appear in the vast majority of the novels over a period of many years, we become very attached to them and we follow the ups and downs of their professional and private lives.

- Not all of the characters are positive, however. In other words, McBain isn't interested in writing a hymn of praise to the police. Instead, he shows them as fallible and imperfect individuals trying to do a difficult job the best they can.

- The significance of McBain's police procedurals lies in the fact that he humanizes the police. Instead of the two-dimensional, slow-witted figures in many early examples of mystery and suspense fiction, now the police are three-dimensional, complex, and imperfect human beings that we're meant to identify with. In the first novel in the series, *Cop Hater*, McBain takes the humanization of the police detective to the extreme. Rather than being a representative of the state, a figure associated with violence and even brutality, in *Cop Hater*, the police detective is a vulnerable, victimized figure.

AN AFRICAN AMERICAN PERSPECTIVE

- Not all writers in the genre of mystery and suspense fiction saw the police in such a positive light. African American writer Chester Himes experienced police brutality firsthand as a young man. Given his background, it's understandable that Himes had a somewhat jaundiced view of the police, and this helps explain an extraordinary novel he wrote entitled *Run Man Run*.

- The main character in the novel is a black law student by the name of Jimmy Johnson who moonlights as a night porter in a New York City luncheonette. When Johnson witnesses drunken detective Matt Walker killing two of his coworkers, he identifies

Walker as the killer to the police. Not only do the police not believe Johnson, they also commit him to Bellevue Hospital for psychiatric evaluation while they investigate the murders.

- Once Johnson is released, Walker begins to hunt him down, and Johnson spends the rest of the novel in a state of constant fear. Not only is he terrified that Walker will eventually catch him and kill him, but he also knows there's no one he can turn to for help, especially not the so-called justice system.

GRAVE DIGGER JONES AND COFFIN ED JOHNSON
- It might seem surprising to learn that Himes published *Run Man Run*, an indictment of police corruption and brutality, at the same time he was writing a highly influential series of police procedural novels featuring his two black homicide detectives, Grave Digger Jones and Coffin Ed Johnson.

- Himes chooses black police officers to anchor his Harlem Domestic series because he was interested in exploring the tensions inherent in black men working for a system that, in Himes's opinion, was racist. Because they work for The Man, Grave Digger and Coffin Ed are not trusted by many residents of Harlem, despite the fact that they have a legendary reputation for both violence and successful investigations.

- Himes finds several other ways to communicate the fact that Grave Digger and Coffin Ed are outsiders in Harlem. For example, both live in a predominantly white suburb on Long Island. But the most significant and certainly the most serious way in which Himes demonstrates the difficulties and limitations of Grave Digger and Coffin Ed's situation as black police detectives in Harlem is the fate that he reserves for them by the end of the series.

- As the series progresses—and especially as the political atmosphere in Harlem becomes more charged and militant as the 1950s give way to the 1960s—Grave Digger and Coffin Ed become more and more powerless and irrelevant. And, in *Plan B*, the last and unfinished novel in the series, Himes kills his detectives off as the ultimate sign that they have outlived their usefulness.

QUESTIONS TO CONSIDER
1. What factors led to the rise of the police procedural?

2. How do police procedurals differ from narratives featuring either classic detectives or hard-boiled private eyes?

SUGGESTED READING
Dove, *The Police Procedural.*

Panek, *The American Police Novel.*

POLICE AS PROTAGONIST

A nyone not familiar with the history of mystery and suspense fiction might assume that police and other law enforcement figures would have been at the center of the genre right from the very beginning. In a sense, they'd be right. The police are indeed a presence not only in the genre-founding tales of Edgar Allan Poe but also in the work of other early luminaries such as Wilkie Collins, Anna Katharine Green, Sir Arthur Conan Doyle, and Agatha Christie.

But as we've already discussed in this course, the police aren't the protagonists in the work of these writers. For the most part, that honor belongs to the amateur detective. What role do the police play then? By and large, they are the antagonists in early mystery and suspense narratives—not in the sense that they're bad or criminal, but in the sense that, compared to the detective, they're usually dismissed as slow, unimaginative, even downright stupid.

In this lecture, we'll examine how and why the status of the police in mystery and suspense fiction began to change. With the emergence of what became known as the police procedural, the police become protagonists of their own variety of mystery and suspense fiction. We'll explore the appeal of the police procedural and how it differs from other types of the genre. If detectives dominated the early stages of the genre, when the police become protagonists the official forces of law and order take center stage in a way that innovates and updates the genre as a whole.

As we move through the history of the police procedural, we'll also see that portrayals of the police in procedurals aren't always positive. Some examples of the genre emphasize systemic corruption that's opposed by a maverick officer. But it's also significant for the way it opens the door for other branches of law enforcement—FBI agents, profilers, forensic scientists, and so on—to become the heroes of their own narratives.

The precise origins of the police procedural are difficult to pin down, but a compelling candidate emerges in 1931 when Belgian novelist Georges Simenon published *The Strange Case of Peter the Lett* also known as *The Case of Peter the Lett, Maigret and the Enigmatic Lett,* and *Pietr the Latvian*. This was the novel in which Simenon introduced one of the most famous characters in mystery and suspense fiction. Inspector Jules Maigret of the Parisian police, usually known to everyone including his wife. simply as Maigret.

The Maigret novels number in the dozens, the last one of which, *Maigret and Monsieur Charles*, was published in 1972. What is it that makes them so compelling a candidate for the origin of the police procedural? Well, the obvious answer to that question is Maigret's professional identity as a police officer rather than as a genius amateur detective. But not surprisingly, there's more to it than that.

In Maigret, Simenon created the minimal hero who possessed none of the flamboyant traits we associate with either the gifted amateur detective or the hard-boiled private eye. As critic S.K. Oberbeck put it.

> He exhibits no flashing forensics, slight deductive genius, rarely encounters personal violence and never steps out with the dolls. If anything, Maigret is utterly bourgeois, egoless, sympathetic and understanding toward criminals, a man whose home life is unruffled domesticity and who wearily laments his shortcomings.

Instead of relying upon abstruse scientific or technical knowledge, Maigret usually investigates his cases by means of intuition, a knowledge of human nature, and vast amounts of patience. He does a huge amount of waiting in many of the novels. The way the Maigret novels are rooted in the mundane details of police procedure is the best reason to describe these novels as police procedurals.

As one critic has pointed out, Maigret rarely carries a gun, rarely throws a punch or takes one, and hardly ever is involved in a chase either on foot or in a car. Instead, in novel after novel, we see him do his job slowly and effectively, occasionally complaining about being cold, tired, thirsty or hungry, but otherwise seemingly unflappable.

The other characteristic that brings the Maigret novels very close to being police procedurals is the recurring presence of Maigret's police colleagues in the series. Four colleagues in particular—Lucas, Janvier, Lapointe, and Torrence, who become known as the Faithful Four—appear in novel after novel, which means that in some ways the Maigret novels could be said to have a collective, rather than an individual, protagonist.

This is a crucial point because individualism, in one form or another, is such a major component of a large amount of mystery and suspense fiction. Whether we're talking about genius detectives like Poe's Auguste Dupin or Conan Doyle's Sherlock Holmes on the one hand, or hard-boiled private eyes like Dashiell Hammett's Sam Spade and Raymond Chandler's Philip Marlowe on the other, the protagonists of many mystery and suspense narratives tend to be loners. Why is this?

Partly because there is a persistent strain of romanticism that runs through many examples of mystery and suspense fiction, both classical and hard-boiled alike. This romanticism consists of the belief that a single individual, despite all appearances to the contrary, can make a difference and restore a world disrupted by crime to something resembling a state of calm.

In this sense, police procedurals can be thought of as radically anti-romantic, and this is a big part of their appeal. The collective protagonist that tends to dominate this type of mystery narrative suggests that one person cannot go it alone, but instead needs the help of others, of a team, in order to get something done. In other words, for all the vaunted realism of hard-boiled crime fiction, it might be the police procedural that is the first truly realistic form of mystery and suspense fiction.

Having constructed what I hope is a fairly convincing case for why Simenon's Maigret novels should be viewed as police procedurals, I now want to dismantle that case a little and complicate the picture. Why? Because it's not quite accurate to say that these novels have a collective protagonist. After all, they are known collectively as the Maigret novels for a reason. Despite the fact that they have a number of recurring characters, there's no doubt Maigret towers above the others in terms of being the protagonist, the most important character in the series and the one to whom we're most attached.

Moreover, as the famous American mystery critic Anthony Boucher once noted, Simenon's work differs from most examples of mystery fiction in that it does not rely on "The well-shaped plot and the devious gimmick though he could be very good at these when he chose to lay stress on the ambience and milieu of the crime and on the ambivalent duel... between the murderer and Maigret."

Boucher's reference to the ambivalent duel is particularly important, I think because it suggests that, in many ways, Maigret resembles the figure of the classical detective more closely than we might think. As I said earlier, Maigret is definitely not flamboyant or eccentric in the manner of a Dupin or a Holmes instead, he is almost aggressively stolid and bourgeois. But he does share with these figures a very dominant personality.

In novel after novel, Maigret remains relatively unchanged as the world around him changes, and this fact suggests that Simenon is reworking the individualism of the detective rather than rejecting it altogether. Maigret is the calm center around which Simenon's fictional world turns, and this gives this character an almost superhuman status, despite his ordinariness. The focus on police procedure and the presence of recurring characters notwithstanding, there are qualities of the Maigret novels that make them not quite fit as police procedurals in the accepted sense of the term.

The same might be said of the work of a writer who is not widely read by fans of mystery and suspense fiction, but who should really be acknowledged as a master of what come close to being police procedurals. John Creasey was born in England in 1908 and went on to have an incredibly prolific career under several pseudonyms writing a wide variety of different types of mystery and suspense fiction, including spy novels and novels featuring a criminal protagonist.

After reportedly being challenged by his neighbor, a retired Scotland Yard detective, to write about us as we are, Creasey published under his own name a series of realistic crime novels featuring Roger West of the London Metropolitan Police. The first novel in the series, *Inspector West Takes Charge*, appeared in 1942 and the series eventually included more than forty novels, the last of which was *A Sharp Rise in Crime*, published in 1978.

For their time, the Inspector West novels were an unusually detailed and realistic look at the ways in which Scotland Yard detectives actually conducted cases. But their realism was undermined by two factors. First, the plots tended to be rather melodramatic. And second, in order to get around problems in legal procedure, Creasey frequently had West use the services of an amateur detective friend who was able to subvert the law in a way that West, as a police officer, could not.

In the mid-1950s, Creasy launched another series of police procedural novels inspired by the American television show *Dragnet*, which had debuted in 1951 and starred Jack Webb in the role of Sergeant Joe Friday, a Los Angeles, police detective. Writing under the pseudonym of J. J. Marric, and with the aim of writing a more down-to-earth type of police novel, Creasy created his protagonist George Gideon, a

Detective Superintendent in the Criminal Investigation Division at Scotland Yard.

The first novel in the series, *Gideon's Day*, was published in 1955. It's a detailed look at a day in the working life of a senior police officer, which involves supervising several unrelated cases being investigated by his subordinates. Unlike the Maigret novels, which normally focus on a single crime that is investigated personally by Maigret himself, the Gideon novels, like many later examples of police procedurals, usually follow several autonomous plot lines simultaneously. This is part of what gives this genre a greater degree of realism than some other types of mystery and suspense fiction.

As J. J. Marric, Creasey got some of the best reviews in his long career for the Gideon novels. One novel in the series, *Gideon's Fire*, which was published in 1961, even won an Edgar Award from the Mystery Writers of America for the Best Mystery Novel. This demonstrates the extent to which the popularity of the police procedural genre had grown by the 1960s.

Although Creasey benefited from the police procedural's popularity, it would be a stretch to say he contributed significantly to that popularity, at least among American audiences. Remember that Creasey was inspired to write the Gideon series by the success of *Dragnet*. This indicates not only the influence of this particular television show on later examples of police procedurals but also the status of American police procedurals more generally as the last word in realism.

Just as the hard-boiled crime fiction that began to appear in American pulp magazines in the 1920s redefined what was meant by realism in mystery and suspense fiction as a whole, so the American version of the police procedural was considered to be grittier and more realistic than its transatlantic cousins. More than any other author, Ed McBain epitomizes the realism of the American police procedural.

Ed McBain was one of several pen names of Evan Hunter, who was born as Salvatore Albert Lombino in New York City in 1926 before legally adopting the name Evan Hunter in 1952. After serving in the U.S. Navy in World War II, he graduated from Hunter College and began to publish short stories while working at a literary agency. As Evan Hunter, he gained some attention in 1954 when he published *Blackboard Jungle*, a novel about juvenile delinquency in the New York City public high school system, where he'd briefly worked as a teacher.

Hunter achieved true and lasting success as Ed McBain, however, when he published *Cop Hater* in 1956, the first novel in a series that would eventually feature dozens of titles. These are collectively known as the 87th Precinct series. Like J. J. Marric's Gideon series, the 87th Precinct novels were also inspired by Dragnet, as we can tell from the fact that each novel begins with the same disclaimer. "The city in these pages is imaginary. The people, the places are all fictitious. Only the police routine is based on established investigatory technique."

Fans of *Dragnet* may recognize the phrasing of McBain's disclaimer because it echoes the statement made at the start of every episode of the television show. "The story you are about to see is true. The names have been changed to protect the innocent." But note the differences as well as the similarities. McBain emphasizes the fictional status of his narrative rather than its truth, and in doing so, he both acknowledges his inspiration while also announcing that he's changed the rules of the game.

Taken together, the 87th Precinct novels undoubtedly form one of the most significant contributions, if not the most significant, to the police procedural genre in the history of mystery and suspense fiction. What are the qualities that make the 87th Precinct novels so important?

Let's begin to answer that question by describing the main characteristics of the novels in the series. As its collective title indicates, every novel in the series is based on the work of a group of police detectives in the 87th Precinct in Isola, a district of a large fictional city based on the New York City borough of Manhattan. The other parts of McBain's fictional city—Calm's Point, Majesta, Riverhead, and Bethtown—correspond to New York's other boroughs—Brooklyn, Queens, the Bronx, and Staten Island.

You might think that, in a quest for greater realism, McBain would've chosen to set his work in an actual city rather than a fictional one, as Simenon and Creasey did before him. But I think the fictive setting of Isola is a big part of the success of the series. Even though it becomes clear to us pretty quickly that McBain's writing about New York City, the fictionalized setting gives us the freedom to see Isola as any city in the general sense. In other words, fictionalizing the urban setting makes the 87th Precinct series more relatable to a wider range of readers.

That's why a number of novels in the series have been adapted into films set in a wide variety of locations. For example, Akira Kurosawa's 1963 film, *High and Low*, which is based on McBain's *King's Ransom*, is set in Tokyo. *Without Apparent Motive*, directed by Philippe Labro and released in 1971, is set on the French Riviera, and is based on *Ten Plus One 1963*, while Claude Chabrol's *Les Liens de sang*, released in 1978, is based on McBain's *Blood Relatives*, but is set in Montreal.

These films both confirm the argument, which I've made in other lectures in this series, about the centrality of urban settings to mystery and suspense narratives, while also indicating the flexible appeal of the 87th Precinct novels to readers and filmmakers alike. Apart from the setting, the success of the 87th Precinct novels is also a product of its cast of recurring characters, which includes detectives Steve Carella, Meyer Meyer, Bert Kling, Cotton Hawes, Arthur Brown the squad's only black detective, Eileen Burke the only female detective, and some detectives who are generally disliked by their colleagues because they are either corrupt or boorish, such as Roger Havilland, Andy Parker, and Richard Genero.

Although there are many other recurring characters, this brief list indicates several important points about McBain's use of these characters. First, they are, on the whole, a diverse group, which means that the 87th Precinct novels do try to replicate the diversity of an actual city. Second, because all of these characters appear in the vast majority of the novels over a period of many years, we become very attached to them, and we follow the ups and downs of their professional and private lives. Third, not all of the characters are positive. In other words, McBain isn't interested in writing a hymn of praise to the police. Instead, he shows them as fallible and imperfect individuals trying to do a difficult job the best they can.

We can summarize the importance of McBain's characters for the police procedural genre as a whole by saying that he attempts to humanize the police. Instead of the two-dimensional, slow-witted figures who are designed to be the butt of the joke in many early examples of mystery and suspense fiction, now the police are three-dimensional, complex, and imperfect human beings that we're meant to identify with.

It's interesting to consider the first novel in the series, *Cop Hater*, from this perspective. The novel revolves around Steve Carella's investigation into the murders of a number of his police detective colleagues. Because the killer apparently has a grudge against all cops, Carella himself could be a potential victim. So part of the novel's suspense comes from whether Carella can find the murderer before he becomes the killer's next victim.

By choosing this plot, McBain takes the humanization of the police detective to the extreme. Rather than being a representative of the state, a figure associated with violence and even brutality, in Cop Hater, the police detective is a vulnerable figure, either an actual or potential victim.

If McBain often emphasizes the human and vulnerable sides of the police, rather than their potential capacity for violence and even brutality, not all writers in the genre saw the police in such a positive light. African-American writer Chester Himes not only experienced police brutality first-hand as a young man but also served a long prison sentence for armed robbery in the Ohio State Penitentiary.

Given this background, it's understandable that Himes had a somewhat jaundiced view of this police, and this helps to explain an extraordinary novel he wrote entitled *Run Man Run*, which was originally published in French in 1959 and then translated into English in 1966, and that has been aptly described by critics as a study in terror.

The main character in the novel is a black law student by the name of Jimmy Johnson who, in order to pay for his schooling, works as a night porter in a New York City luncheonette. When Johnson witnesses drunken detective Matt Walker killing two of his co-workers, he identifies Walker as the killer to the police. Not only do the police not believe Johnson, they also commit him to Bellevue Hospital for psychiatric evaluation while they investigate the murders.

Once Johnson is released, Walker starts to hunt him down so that he can kill him and thereby remove a troubling witness. Johnson spends the rest of the novel in a state of constant fear. Not only is he terrified that Walker will eventually catch him and kill him, but he also knows there's no one he can turn to for help, especially not the so-called justice system.

It might seem surprising to learn that Himes published this indictment of police corruption and brutality in the middle of also writing a highly influential series of police procedural novels featuring his two black homicide detectives Gravedigger Jones and Coffin Ed Johnson. What can explain this apparent contradiction?

Himes chooses black police officers to anchor his Harlem Domestic series because he was interested in exploring the tensions inherent in black men working for a system that, in Himes's opinion, is unambiguously racist. Because they work for the Man, Gravedigger, and Coffin Ed are not trusted by many residents of Harlem, despite the fact that they have a legendary reputation for both violence and getting to the bottom of whatever cases they're investigating.

But from the perspective of their white colleagues and superiors, Gravedigger and Coffin Ed are also not to be trusted, this time, because their success and effectiveness make them the targets of envy, resentment, and suspicion about the extra-legal methods they might use to achieve their results.

Himes finds several other ways to communicate the fact that although Gravedigger and Coffin Ed are in Harlem and care passionately about the welfare of the poor and vulnerable members of that community they are in some ways not of Harlem. For example, they live not in Harlem but in a predominantly white suburb on Long Island. This is a powerful symbol of how their status as detectives separates them ideologically as well as physically from Harlem.

It's also notable that Gravedigger and Coffin Ed have to rely extensively on informants and stool pigeons in order to do their job effectively. Why? Partly because they're so well-known in Harlem that they can't go anywhere without being recognized and partly because there's enough hostility directed toward them from Harlem residents that many people don't want to cooperate with them.

But the most significant and certainly the most serious way in which Himes demonstrates the difficulties and limitations of Gravedigger and Coffin Ed's situation as black police detectives in Harlem is the fate that he reserves for them by the end of the series. As its name implies, there's a sense in which Himes' Harlem Domestic series was always more about Harlem than it was about his detectives. Even the early novels in the series contain many episodes in which neither Gravedigger nor Coffin Ed are present.

As the series progresses, however, and especially as the political atmosphere in Harlem becomes more charged and militant as the 1950s give way to the 1960s, Gravedigger and Coffin Ed become more and more powerless and irrelevant. By the time we get to the last novel in the series, *Blind Man with a Pistol*, which was published in 1969, race riots have broken out in Harlem and Himes's ace police detectives are reduced to shooting rats as they escape a burning building rather than doing anything to control the chaos unfolding around them.

With all this in mind, it should come as no surprise that in *Plan B*, the last and unfinished novel in the series, published in France in 1983 but not appearing in English until 1993, Himes kills his detectives off as the ultimate sign that they have outlived their usefulness. The major violence in *Plan B* is committed not by Gravedigger and Coffin Ed but instead by the citizens of Harlem themselves as they rise up in an organized revolutionary movement in an attempt to overthrow the racist status quo.

The police procedural began as an attempt to introduce a new kind of realism to mystery and suspense fiction by focusing on the everyday work routines of law enforcement professionals in the novels of writers like Georges Simenon, John Creasey, and Ed McBain. By the time we get to Chester Himes, the police procedural has apparently been exhausted, overtaken by a level of violence that cannot be accommodated within the limits of the genre. According to Himes at least, that violence is capable of burning down not only the police procedural but also the cities in which it is customarily set.

NATIVE AMERICAN MYSTERIES

Native American writers have taken some traditional elements of mystery and suspense fiction and adapted them for their own purposes, demonstrating both the limits and the flexibility of the genre. In this lecture, we'll understand how many Native American mysteries complicate the spatial and thematic limits of traditional mystery and suspense fiction; incorporate mythical and cultural elements into the narratives; and provide an example of how the genre contemplates the meaning of justice.

TONY HILLERMAN

- One figure currently towers above every other writer in the field of Native American mystery and suspense fiction—and he's white, not Native American. Tony Hillerman was born in Sacred Heart, Oklahoma, in 1925. Growing up, most of Hillerman's playmates were children from the Potawatomi and Seminole tribes, and this experience gave him an early familiarity with Native American cultures.

- Hillerman served in World War II, where he was injured and received the Purple Heart. After being hospitalized for several months in France, he then returned to the United States and began working for a company that transported oil-field equipment. During this period, Hillerman visited a Navajo reservation where he witnessed the Enemy Way ceremony.

- The purpose of this ceremony, designed for members of the Navajo tribe who had served in the war, was to cleanse them of any negative influences resulting from the war. Hillerman later noted that witnessing this ceremony made him want to learn more about Navajo culture, which would later turn out to be a major part of his mystery fiction.

- For many years, Hillerman worked as a journalist; it wasn't until he was in his mid-40s that he began to write his first novel. The result of Hillerman's labors was *The Blessing Way*, which was published in 1970. The novel is significant for several reasons, some of which have to do with Hillerman's subsequent career and some of which are concerned with Hillerman's later influence on Native American mystery and suspense fiction as a whole.

JOE LEAPHORN

- Like many of Hillerman's later novels, *The Blessing Way* is set on a Navajo reservation, an area covering some 16 million acres in the Four Corners area, where New Mexico, Arizona, Utah, and Colorado meet.

- This setting is significant for a couple of reasons. Many of Hillerman's novels would later be praised for their exploration of the Native American cultures of the southwestern region of the United States and for their detailed and evocative descriptions of landscape. Hillerman's work is distinctive because it uses neither city nor rural settings. Moreover, given that Hillerman's mystery novels are police procedurals, the size and variety of the setting is also significant as it relates to police jurisdiction.

- In *The Blessing Way*, Hillerman introduces Joe Leaphorn, a detective in the Navajo Tribal Police. This might seem like an odd choice for a Native American mystery novel, as the police officer would be regarded by many as a default representative of the dominant power structure. In fact, however, Leaphorn and his colleagues in the Navajo Tribal Police often find themselves in conflict with other law enforcement organizations.

- This is where the issue of jurisdiction comes in. Because Hillerman uses the Four Corners setting, many of the cases that Leaphorn investigates necessarily cross state lines. This means that regular police departments can't investigate them due to jurisdictional limitations. The Navajo Tribal Police can, though—a fact that often leads to conflict.

- Much of Hillerman's work focuses on questions of identity and belonging. Leaphorn distinguishes himself throughout the series not only by his talents as a detective but also by his ability to move adroitly between the white and Native American cultures. He's able to occupy the liminal space between them, using that ability to his advantage.

STACE RED HAWK
- Unlike Tony Hillerman, some Native American writers turn to mystery and suspense fiction occasionally to address the concerns that animate their other work. Linda Hogan, for example, who was born in 1947 and is a member of the Chickasaw, is known primarily as a poet, although she has also written novels, short stories, plays, and essays.

- Despite writing in a variety of genres, Hogan addresses the same group of concerns in much of her work: environmentalism, social justice, the significance of nature, and the regenerative power of women. Hogan combines many of these concerns in her single mystery novel, *Mean Spirit*, which was published in 1990 and nominated for the Pulitzer Prize the following year.

- Hogan sets *Mean Spirit* in northeastern Oklahoma in the 1920s, during a period known as the Osage oil boom, which was triggered by the discovery of huge amounts of oil underneath land that was owned by Native Americans. Since the income from the oil was divided equally among all Osage tribe members, this meant that during this period, a white man could become

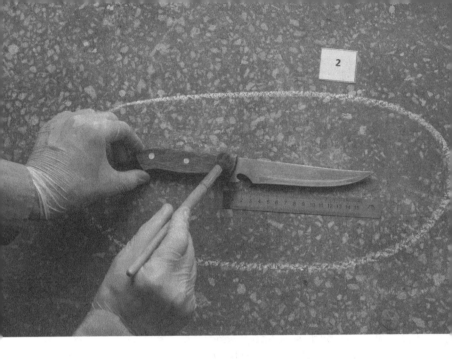

very rich by marrying an Osage woman. Against this historical background, Hogan tells the story of two families, the Blankets and the Grayclouds.

- Thanks to the oil boom, Grace Blanket has become the richest woman in town, but this leads to her murder by a group of white men who want her wealth. Because Grace's daughter, Nola, witnessed the murder, she is now in danger and is sent to live with the Graycloud family. When members of that family start dying off in mysterious circumstances, the desperate family writes to the federal government in Washington, D.C., begging for help.

- Help comes in the somewhat unlikely form of Stace Red Hawk, a Lakota Sioux who works for the FBI. In fact, when Red Hawk first enters the narrative, we have good cause to wonder where exactly his loyalties lie. Ultimately, the situation in Osage territory will force Red Hawk to choose sides. As his investigation gradually uncovers an elaborate scheme involving intimidation, fraud, and murder, Red Hawk not only solves the mystery but also comes to feel an increasing degree of closeness to both the other Native American characters and to the land.

SHERMAN ALEXIE

- Although Native American author Sherman Alexie has written in a number of different genres, his single mystery narrative is quite different from the rest of his work. Sherman Alexie was born in 1966 in Spokane, Washington, and grew up on a Spokane reservation. Alexie is of mixed ancestry—his father was a member of the Coeur d'Alene tribe, while his mother was of Colville, Choctaw, Spokane, and European American ancestry.

- According to critic Sarah Quirk, Alexie asks the same series of questions in all his work: "What does it mean to live as an Indian in this time? What does it mean to be an Indian man? Finally, what does it mean to live on an Indian reservation?"

- A wonderful sense of humor pervades much of Alexie's work—a humor that arises from an appreciation of both the absurdity of life and the importance of humor as a survival mechanism for Native Americans. As Quirk explains, for Alexie, humor is "a means of cultural survival for American Indians—survival in the face of the larger American culture's stereotypes of American Indians and their concomitant distillation of individual tribal characteristics into one pan-Indian consciousness."

INDIAN KILLER

- Alexie's sole mystery novel, *Indian Killer*, is distinctly different from the rest of his oeuvre. Rejecting the humor that characterizes so much of the rest of his work, in this novel, Alexie is at his angriest.

- Published in 1996, *Indian Killer* tells the story of a young Native American man named John Smith—a deeply ironic name because John Smith was the English soldier and explorer who is famous for helping found Jamestown, the first permanent English settlement in North America.

- Filled with anger, Smith becomes convinced that at the end of the 20th century, Native Americans had become too docile and as a result whites were no longer afraid of them. In Alexie's chilling words, "John wanted to change that. He wanted to see fear in every pair of blue eyes." Smith embarks on a murder spree in which he kills white men at random and also scalps them.

- And yet, we never actually see John Smith commit any murders. Although he talks and thinks obsessively about wanting to do so, we never see him come into contact with the victims. What's more, the investigative part of the narrative is told from a third-person point of view that gives nothing away about who the actual perpetrator might be. The identity of the killer remains a mystery at the end of the book.

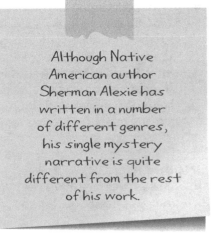

Although Native American author Sherman Alexie has written in a number of different genres, his single mystery narrative is quite different from the rest of his work.

- At this point, we begin to appreciate just how subversive Alexie's use of the mystery novel is. Upending our typical assumptions about guilt, innocence, and justice, the inconclusiveness of *Indian Killer*'s ending encourages us to look in the mirror and examine ourselves rather than making John Smith the scapegoat—no matter how superficially satisfying that ending might be.

TAY-BODAL

- Mardi Oakley Medawar makes a highly valuable and entertaining contribution to Native American mystery and suspense fiction. She is of Cherokee descent and was born in Louisiana. Medawar has published one mystery novel with a contemporary setting, *Murder on the Red Cliff Rez*, set on the Red Cliff reservation in Wisconsin. The majority of her mystery novels, however, are set in the 19th century and deal mostly with the Kiowa and Crow tribes.

- Medawar's historical mysteries are known collectively as the Tay-Bodal Mystery series, named after the series' protagonist. Although the series takes place during the period of Indian removal and the realization of the ideology of manifest destiny, the series is suffused with both humor and an optimism about the ability of Native Americans to survive.

- Much of this humor and optimism is generated by Tay-bodal, who, while unmistakably Native American, also possesses elements of the classic detectives of old. For example, like C. Auguste Dupin and Sherlock Holmes, Tay-bodal is something of an outsider in the Kiowa tribe. More interested in healing, herbs, medicine, and the mysteries of the human body than in tribal councils and war parties, Tay-bodal is regarded as extremely eccentric by his fellow tribe members.

- And yet Tay-bodal proves to be a highly successful detective. Through the character of Tay-bodal, Medawar is able to combine commentary about key events in the history of the American West with fundamental information about Native American cultures.

QUESTIONS TO CONSIDER

1. How do Native American mysteries address issues of social justice?

2. What is distinctive about the use of setting and space in many Native American examples of the genre?

SUGGESTED READING

Browne, *Murder on the Reservation.*

Macdonald, Macdonald, and Sheridan, *Shaman or Sherlock?*

NATIVE AMERICAN MYSTERIES

Native American mystery and suspense writers remain understudied, but they are a crucial example of how the genre is able to explore new settings, examine the limits of more traditional examples of the genre, and contemplate the meaning of justice. For example, just as some African-American writers consider the context of slavery in their mystery and suspense narratives, so some Native American writers contemplate the meaning of crime and justice when considered against the background of Native American genocide.

In addition, many Native American mysteries complicate the spatial and thematic limits of traditional mystery and suspense fiction by using settings that span several states, as well as incorporating mythical and cultural elements that aren't found in many other examples of the genre. In these ways, Native American mystery and suspense fiction writers take some traditional elements of the genre and adapt them for their own purposes, demonstrating both the limits and the flexibility of the genre.

One figure currently towers above every other writer in the field of Native American mystery and suspense fiction, and he's not Native American but white. I'm referring to Tony Hillerman, who was born in Sacred Heart, Oklahoma, in 1925. Hillerman and his siblings were among a very small number of white children who attended a school in Sacred Heart called St. Mary's Academy, which was actually a boarding school for Native American girls. Growing up, most of Hillerman's playmates were children from the Potawatomi and Seminole tribes, and this experience gave him an early familiarity with Native American cultures.

Hillerman served as a mortar gunner in World War II, where he was injured and received the Purple Heart. After being hospitalized for several months in France, he then returned to the U.S. and began working for a company that transported oil-field equipment. During this period, Hillerman visited a Navajo reservation where he witnessed the Enemy Way ceremony.

This ceremony was designed for members of the Navajo tribe who had served in the war, and its purpose was to cleanse them of any negative influences they had encountered during their wartime experiences. Hillerman later said that witnessing this ceremony made him want to learn more about Navajo culture, which would later turn out to be a major part of his mystery fiction.

Hillerman had always wanted to write fiction. For many years he worked as a journalist, but it wasn't until the late 1960s, when he was in his mid-40s, that he began to write his first novel. Although Hillerman later said he'd always wanted to write a mainstream novel, he decided to write a mystery novel because he thought it would be an easier sell for a first-time author.

The result of Hillerman's labors was *The Blessing Way*, which was published in 1970. The novel is significant for several reasons, some of which have to do with Hillerman's subsequent career, and some of which are concerned with Hillerman's later influence on Native American mystery and suspense fiction as a whole.

First of all, let's consider the setting. Like many of Hillerman's later novels, *The Blessing Way* is set on the Navajo reservation, an area covering some 16 million acres in what is known as the Four Corners area, where the states of New Mexico, Arizona, Utah, and Colorado meet.

This setting is significant for a couple of reasons. Many of Hillerman's novels would later be praised for their exploration of the Native American cultures of the southwestern region of the United States and for their detailed and evocative descriptions of landscape. This means that Hillerman's work is distinctive compared to most other examples of the genre because it uses neither city nor rural settings. Instead, a typical Hillerman novel ranges over a much larger and more various landscape, which is one of the reasons his work is so appealing and popular with so many readers.

Moreover, given that Hillerman's mystery novels are police procedurals—which I'll say more about in a moment—the size and variety of the setting is also significant for more pragmatic reasons having to do with police jurisdiction. In *The Blessing Way*, Hillerman introduces Joe Leaphorn, who would go on to become one of his two main series characters. Leaphorn is a detective in the Navajo Tribal Police, which at first glance might seem like an odd choice for a Native American mystery novel.

Why? For the same reason that it's odd that African-American writer Chester Himes would have chosen to write a series of police procedural novels featuring black detectives. In as much as police officers would be regarded by many as default representatives of the dominant—i.e., white—power structure, why would Himes and Hillerman want to make their protagonists cops?

In Himes's case, the reason has to do with his desire to explore the tensions inherent in black men working for a system that is inherently racist. And I believe there's some of the same impulse present in Hillerman's decision. More significant, however, is the fact that Leaphorn and his colleagues in the Navajo Tribal Police often find themselves in conflict with, rather than working hand in hand with, other law enforcement organizations.

This is where we come back to the issue of jurisdiction. Because Hillerman uses the Four Corners setting, many of the cases that Leaphorn investigates necessarily cross state lines. This means that regular police departments can't investigate them due to jurisdictional limitations. The Navajo Tribal Police can, though—a fact that often leads to conflict. Leaphorn and his colleagues often also find themselves at odds with the FBI, who are not bound by jurisdictional limitations either, but who, from Leaphorn's point of view, often try to take over his investigations, ignoring the fact that the Navajo reservation is sovereign territory.

We can see from the preceding discussion how creatively Hillerman is able to use some of the defining features of the police procedural genre to address larger questions involving conflict between white American and Native American cultures. And this brings us to another reason that *The Blessing Way* is significant.

As in many of his later works, Hillerman's debut novel features a Navajo character who is caught between two cultures, and who belongs to neither of them completely. The character is named Luis Horseman, and at one point Leaphorn thinks to himself about Horseman, "Just another poor soul who didn't quite know how to be a Navajo and couldn't learn to act like a white."

This remark is typical of the way in which much of Hillerman's work focuses on questions of identity and belonging. Leaphorn distinguishes himself throughout the series not only by his abilities as a detective but also by his ability to move adroitly between the white and Native American cultures. He's able to occupy the liminal space between them, and he frequently uses that ability to his advantage.

In this respect, it's interesting to compare Leaphorn to Hillerman's other main series character, Jim Chee, another Navajo tribal policeman who is first introduced to readers in Hillerman's 1980 novel, *People of Darkness*. Not only is he some 20 years younger than Leaphorn, but he's also, in Hillerman's words, "less culturally assimilated" than his colleague in the sense that his indigenous religious beliefs are much more traditional.

Beginning with his 1986 novel *Skinwalkers*, which marks the first time the two series protagonists appear in the same book, Hillerman uses the differences between them to develop both characters in more detail. He also inaugurates what would become an ongoing emphasis on generational differences between the two men, which in turn Hillerman uses to reflect on the complexities and changes in Navajo identity that take place over the course of the novels.

Before moving on to look at other Native American mystery and suspense narratives, we need to consider one final aspect of Hillerman's work that makes it extremely influential on other writers. Despite the significance of *The Blessing Way*, Hillerman once said that he found it quite an embarrassing book to look back on because it's filled with inaccuracies about Navajo culture. As a result of diligent and exhaustive research on his part, Hillerman largely avoided this problem in his other books.

Consequently, many of the novels featuring Leaphorn and Chee also possess a valuable pedagogic dimension for non–Native American readers who can learn a great deal about Native American cultures and about issues impacting Native Americans from reading them.

For example, in *Skinwalkers*, Chee—who, as usual, is concerned about conflicts between his Navajo identity and white culture—completes his training and becomes a *yataalii*; a singer qualified to conduct Navajo religious rites such as the Blessing Way and the Enemy Way. In the process, the reader learns a lot about these ceremonies.

And in such novels as *A Thief of Time*, which was published in 1988 and was Hillerman's own favorite among his many books, and *Talking God*, which came out in 1989, Hillerman explores a wide range of issues of concern to contemporary Native Americans, including the theft of Native American artifacts and the refusal of some museums to return Native American skeletons in their collections to tribal members.

Over the course of a long, prolific, and successful career, then, Tony Hillerman set the bar very high for other authors of Native American mystery and suspense fiction. How did they respond? The short answer to the question is, given the diversity of Native American cultures, in a variety of ways.

Unlike Tony Hillerman, the vast majority of whose work consists of mysteries, other writers have only turned to mystery and suspense fiction occasionally to address the concerns that animate their other work. Linda Hogan, for example, who was born in 1947 and is a member of the Chickasaw Nation, is known primarily as a poet—although she has also written novels, short stories, plays, and essays.

Despite writing in a variety of genres, Hogan addresses the same group of concerns in much of her work—environmentalism, social justice, what nature can teach human beings, and the regenerative power of women. Hogan combines many of these concerns in her single mystery novel, *Mean Spirit*, which was published in 1990 and nominated for the Pulitzer Prize in Fiction the following year.

Hogan sets *Mean Spirit* in northeastern Oklahoma in the 1920s, during a period known as the Osage Oil Boom, but which the Osage themselves call the Reign of Terror or the Great Frenzy. The boom was triggered by the discovery of huge amounts of oil underneath land that was owned by Native Americans.

Since the income from the oil was divided equally among all Osage tribe members, this meant that during this period a white man could become very rich from marrying an Osage woman. In fact, in *Mean Spirit*, Hogan quotes directly from an actual letter written by a white man in Missouri to an Indian agent in Oklahoma asking the agent to help him find an Osage wife. Part of the letter reads as follows: "not a full blood, but one as near white as possible." In exchange for helping him find a woman, the man offers to pay a fee. "For every $5,000 she is worth, I will give you $25." Against this historical background of white greed and exploitation of Native Americans in general, and Native American women in particular, in *Mean Spirit*, Hogan tells the story of two families—the Blankets and the Grayclouds.

Thanks to the oil boom, Grace Blanket has become the richest woman in town, but this leads to her murder by a group of white men who want her wealth. Because Grace's daughter, Nola, witnessed the murder, she is now in danger and is sent to live with the Graycloud family to protect her. When members of that family start dying off in mysterious circumstances, the desperate family writes to the federal government in Washington, D.C., begging for help.

Help comes in the somewhat unlikely form of Stace Red Hawk, a Lakota Sioux who works for the U.S. Bureau of Investigation. Why do I say unlikely? Well, Tony Hillerman's Jim Chee rejects the possibility of becoming an FBI agent even though he's been accepted into the FBI Academy because he doubts that he can be both Navajo and a representative of the federal government. So, when Red Hawk first enters the narrative, we have good cause to wonder where exactly his loyalties lie.

And indeed, it turns out that Red Hawk does feel some conflict between his two identities. Ultimately, the situation in Osage territory will force Red Hawk to choose sides. As his investigation gradually uncovers an elaborate scheme involving intimidation, fraud, and murder, Red Hawk not only solves the mystery but also comes to feel an increasing degree of closeness to both the other Native American characters and to the land.

I'm aware that if you haven't read *Mean Spirit*, then this narrative resolution might sound a little too pat and hokey. But it works, and the reason it works is because Hogan is accomplished at describing Native American beliefs and values in such a way that they constitute a persuasive and much healthier alternative to the violence, materialism, and greed that define the dominant culture.

By using the form of the historical mystery in *Mean Spirit*, Hogan is able to go back in time and explore an episode that still resonates for Native Americans and whites today. In fact, if anything, the deeply moral choice between exploiting the resources of the land and the people who live on that land on the one hand, and finding a way to live in harmony with nature on the other is even more relevant in the 21st century than it was in the 1920s. In this way, Hogan reminds us of how effective mystery and suspense fiction can be in dramatizing issues of justice not just in the narrow legal sense, but also in a much broader and more ethical sense.

Sherman Alexie is another good example of a Native American author who writes in a number of different genres, and who has written a single mystery narrative to explore questions of identity and social justice. But as we'll see, Alexie's mystery novel isn't just very different from Hogan's *Mean Spirit*, it's also quite different from the rest of Alexie's work.

Sherman Alexie was born in 1966 in Spokane, Washington, and grew up on the Spokane Reservation. Alexie is of mixed ancestry—his father was a member of the Coeur d'Alene tribe, while his mother was of Colville, Choctaw, Spokane, and European American ancestry. Due to major surgery he had to have as a small child, and the resulting side effects, Alexie was unable to participate in many of the rituals that mark the maturation of a young Native American man. And so he grew up a somewhat solitary child, with a reputation for devouring any book he could get his hands on.

Alexie's writing career began with the publication in 1992 of his first collection of poems entitled *The Business of Fancydancing*. Since then, he's published many other collections of poems but is also well-known for his short stories. His first collection of stories, *The Lone Ranger and Tonto Fistfight in Heaven*, was published in 1993. Alexie would revisit some of the characters in this collection in his first novel, *Reservation Blues*, which came out in 1995.

As this brief summary indicates, Alexie is a prolific author who writes in a variety of genres. But according to critic Sarah Quirk, Alexie asks the same series of questions in all of his work—What does it mean to live as an Indian in this time? What does it mean to be an Indian man? Finally, what does it mean to live on an Indian reservation?

Alexie's answers to these questions are both honest and painful, but rarely optimistic. Throughout his work, his characters struggle with feelings of powerlessness and exclusion in relation to white society, a struggle that often results in various forms of self-destructive behavior, especially alcoholism.

And yet, if these words suggest that Alexie's work is characterized by sadness, in fact, a wonderful sense of humor pervades much of his work. Some of this humor comes from his frequent use of pop culture references, especially pop cultural appropriations of Native Americans. But it also comes from an appreciation of both the absurdity of life and the importance of humor as a survival mechanism for Native Americans.

As Quirk explains, for Alexie, humor is "a means of cultural survival for American Indians—survival in the face of the larger American culture's stereotypes of American Indians and their concomitant distillation of individual tribal characteristics into one pan-Indian consciousness."

I've done my best to reconstruct the outline and tenor of Alexie's work not only as a way of encouraging you to explore that work, but also to emphasize how different his only mystery novel, *Indian Killer*, is from the rest of his oeuvre. Rejecting the humor that characterizes so much of the rest of his work, in this novel Alexie is at his angriest.

Published in 1996, *Indian Killer* tells the story of a young Native American man ironically named John Smith. How is this ironic? Because Alexie's character shares a name with the English soldier and explorer who is famous for helping found Jamestown, the first permanent English settlement in North America.

Alexie's John Smith got his name because he was adopted by a white American couple, a fact that accentuates how cut off Smith is from his own Native culture. This is accentuated even more when we learn that Smith has no idea who his birth parents are, and consequently has no idea tribe he belongs to.

Filled with anger by both his own treatment and the treatment of other Native Americans at the hands of whites, Smith becomes convinced that at the end of the 20th century, Native Americans have become too docile and as a result, whites are no longer afraid of them. In Alexie's chilling words, "John wanted to change that. He wanted to see fear in every pair of blue eyes."

Consequently, Smith embarks on a murder spree in which he kills white men at random and also scalps them. Alexie reverses the assumed meaning of the book's title *Indian Killer*, which most readers—at least before reading the book—would assume refers to someone who kills Indians. Instead, we realize that Alexie is using the term to mean an Indian who kills.

And yet, here's the twist, we never actually see John Smith commit any murders. Although he talks and thinks obsessively about wanting to do so, we never see him come into contact with the victims, and the investigative part of the narrative is told from a third-person point of view that gives nothing away about who the actual perpetrator might be.

And at the end of the novel, Smith kills himself by jumping off a skyscraper, so we never get a chance to find out the truth from him. Moreover, Alexie never confirms whether or not Smith is the killer, and so the identity of the killer remains a mystery when we finish the book.

Why does Alexie do this? The best way of answering this question is to contemplate how we'd feel if Alexie had confirmed that Smith was the killer. Without the ambiguity concerning whether or not Smith was the murderer, *Indian Killer* becomes a less complex and less interesting book. We may or may not feel sympathy for Smith's anger and frustration at the situation of Native Americans, but very few of us would endorse Smith's actions, no matter how sympathetic we feel.

But because we don't know one way or another, we're left to ponder another question: Why did we assume that Smith was indeed the killer? Partly because Alexie did everything in his power to make us think that. But perhaps also because, we might think to ourselves, something about the idea of a bloodthirsty Indian killing white men at random just makes sense to us.

At this point, we begin to appreciate just how subversive Alexie's use of the mystery novel is. Upending our typical assumptions about guilt, innocence, and justice, the inconclusiveness of *Indian Killer*'s conclusion encourages us to look in the mirror and examine ourselves rather than making John Smith the scapegoat, no matter how superficially satisfying that ending might appear to be.

Alexie sets *Indian Killer* in the present and in the urban setting of Seattle as a way of emphasizing the fact that Native American issues are still very much relevant and pressing today, and not something that can be safely confined to the past.

The last author I want to discuss in this lecture, Mardi Oakley Medawar, takes a very different approach to these issues but is still able to make a valuable and entertaining contribution to Native American mystery and suspense fiction.

Medawar is of Cherokee descent and was born in Louisiana. She's published one mystery novel with a contemporary setting, *Murder on the Red Cliff Rez*, which was published in 2002 and is set on the Red Cliff Reservation in Wisconsin, where Medawar now lives. The majority of her mystery novels, however, are set in the 19th century and deal mostly with the Kiowa and Crow tribes.

Medawar's historical mysteries are known collectively as the "Tay-Bodal Series" and are named after the series' protagonist. Beginning with the publication of *Death at Rainy Mountain* in 1996. The series also consists of *Witch of the Palo Duro*, *Murder at Medicine Lodge*, and concludes with *The Ft. Larned Incident*, which was published in 2000.

Although the series takes place during the period of Indian Removal and the realization of the ideology of Manifest Destiny, the series is suffused with both humor and an optimism about the ability of Native American ways to survive. Much of this humor and optimism is generated by Tay-Bodal, who while unmistakably Native American also possesses elements of the classical detectives of old.

For example, like Auguste Dupin and Sherlock Holmes, Tay-Bodal is something of an outsider in relation to the Kiowa tribe he's a member of. More interested in healing, herbs, medicine, and the mysteries of the human body than in tribal councils and war parties, Tay-Bodal is regarded as being very eccentric by his fellow tribe members.

And yet, throughout the mysteries he appears in, Tay-Bodal proves his worth, whether it's by solving the murder of a candidate for the position of tribal chief or by clearing the name of Kiowa chief White Bear after a U.S. soldier is murdered during treaty talks. Through the character of Tay-Bodal, Medawar is able to combine commentary about key events in the history of the American West with information about Native American cultures.

This combination has, in one way or another, characterized the work of every writer we've looked at in this lecture. The variety of their work reminds us that there is no one infallible or correct way to manage the interaction between Native American history and culture on the one hand, and mystery and suspense fiction on the other. Like both African-American and Latino varieties of the genre, examples of Native American mystery and suspense fiction are extremely adept at exploring issues of cultural identity and interaction. In doing so, they add a thought-provoking and valuable dimension to the genre as a whole.

THE EUROPEAN MYSTERY TRADITION

U nlike many Anglo-American critics, Europeans regarded mystery and suspense fiction as a legitimate and serious form of literature. American hard-boiled mystery fiction in particular was enormously popular and influential throughout Europe. Albert Camus, for example, noted that he used James M. Cain's *The Postman Always Rings Twice* as a model for his existentialist novel *The Stranger*. Similarly, André Gide, celebrated French novelist and winner of the Nobel Prize, was a great admirer of Dashiell Hammett's work. In this lecture, we'll explore the richness and variety of European mystery and suspense fiction—a legacy inherited from the British and the Americans.

SÉRIE NOIRE

- In 1931, Belgian writer Georges Simenon began publishing the first of what would eventually be 75 novels and 28 stories featuring Inspector Maigret. While the Maigret novels are technically police procedurals, Simenon's works owe a significant debt to writers such as Sir Arthur Conan Doyle and Agatha Christie.

- Like Sherlock Holmes and Hercule Poirot before him, the figure of Maigret dominates his narratives, a fact that makes him closer to the archetype of the great amateur detective than to the relatively anonymous member of a law enforcement organization.

- A landmark year in French mystery and suspense fiction was 1945, when Marcel Duhamel founded the imprint Série noire, which was dedicated to publishing translations of American hard-boiled writers such as James M. Cain, Dashiell Hammett, and Raymond Chandler. Consequently, the work of these writers became very popular and influential in France.

BOILEAU-NARCEJAC

- Boileau-Narcejac is the collective nom de plume of Pierre Boileau and Pierre Ayraud, or Thomas Narcejac. Beginning in 1952, Boileau-Narcejac published many successful thrillers, many of which revolved around elaborate murder conspiracies and explored interpersonal relationships and questions of identity.

- Boileau-Narcejac also published a series of detective novels for young readers known as the Sans Atout series, about a young boy detective. What's more, Boileau-Narcejac wrote five authorized sequels to Maurice Leblanc's series about the gentleman thief Arsène Lupin.

- Their best-known work, however, consists of two novels that were adapted into famous films. *She Who Was No More* was adapted by the noted film director Henri-Georges Clouzot and released under the title *Les diaboliques* in 1955. Boileau-Narcejac's 1954 novel *D'entre les morts* subsequently became the basis for Alfred Hitchcock's 1959 film *Vertigo*.

FRIEDRICH DÜRRENMATT

- Born in 1921, Swiss writer Friedrich Dürrenmatt was known primarily as a playwright whose work often reflected on World War II. But he was also the author of philosophical crime novels, including *The Judge and His Hangman* and *Suspicion*, both of which deal with Swiss complicity with the Nazis.

- These novels feature Inspector Bärlach, a Swiss police officer who was sent to work in Germany in the early 1930s but who returned to Switzerland after a dispute with a Hitler official. Dürrenmatt uses Bärlach to explore the moral consequences of Switzerland's neutrality during World War II, a policy that Dürrenmatt regarded as a lie.

- In his 1958 novel *The Pledge*, Dürrenmatt makes possibly his greatest contribution to mystery fiction. Tellingly subtitled *Requiem for the Detective Novel*, *The Pledge* systematically undoes the moral certainties of mystery fiction by showing how Matthias, a retired homicide detective, uses a young girl as bait in an attempt to capture a killer who has eluded him for years. In Dürrenmatt's hands, mystery fiction becomes almost the antithesis of justice and resolution rather than its apotheosis.

INFLUENCE ON EDGAR ALLAN POE

- Mystery and suspense fiction in Germany has a venerable history. The well-known E. T. A. Hoffmann novella *Mademoiselle von Scudéri*, published in 1819, is a crime story in which Scudéri plays a detective role, an innocent person is exonerated, and a villain is captured. A number of critics have argued that Hoffmann's story was an important influence on Edgar Allan Poe when he came to write his mystery tales in the 1840s.

- Probably better known to English-speaking readers, however, is Erich Kästner, who published *Emil and the Detectives* in 1929, launching an enormously popular children's series.

- It took German mystery and suspense fiction writers a considerable period of time to figure out how to address the experience and the legacy of World War II in their work. According to the critic Katharina Hall, "German reunification in 1990 prompted a wide-ranging public discussion about the country's uneasy double past of fascism and communism." Thanks to this discussion, Germany is currently in the middle of a boom in historical mystery fiction.

It Happened in Berlin

- Beginning in 2007 and now consisting of dozens of novels, the series collectively titled It Happened in Berlin uses the investigations of a German police inspector to chart the complex history of Germany over the course of the 20th century.

- The project, which was dreamed up by well-known German crime writer and sociologist Horst Bosetzky, has been dubbed a *Kettenroman*, or chain novel, because the series is actually written by a collective of authors, with Bosetzky doing the editing. Once completed, the series will constitute an exhaustive chronicle of Germany's recent history, with Berlin at its center.

- Even German writers primarily known for writing literary fiction have found the mystery and suspense fiction genre a useful way of exploring a range of issues. Bernhard Schlink has written a trilogy of novels that feature a detective named Self and deal with Germany's past history.

THE ANTI-DETECTIVE NOVEL

- Italian mystery and suspense fiction has addressed issues of importance to Italian society and culture. Not surprisingly, the impact of organized crime and the Mafia are at the top of that list. Although there were a few mystery writers working in Italy in the 19th century, the genre didn't really take off until 1929, when the publishing house Mondadori began to publish translations of American and British mysteries.

- Mondadori's books were distinguished by their yellow covers; for this reason, they became known as *i libri gialli*, meaning "yellow books." Eventually, *giallo* became a shorthand term for the crime fiction genre as a whole, a term that eventually expanded to include films, especially horror and suspense films.

- Thanks to the popularity of Mondadori's *gialli* translations, some Italian writers started producing their own works of mystery and suspense fiction. Unfortunately, the genre was first curtailed and then banned outright in 1943 by Benito Mussolini's fascist government, who felt that it was unpatriotic in the way it portrayed the state.

- After World War II ended, however, the popularity of the genre grew rapidly. A particularly significant author during this period was Carlo Emilio Gadda, whose 1957 novel *That Awful Mess on Via Merulana* was set in fascist Italy of the 1920s and provided a searing commentary on that period of Italian history. Gadda's work, which influenced many

> Even German writers primarily known for writing literary fiction have found the mystery and suspense fiction genre a useful way of exploring a range of issues.

later authors, came to be known as the anti-detective novel, which referred to a type of crime fiction where the solution is either highly ambiguous or altogether absent.

THE NAME OF THE ROSE

- A significant example of Italian anti-mystery fiction is Umberto Eco's celebrated 1980 novel *The Name of the Rose*. As befits a crime novel from Eco, who was a widely known postmodern literary theorist, this novel combines semiotics, philosophy, medieval studies, and biblical analysis with an old-fashioned murder mystery set in a 14th-century Italian monastery.

- The novel's protagonist, a Franciscan friar named William of Baskerville, travels to a monastery in northern Italy with his assistant, Adso of Melk, to attend a theological disputation. Once there, William learns that a suspicious death has recently occurred, which is soon followed by other deaths at the monastery. The abbot asks William to investigate the killings, which seem to revolve around the existence of a fabled book thought to have been lost: the Greek philosopher Aristotle's writings on comedy. At the novel's climax, William tries but fails to find this book in the monastery's labyrinthine library.

- As this brief summary suggests, *The Name of the Rose* is a highly self-reflexive novel, not only in the way that it is a book about books, but also in the sense that it is a mystery novel filled with allusions to other mystery novels. Following are two examples: William of Baskerville's name is an obvious tribute to Sir Arthur Conan Doyle's Sherlock Holmes novel *The Hound of the Baskervilles*, while the library labyrinth is a more elliptical nod to the work of the great Argentinean author of experimental mystery fiction, Jorge Luis Borges.

SOCIAL COMMENTARY

- Less well known than Eco but probably more important to Italian crime fiction is Leonardo Sciascia, who was born in Sicily in 1921. Sciascia has combined the Mafia, crime, and Italian politics together in a series of best-selling books—a fact that has made him a high-profile and controversial character.

- In Sciascia's 1971 novel *Equal Danger*, a detective is sent to Sicily to investigate a series of murders of judges. Sciascia focuses on how and why the authorities are both unable and unwilling to conduct such investigations properly because of their own corruption. Not surprisingly, the detective fails to solve this case, which illustrates the extent to which many of Sciascia's novels can also be described as anti-detective novels.

- Andrea Camilleri, another writer based in Sicily, enjoyed a long career as a film and theater director before writing novels. In 1994, he published *The Shape of Water*, the first in what would become a long series of novels featuring Inspector Montalbano, a police detective in the police force of Vigàta, an imaginary Sicilian town.

- One of the most notable features of Camilleri's Montalbano novels is the way in which they persistently and aggressively address a variety of social problems in contemporary Italy. Indeed, Camilleri has remarked that social commentary was "always my aim."

MANUEL VÁZQUEZ MONTALBÁN

- Montalbano's name is an homage to the writer Manuel Vázquez Montalbán, the dean of Spanish mystery writers. Like the other countries we've looked at in this lecture, Spain has had a long and fractious history when it comes to mystery and suspense fiction. In general, the genre had to wait until after the fall of the Franco regime in 1975 to truly come into its own.

■ During this period, a number of authors came to the fore, but Montalbán and his fictional private detective Pepe Carvalho are undoubtedly at the head of the pack. Carvalho is a rich and complex character who combines elements of the classic detective and the hard-boiled detective. Beginning in 1972 with the publication of *I Killed Kennedy*, Montalbán uses Carvalho to explore various aspects of Spanish society in the last half of the 20th century.

QUESTIONS TO CONSIDER

1. How does European mystery and suspense fiction combine experimentation with social commentary?

2. Do examples of the genre from different European countries have anything in common? If so, what?

SUGGESTED READING

Forshaw, *Euro Noir*.

Geherin, *The Dragon Tattoo and Its Long Tail*.

THE EUROPEAN MYSTERY TRADITION

D id you know that mystery and suspense fiction began in Europe? Not literally, because Edgar Allan Poe was living in the United States when he wrote the three mystery tales that inaugurated the genre. But certainly metaphorically, in the sense that each one of those tales—"The Murders in the Rue Morgue," "The Mystery of Marie Rogêt," and "The Purloined Letter"—was set in France.

Why did Poe choose a French setting and a French detective to launch a new genre? The jury is still out on that question. It may have had something to do with the fact that Poe felt Paris possessed an air of romance and mystery that American cities of the 1840s lacked. Or it may have been simply a result of a calculation on Poe's part that a foreign setting might make the stories more appealing to readers.

Whatever the reason, it turned out to be a very appropriate choice because France in particular and Europe, in general, have a long history of taking mystery and suspense fiction more seriously than many Anglo-American readers and critics.

Albert Camus, for example, once said that he used James M. Cain's *The Postman Always Rings Twice* as a model when he was writing his classic existentialist novel *The Stranger*. Similarly, famous French novelist and winner of the Nobel Prize André Gide was a big fan of Dashiell Hammett's work, saying of *Red Harvest* that it was a remarkable achievement, the last word in atrocity, cynicism, and horror.

Thanks to praise from literary giants like Camus and Gide, who clearly regarded mystery and suspense fiction as a legitimate and serious form of literature, American hard-boiled mystery fiction, in particular, was enormously popular and influential throughout Europe, and consequently, the genre has a long and complicated history in this region.

Although it's impossible to do justice to this history in the space of a single lecture, what I can do is give you a sense of the richness and variety of European mystery fiction. In the process, we'll see exactly what European writers did to the legacy of mystery and suspense fiction that they inherited from their Anglo-American cousins.

As I've already indicated, the logical place to begin our journey is France. Although examples of mystery and suspense fiction had been published in France prior to 1931, that year changed everything because that's when Georges Simenon began publishing the first of what would eventually be 75 novels and 28 stories featuring Inspector Maigret.

Technically speaking, the Maigret novels are police procedurals. Maigret is a police inspector, most of the novels follow the details of Maigret's investigations quite closely, and the novels also include Maigret's work colleagues as series characters. Nevertheless, I think it's more accurate to describe Simenon's invention as owing a significant debt to writers like Sir Arthur Conan Doyle and Agatha Christie.

Like Sherlock Holmes and Hercule Poirot before him, the figure of Maigret dominates the narratives in which he appears, which makes him closer to the archetype of the Great Amateur Detective, rather than relatively anonymous member of a law enforcement organization. Maigret deservedly occupies a place near the top of the genre's pantheon of famous detectives.

After the first appearance of Maigret in 1931, the next landmark year in French mystery and suspense fiction comes in 1945 when Marcel Duhamel, an editor at the prestigious French publishing house of Gallimard, founded the imprint Série Noire. This new imprint was dedicated to publishing translations of American hard-boiled writers like Cain, Hammett, and Chandler, and the work of these writers consequently became very popular and influential in France.

An early sign of this influence is an extraordinary novel published in 1946 by Boris Vian, writing under the pseudonym of Vernon Sullivan, called *I Spit on Your Graves*. Although not published by Série Noire, Vian's novel is exactly the kind of work that Duhamel wanted to encourage. Boris Vian was born in Paris in 1920 and died at the age of 39 while heckling the premiere of a film version of *I Spit on Your Graves*. Vian wrote the novel in two weeks after accepting a bet that he could write a best-seller in that amount of time. Vian won the bet, the book was a huge success and also hugely controversial. Why?

Vian used the pseudonym Vernon Sullivan but also wrote an introduction to the novel under his own name in which he explained that Sullivan was an African-American writer whose work was too controversial to be published in the United States. Graves tells the story of Lee Anderson, a light-skinned black man who leaves town after his brother is lynched. Able to pass as white, Anderson seeks revenge for his brother's murder by seducing and then murdering two rich white sisters. The novel ends with Anderson being shot dead by the police and then being hanged by the local townspeople for good measure.

The success of Graves demonstrates not only the market for sensational hard-boiled American crime fiction in post–World War II France but also the fact that the French would believe practically anything about the United States. African-American expatriate writer Chester Himes would take advantage of this fact when he began writing and publishing his absurdly over-the-top crime novels in France in the 1950s, but in the meantime, there was also plenty of inventive and challenging mystery and suspense fiction being written by French writers using French settings.

A good example is the long and prolific career of Boileau-Narcejac, the collective nom de plume of Pierre Boileau and Pierre Ayraud, aka Thomas Narcejac. Before ever working together, both these men had individually won the Prix du Roman d'Aventures, awarded each year for the best work of detective fiction. Coincidentally, both their winning novels were "locked room" mysteries. When they started working together, they became even more successful.

Beginning in 1952 with the publication of *Celle qui n'était plus* published in translation as *The Woman Who Was No More*, as Boileau-Narcejac they published many successful thrillers, many of which revolved around elaborate murder conspiracies and explored interpersonal relationships and questions of identity.

They also published a series of detective novels for young readers known as the Sans Atout series, about a young boy detective, and five authorized sequels to Maurice Leblanc's series about the gentleman thief Arsène Lupin.

Their best-known work, however, is probably their two novels which were adapted into very famous films, *She Who Was No More*, which was adapted by the great film director Henri-Georges Clouzot and released under the title *Les Diaboliques* in 1955, and their 1954 novel *D'entre les morts*, which became the basis for Alfred Hitchcock's 1959 film *Vertigo*.

There is so much great French mystery and suspense fiction that I would like to tell you about, including the work of Jean-Claude Izzo, Jean-Patrick Manchette, Fred Vargas, and Véronique Desnain, but before we move on, let me tell you a little bit about a novel that I guarantee is like nothing you've ever read before, Georges Perec's *La Disparition*.

Perec was a member of a French group named Oulipo, which was made up of writers and mathematicians who practiced what are known as constrained writing techniques. In particular, members of Oulipo were fond of lipograms, which are pieces of writing in which a particular letter or group of letters are avoided.

Most lipograms are usually just a few sentences or paragraphs long, but in *La Disparition* Perec wrote a 300-page mystery novel without using the most common letter in the French language—the vowel e. The book's title literally means The Disappearance, but it was translated by Gilbert Adair into English as *A Void,* after all, the title mustn't contain an e.

The plot involves a group of friends looking for a missing companion by the name of Anton Vowl, spelled v-o-w-l. As the last name Vowl implies, the novel is filled with jokes and puns and is a parody of noir fiction. But there's much more than playfulness and humor at stake here.

Both Perec's parents disappeared during World War II, his father in combat and his mother in the Holocaust. *La Disparition* has been interpreted as an expression of Perec's sense of loss and incompleteness and his attempt to come to terms with those feelings.

With that combination of playful experimentation and tragic events in mind, we're now going to jump over to Switzerland and discuss briefly the work of Friedrich Dürrenmatt. Born in 1921, Dürrenmatt was known primarily as a playwright whose work often reflected upon World War II. But he was also the author of philosophical crime novels, including *The Judge and his Hangman* and *Suspicion*, both of which deal with such subjects as Swiss complicity with the Nazis.

These novels feature Inspector Bärlach, a Swiss police officer who was sent to work in Germany in the early 1930s but who returned to Switzerland after a dispute with a Hitler official. Dürrenmatt uses Bärlach to explore the moral consequences of Switzerland's neutrality during the Second World War, a policy that Dürrenmatt regarded as a lie.

But it's in his 1958 novel The Pledge that Dürrenmatt makes possibly his greatest contribution to mystery fiction. Tellingly subtitled Requiem for the Detective Novel, The Pledge systematically undoes the moral certainties of mystery fiction by showing how Matthias, a retired homicide detective, uses a young girl as bait in an attempt to capture a killer who has eluded him for years. In Dürrenmatt's hands, mystery fiction becomes almost the antithesis of justice and resolution rather than its apotheosis.

The way in which both Perec and Dürrenmatt use mystery and suspense fiction give us a convenient way to now move to Germany and see how their writers addressed the experience of World War II.

Mystery and suspense fiction in Germany has a venerable history. The well-known E.T.A. Hoffmann novella Mademoiselle von Scudéri, published in 1819, is a crime story in which Scudéri plays a detective role, an innocent person is exonerated, and a villain is captured. A number of critics had argued that Hoffmann's story was an important influence on Edgar Allan Poe when he came to write his mystery tales in the 1840s.

Probably better known to English-speaking readers, however, is the work of Erich Kästner, who launched one of the most popular children's mystery series in 1929 with Emil and the Detectives. Kästner followed this very successful book with Emil and the Three Twins in 1934. Unfortunately, this book was not nearly so popular because of the Nazis, who banned the publication of Kästner's work in Germany. They exempted Emil and the Detectives from this ban, though, because it was seen as too popular and too harmless to go to the trouble of banning it.

It's fair to say that it took German mystery and suspense fiction writers a considerable period of time to figure out how to address the experience and the legacy of World War II in their work. This shouldn't be surprising because in fact relatively few examples of mystery and suspense fiction are set during a time of war. Even fewer take the opportunity to examine how in any crime novel set during wartime, the focus on a single murder and its investigation may be altered by the fact that thousands, if not millions, of war-related murders are taking place around the one murder ostensibly at the center of the narrative.

Such examples of the genre do exist, of course, I'm thinking of the work of such writers as Martin Limón, Philip Kerr, J. Robert Janes, and James R. Benn, but they are few and far between. It seems that most mystery and suspense fiction writers prefer to avoid war altogether because they fear it might render an individual murder meaningless in a way that destroys both the spoken and unspoken rules of the genre.

According to the critic Katharina Hall, "German reunification in 1990 prompted a wide-ranging public discussion about the country's uneasy double past of fascism and communism." Thanks to this discussion, Germany is currently in the middle of a boom in historical mystery fiction.

In Hall's words,

> The capacity of the state to persecute dissenting citizens—Nazi Germany, East Germany—the actions of individuals or groups against the state—Nazi resisters, left-wing terrorists, right-wing neo-Nazis—and the government's sometimes over-zealous response—an increase in security measures, laws and trials—all provide rich material for the historical crime author's pen.

Let's look at a few examples of this work. Beginning in 2007, and now consisting of dozens of novels, the series with the collective title *It Happened in Berlin* uses the investigations of a German police inspector, and later his nephew, to chart the complex history of Germany over the course of the 20th century.

The project was dreamed up by well-known German crime writer and sociologist Horst Bosetzky and has been dubbed a Kettenroman, or chain novel, because the series is actually written by a collective of authors, with Bosetzky doing the editing. Once completed *It Happened in Berlin* will constitute an exhaustive chronicle of Germany's recent history, with Berlin at its center.

Less ambitious but equally compelling is Ferdinand von Schirach's 2011 novel *The Collini Case*, which uses the apparently motiveless murder of an elderly businessman to explore West Germany's failure to prosecute former Nazi war criminals more aggressively.

It's worth noting that this story also has a personal dimension for von Schirach. His grandfather was Baldur von Schirach, leader of the Hitler Youth organization. In The *Collini Case*, therefore, we see the author attempting to come to terms with both his family's and the nation's past.

Even German writers primarily known for writing literary fiction have found the mystery and suspense fiction genre a useful way of exploring a range of issues. Bernhard Schlink, for example, is probably best-known for his literary novel *The Reader*, but he has also written a trilogy of novels featuring a detective named Self, which consists of *Self's Punishment* which addresses the legacy of the Nazi past, *Self's Deception* which focuses on terrorist acts committed in 1970s Germany by groups like the Baader-Meinhof Group, and *Self's Murder* which revolves around the collapse of East Germany.

Finally, some German writers have used mystery and suspense fiction to address much more recent issues. The work of Jakob Arjouni, for example, features the Turkish-German private investigator Kemal Kayankaya. In novels such as *Kismet* and *Brother Kemal*, Arjouni discusses issues whose implications are still highly relevant for 21st-century Germany, including the impact of the fall of Communism and the Balkan Wars, as well as immigration and religious intolerance.

Italian mystery and suspense fiction has also addressed issues of great importance to Italian society and culture. Not surprisingly, the impact of organized crime and the mafia are at the top of that list. Although there were a few mystery writers working in Italy in the 19th century, the genre didn't really take off until 1929 when the publishing house Mondadori began to publish translations of American and British mysteries in the same way Série Noire did in France after World War II.

Mondadori's books were distinguished by their yellow covers, and for this reason, they became known as i libri gialli or the yellow books. Eventually, giallo became a shorthand term for the crime fiction genre as a whole, a term that eventually expanded to include films, especially horror, and suspense films.

Thanks to the popularity of Mondadori's gialli translations, some Italian writers started producing their own works of mystery and suspense fiction. Unfortunately, before the genre could really get off the ground in Italy, it was first curtailed and then banned outright in 1943 by Benito Mussolini's fascist government, who felt that it was unpatriotic in the way it portrayed the state.

After World War II ended, the popularity of the genre grew rapidly. A particularly significant author during this period was Carlo Emilio Gadda, whose 1957 novel *That Awful Mess on Via Merulana* was set in fascist Italy of the 1920s and provided a searing commentary on that period of Italian history. Gadda's work influenced many later Italian crime fiction authors for the way it constituted what came to be known as an anti-detective novel, which referred to a type of crime fiction where the solution is either highly ambiguous or altogether absent.

A significant later example of this thread of Italian anti-mystery fiction known to many English-speaking readers is Umberto Eco's famous 1980 novel *The Name of the Rose*. As befits a crime novel from Eco, who was a widely-known postmodern literary theorist, this novel combines semiotics, philosophy, medieval studies, and biblical analysis with a good old-fashioned murder mystery set in a 14th-century Italian monastery.

The novel's protagonist, a Franciscan friar named William of Baskerville, travels to a monastery in Northern Italy with his assistant, Adso of Melk, to attend a theological disputation. Once there, Williams learns that a suspicious death has recently taken place, one that is followed by other deaths at the monastery. The Abbott asks William to investigate the killings, which all seem to revolve around the existence of a fabled book thought to have been lost, the Greek philosopher Aristotle's writings on comedy. At the novel's climax, William tries but fails to find this book in the monastery's labyrinthine library.

As this brief summary suggests, *The Name of the Rose* is a highly self-reflexive novel, not only in the sense that it is a book about books, but also in the sense that it is a mystery novel filled with allusions to other mystery novels. To give just two examples, William of Baskerville's name is an obvious tribute to Sir Arthur Conan Doyle's Sherlock Holmes novel *The Hound of the Baskervilles*, while the library labyrinth is a more elliptical nod the work of the great Argentinian author of experimental mystery fiction, Jorge Luis Borges.

Less well-known than Eco, but probably more important to Italian crime fiction is the work of Leonardo Sciascia, who was born in Sicily in 1921. Much of his crime fiction, beginning with *The Day of the Owl* in 1961, discusses the influence of the mafia in the daily life of both Sicily in particular and Italy in general, and how it's able to sustain its power thanks, in part, to the corruption of the Italian political establishment.

Sciascia later acquired first-hand knowledge of that system because he served as a politician during the 1970s and was involved in the investigation into the government's handling of the kidnapping of the Italian politician Aldo Moro in 1978 by the Red Brigades.

The way in which Sciascia linked the mafia, crime, and Italian politics together in a series of best-selling books made him a high-profile and controversial character, perhaps partly because he felt no compulsion to offer happy endings or anything approaching justice at the end of his novels.

A good example of this tendency in his work is his 1971 novel *Equal Danger*, in which a detective is sent to Sicily to investigate a series of murders of judges. Sciascia focuses on how and why the authorities are both unable and unwilling to conduct such investigations properly because of their own corruption. Not surprisingly, the detective fails to solve this case, which illustrates the extent to which many of Sciascia's novels can also be described as anti-detective novels.

Sciascia's persistent focus on the setting of Sicily indicates the extent to which, as critic G. J. Demko has pointed out, mass-market mystery writers in Italy tend to have a very regional voice. Probably the best-known example of this fact in contemporary Italian mystery fiction is another Sicily-based writer by the name of Andrea Camilleri.

Camilleri enjoyed a long career as a film and theater director before writing his first novel in his 50s. Even so, he didn't become a best-selling writer until he was nearly 70, when in 1994 he published *The Shape of Water*. The book was first in what would become a long series of novels featuring Inspector Montalbano, a police detective in the police force of Vigàta, an imaginary Sicilian town.

One of the most notable features of Camilleri's Montalbano novels is the way in which they address persistently and aggressively a variety of social problems in contemporary Italy. Indeed, Camilleri has remarked

That social commentary... was always my aim. In many crime novels, the events seem completely detached from the economic, political, and social context in which they occur... In my books, I deliberately decided to smuggle into a detective novel a critical commentary on my times. This also allowed me to show the progression and evolution in the character of Montalbano.

We can see this evolution in Montalbano in the form of frequent inner monologues in which he questions what it means to be a good detective in a society like Italy, where solving a case can actually put your life in danger. In this way, Camilleri reminds us that mystery and suspense fiction can not only reflect a society but also hopefully contribute to changing that society.

Montalbano also gives us a way of moving to the final stop of our European tour because his name is an homage to the writer Manuel Vázquez Montalbán, the dean of Spanish mystery writers. Like the other countries we've looked at in this lecture, Spain has a long and fractious history when it comes to mystery and suspense fiction. A notable early example of the genre is the story El Clavo, written by Pedro Antonio de Alarcón and published in 1853.

In general, however, the genre had to wait until after the fall of the Franco regime in 1975 to truly come into its own. During this period, a number of authors came to the fore, including Eduardo Mendoza and Andreu Martín, but Montalbán and his fictional private detective Pepe Carvalho are undoubtedly at the head of the pack.

Carvalho is a rich and complex character that combines elements of the classical detective like Rex Stout's Nero Wolfe, he is a gastronome and the hard-boiled detective he's thoroughly at home on the mean streets of Barcelona. Beginning in 1972 with the publication of *I Killed Kennedy*, Montalbán uses Carvalho to explore various aspects of Spanish society in the last half of the 20th century.

In *Murder in the Central Committee*, for example, Montalbán addresses the complexities of the transitional period in Spanish history between the death of General Franco and the restoration of a constitutional democracy. And in *An Olympic Death*, he examines a subject dear to his heart, born in Barcelona and a passionate FC Barcelona supporter, in this novel Montalbán uses the conventions of mystery fiction to examine the largely negative changes that took place in his native city during the 1992 Olympic Games.

A final significant detail about Pepe Carvalho is that he's a great traveler. Many of Montalbán's novels featuring his private eye take place in other countries, including *The Buenos Aires Quintet* in Argentina and *The Birds of Bangkok* in Thailand.

This is an appropriate detail with which to end this lecture because it reminds us of where we started. Our European tour has demonstrated that mystery and suspense fiction has an unparalleled ability to travel to a wide range of countries. It is able to both address specific issues in any one of those countries in an entertaining and thought-provoking manner, while also remaining true to the genre's core elements that appeal to its legions of fans.

NORDIC NOIR

Today, Nordic noir is at the forefront of international mystery fiction. Nordic noir —which refers to crime fiction authored by writers living and working in Sweden, Norway, Denmark, Iceland, and Finland—has something for every fan of the genre, from police procedurals to private-eye stories. The boom in Nordic noir is a notable example of a phenomenon we've discussed in previous lectures: the ability of mystery and suspense fiction writers to combine core features of the genre with local innovations. In this sense, the success of Nordic noir mirrors the success of the genre as a whole.

WHEN MAJ MET PER

- The history of Scandinavian crime fiction goes back to the summer of 1962, when Maj Sjöwall met Per Wahlöö. At the time they met, they were both working as journalists, and they discussed writing a series of crime novels together. According to Sjöwall, "We wanted to describe society from our left point of view.... We wanted to show where Sweden was heading: towards a capitalistic, cold and inhuman society, where the rich got richer, the poor got poorer."

- Sjöwall and Wahlöö planned out the entire series before they even began writing. It was to consist of 10 books, under the collective title of The Story of a Crime. The crime was Swedish society's abandonment of the poor and vulnerable. Each novel in the series revolves around cases investigated by detective Martin Beck and his colleagues in the homicide division of the Swedish national police.

- An important question is why the authors chose to write about police officers if the aim was to expose the decay of Swedish society and describe the plight of vulnerable and poverty-stricken people. The reason is that police officers, perhaps more than any other group in society, see the consequences of that decay vividly on a daily basis. In that sense, writing police procedurals was a logical choice for Sjöwall and Wahlöö.

SOCIALLY CONSCIOUS AND PROGRESSIVE

- Although the last word in *The Terrorists*—the final novel in the Sjöwall and Wahlöö series—is "Marx," which some readers have interpreted as a faith in Marxism to solve problems, the series is very far from being politically dogmatic. Instead, the novels show that Martin Beck and his colleagues are doing a difficult job under very challenging circumstances.

- The way in which Sjöwall and Wahlöö humanize their police protagonists is one reason that the Story of a Crime novels are so influential. But even more significant is how the authors use the form of the police procedural to examine a wide variety of social problems Swedish society was struggling with during the 1960s and 1970s.

- Although the main crime under investigation in any novel in the series is usually murder, Sjöwall and Wahlöö use this crime to introduce a number of related issues, including drug smuggling, political corruption, sexism, and pedophilia. They eventually connect all of these to what they see as the most serious crime committed by the most dangerous criminal: the state's systematic neglect of its citizens, a neglect that has lethal consequences even if it doesn't have murderous intent.

- From its very beginnings, then, we see that Nordic noir constitutes a socially conscious and progressive form of mystery and suspense fiction, and social consciousness has remained its hallmark ever since. Many examples of the genre have used mystery narratives for this purpose, of course, such as Raymond Chandler's critique of the corruption of American society and Paco Ignacio Taibo II's focus on the criminal actions of the Mexican state.

■ Nevertheless, no variety of mystery and suspense fiction has been more consistent than Nordic noir in its focus on the powerful, rather than the powerless, as the main source of criminal activity.

An important question is why the authors chose to write about police officers if the aim was to expose the decay of Swedish society and describe the plight of vulnerable and poverty-stricken people.

HENNING MANKELL'S KURT WALLANDER

■ Jo Nesbø, a Norwegian novelist, has commented, "Maj Sjöwall and Per Wahlöö were the godfathers of Scandinavian crime. They broke the crime novel in Scandinavia from the kiosks and into the serious bookstores." Many authors have benefited from their success, but perhaps none has been influenced more by the Story of a Crime series and its ethos than Henning Mankell.

■ Mankell was born in 1948 in Stockholm, Sweden, and in 1991, he published *Faceless Killers*, the first in what would become a best-selling series of 12 novels featuring Kurt Wallander. Like Sjöwall and Wahlöö's Martin Beck, Wallander is very far from being a heroic figure. Although Wallander is a competent and committed investigator, his personal life is a shambles. He looks to his job as a way to give both his life and the world around him some meaning.

- This means that each of the investigations that Wallander conducts has a deeply personal dimension. But like the work of Sjöwall and Wahlöö, Mankell also uses Wallander's cases to get his readers to think about the complexities of social issues facing Swedish society.

STIEG LARSSON'S MILLENNIUM TRILOGY

- The work of Stieg Larsson, author of the Millennium Trilogy (*The Girl with the Dragon Tattoo*, *The Girl Who Played with Fire*, and *The Girl Who Kicked the Hornet's Nest*) has iconic status in Nordic noir. Like J. K. Rowling's Harry Potter series or E. L. James's *Fifty Shades of Grey*, Larsson's trilogy was read by millions of people who usually didn't read books at all, let alone mysteries.

- Larsson writes an extremely hybrid version of mystery and suspense fiction with elements of the police procedural, private-eye novel, political thriller, serial-killer narrative, conspiracy thriller, and even a kind of romance.

- It's no accident that when Larsson's novels were translated into English, only the second volume in the trilogy, *The Girl Who Played with Fire*, has a title that resembles the original Swedish title. *The Girl with the Dragon Tattoo* was originally titled *Men Who Hate Women*, while *The Air Castle That Was Blown Up* became *The Girl Who Kicked the Hornet's Nest*. By emphasizing the word "girl" in all three translated titles, Larsson underlines the importance of his protagonist Lisbeth Salander and feminism to the trilogy as a whole.

COMIC BOOK SUPERHERO

- In the sole interview that Larsson gave about the Millennium Trilogy, he mentioned that one of the inspirations for the character of Lisbeth Salander was Pippi Longstocking, the nine-year-old hero of the well-known series of children's books by Swedish author Astrid Lindgren that first appeared in 1945. If this seems like a bizarre comparison, consider these facts: Larsson said that Salander was his version of what Pippi might have been if she'd grown up, and he maintained that Lindgren's Pippi is unconventional, assertive, frequently gets angry, and is enormously strong.

- Part of the success of Larsson's trilogy, in other words, derives from the fact that there's more than a little of the comic book superhero about Lisbeth. Salander proves to be successful in responding to the most unusual and dangerous circumstances, capable of defending herself and saving others, and committed to defeating evil and seeing justice triumph.

- Just as we read Ian Fleming's James Bond novels for their combination of realism and fantasy, the same can be said of the way we read the many adventures of Lisbeth Salander in her crusade against misogyny, corruption, and crime. Although Larsson kept his emphasis on political and social progressivism and the critique of the Swedish state, he added layers of adventure, romance, and intrigue that turned his novels into blockbusters.

JO NESBØ

- Jo Nesbø is a best-selling Norwegian author of crime novels who started out as a stockbroker and musician before beginning his writing career. His series protagonist, Harry Hole, is a troubled and alcoholic homicide detective who works in Oslo.

- On the whole, Nesbø eschews Larsson's focus on complex conspiracies involving large numbers of characters. Instead, in a series of novels that began with the publication of *The Bat* in 1997, Nesbø usually has Hole focus on a single complicated case,

Although the main crime under investigation in any novel in the series is usually murder, Sjöwall and Wahlöö use this crime to introduce a number of related issues, including drug smuggling, political corruption, sexism, and pedophilia.

often involving serial killers, that combines elements of the police procedural and the psychological thriller.

■ It's interesting to note that, although he's undoubtedly benefited from the boom in Nordic noir, Nesbø feels somewhat ambivalent about the category. When asked by an interviewer how he felt about Swedish and Norwegian crime novels being lumped in together, Nesbø replied, "It may not seem this way for outsiders, since there are cultural, demographic, and geographical similarities in the stories, but I think the voices are very different. I actually feel more related to the American hard-boiled crime novel than the Scandinavian crime novel, whatever that is."

Two Queens of Norwegian Crime

- Both Karin Fossum and Anne Holt have been described by reviewers as the "queen of Norwegian crime."

- Karin Fossum's successful series featuring police inspector Konrad Sejer is typical of Nordic noir in the way it's rooted in the mundane details of police procedure. But as Fossum explains, the setting of her work is quite different: "I use the setting of a small rural Norwegian community—the kind of place that I know so intimately. I could never write a novel set in a big city, because, frankly, I don't know what it would be like."

- Anne Holt has worked as a lawyer and even served as the Norwegian Minister of Justice. Her books actually owe as much to Agatha Christie as they do to noir conventions. In *1222*, the first novel in the series, retired policewoman Hanne Wilhelmsen finds herself stranded after a train accident, along with 268 other passengers, at a hotel in northern Norway located 1,222 meters above sea level (hence the novel's title). When passengers start to die off, Wilhelmsen has to use her powers of observation (she is paralyzed from the waist down after being shot in a gunfight) to solve the mystery.

- *1222* sounds more like a locked-room mystery in the manner of Christie's *Murder on the Orient Express* than a Nordic noir in the traditional sense. Holt describes her work: "I write about people… not about Scandinavia…. It is never the principal goal for me to describe my own region—it is purely the means to a narrative end."

- Despite Holt's remarks, it's clear that the massive success of Nordic noir comes precisely from the adroit way in which writers in this field are able to combine details of their local cultures with their own variations on the recognized conventions of mystery and suspense fiction.

   1. Why has Nordic noir led the way in the globalization of mystery and suspense fiction?

   2. Why do some of Nordic noir's most well-known practitioners have problems with the term?

SUGGESTED READING

Forshaw, *Death in a Cold Climate.*

Nestingen, *Crime and Fantasy in Scandinavia.*

NORDIC NOIR

One of the most striking and exciting developments in mystery and suspense fiction over the past 20 years has been the rapid spread of the genre across the world, as more and more crime fiction from international authors is appearing in English translations and is being eagerly consumed by curious readers.

Although you can now read examples of the genre from pretty much any country in the world, most people would agree that the rise of international mystery fiction has been spearheaded by what has come to be known as 'Nordic Noir.' This term refers to crime fiction authored by writers living and working in a group of countries that includes Sweden, Norway, Denmark, Iceland, and Finland.

Why has 'Nordic Noir' become so phenomenally popular with readers of mystery and suspense fiction? Perhaps it has something to do with the fact that most people don't think of Scandinavia as a particularly crime-ridden part of the world. Instead, we tend to assume that Scandinavian countries are all liberal democracies with no serious social problems, largely thanks to a well-developed welfare state system that provides a safety net for the poor and vulnerable.

Who could imagine crime being a serious problem in such a context? And yet, judging from the 'Nordic Noir' writers, there's obviously more than enough crime to go around in Scandinavia. Perhaps it's the contrast between our idealized view of the region and the gritty reality that we find so intriguing.

Apart from the relationship between ideal and reality, however, the other main factor that helps explain the success of 'Nordic Noir' is the variety of work produced under that label. Ranging from police procedurals to private eye stories and featuring a wide variety crimes committed by an equally broad range of criminals, 'Nordic Noir' has something for every fan of the genre.

The boom in 'Nordic Noir' is a great example of a phenomenon we've seen in a number of other lectures in this course—namely, the ability of different forms of mystery and suspense fiction to combine core features of the genre with local innovations. In this sense, the success of 'Nordic Noir' mirrors the success of the genre as a whole.

Thanks to the extraordinary popularity of Stieg Larsson's *Millennium* Trilogy, many people assume that 'Nordic Noir' begins when Larsson's main protagonist, Lisbeth Salander, first walks on to the stage in *The Girl with the Dragon Tattoo*, which was originally published in 2005 and first appeared in English translation in 2008.

Although this may be true in relation to the publishing boom aspect of 'Nordic Noir,' the history of Scandinavian crime fiction goes back much further. In fact, I would date its origins to the summer of 1962, when Maj Sjöwall met Per Wahlöö. At the time they met, they were both working as journalists, though Wahlöö had already published a number of novels. After they fell in love and started living together, they discussed writing a series of crime novels together.

According to Sjöwall,

> We wanted to describe society from our left point of view. Per had written political books, but they'd only sold 300 copies. We realized that people read crime and through the stories, we could show the reader that under the official image of welfare-state Sweden there was another layer of poverty, criminality, and brutality. We wanted to show where Sweden was heading: towards a capitalistic, cold, and inhuman society where the rich got richer; the poor got poorer.

They planned the whole series out before they even began writing. It was to consist of 10 books and together, the books would have the collective title *The Story of a Crime*. What was the crime? Swedish society's abandonment of the poor and vulnerable.

Once the series was under way, Sjöwall and Wahlöö settled into an unusual but productive writing routine. Writing at night while their children were asleep, each chapter of the novel was plotted out like a storyboard, and then they wrote alternate chapters, before swapping completed chapters so they could each edit the other's work.

According to Sjöwall, they paid a great deal of attention not only to detail—such as how long it would take for a character to travel from one place to another—in order to give the books a realistic feel, but also to matters of style. "We wanted to find a style which was not personally his, or not personally mine, but a style that was good for the books. We wanted the books to be read by everyone, whether you were educated or not."

They succeeded, to put it mildly. The *Story of a Crime* series, as I indicated earlier, consists of the following 10 books, which were published at the rate of one a year between 1965 and 1975: *Roseanna*, *The Man Who Went Up in Smoke*, *The Man on the Balcony*, *The Laughing Policeman*, *The Fire Engine That Disappeared*, *Murder at the Savoy*, *The Abominable Man*, *The Locked Room*, *Cop Killer*, and *The Terrorists*.

In my view, it is the best series of novels ever published in the mystery and suspense fiction genre, a must-read for anyone and everyone. What are some of the characteristics that make this series such a landmark in 'Nordic Noir?'

First of all, let's consider Sjöwall and Wahlöö's decision to write mystery novels rather than novels in another genre or literary fiction. Granted, they wanted the series to be read widely, but according to Marxist critic Ernest Mandel in his indispensable book *Delightful*

Murder: A Social History of the Crime Story, mystery and suspense fiction is an inherently conservative genre because it's obsessed with the restoration of order in a bourgeois society.

Looked at in this light, Sjöwall and Wahlöö's decision to write police procedurals might seem even more eccentric. Each novel in their series revolves around cases investigated by Detective Martin Beck and his colleagues in the homicide division of the Swedish National Police. Why choose to write about police officers if your aim is to expose how Swedish society is in the process of decaying and as a result, more and more people are becoming vulnerable and falling into poverty?

Because police officers, perhaps more than any other group in society, see the consequences of that decay vividly on a daily basis. In that sense, writing police procedurals was a logical choice on the part of Sjöwall and Wahlöö.

Moreover, although the last word in *The Terrorists*—the final novel in the series—is "Marx," which some readers have interpreted as meaning that the authors believe Marxism is the answer to the problems they examine, the series is very far from being politically dogmatic. Instead, the novels do their very best to show that Martin Beck and his colleagues are doing a difficult job under very difficult circumstances.

In order to avoid making their work into an apology for the police, however, Sjöwall and Wahlöö are also careful to show that many of the problems their police protagonists face come from other police officers. Their superiors, especially, represent a faceless, inefficient, and uncaring bureaucracy that refuses to be responsive to the problems experienced by the other characters in the series—police, criminals, and victims alike.

So, the way in which Sjöwall and Wahlöö humanize their police officer protagonists and then allow their readers to follow the details of their personal and professional lives is definitely one reason that the *Story of a Crime* novels are so influential. But even more significant is how the authors use the form of the police procedural to examine a wide variety of social problems Swedish society was struggling with during the 1960s and 1970s.

Although the main crime under investigation in any novel in the series is usually murder, Sjöwall and Wahlöö use this crime to introduce a number of related issues, including drug smuggling, political corruption, sexism, and pedophilia. They eventually connect all of these to what they see as the most serious crime committed by the most serious criminal—the State's systematic neglect of its citizens, a neglect that has murderous consequences even if it doesn't have murderous intent.

From its very beginnings, then, we see that 'Nordic Noir' constitutes a socially conscious and progressive form of mystery and suspense fiction, and that social consciousness has remained its hallmark ever since. Many examples of the genre have used mystery narratives for this purpose, of course, such as Raymond Chandler's critique of the corruption of American society and Paco Ignacio Taibo II's focus on the criminal actions of the Mexican state. Nevertheless, I think it's fair to say that no variety of mystery and suspense fiction has been more consistent than 'Nordic Noir' in its focus on the powerful, rather than the powerless, being the main source of criminal activity.

Jo Nesbø, a Norwegian novelist whose work we'll look at later in this lecture, has commented that "Maj Sjöwall and Per Wahlöö were the godfathers of Scandinavian crime. They broke the crime novel in Scandinavia from the kiosks and into the serious bookstores." Many authors have benefitted from their success, but perhaps none have been influenced more by the *Story of a Crime* series and its ethos than Henning Mankell.

Mankell was born in 1948 in Stockholm, Sweden, and for the first part of his career, he focused mainly on working in the theater, both in Sweden and in Mozambique, which, over the course of his life, became a kind of second home for him. He published his first novel, *Bergsprängaren*, which focuses on the Swedish labor movement, in 1973.

But it wasn't until 1991 that he turned to crime fiction. In that year, he published *Faceless Killers*, the first in what would become a best-selling series of 12 novels featuring Kurt Wallander, a police inspector who lives and works in the Swedish town of Ystad.

Like Sjöwall and Wahlöö's Martin Beck, Wallander is very far from being a heroic figure. Although he is a competent and committed investigator, Wallander's personal life is a shambles—his wife has left him, he's estranged from his daughter, he drinks too much, and he's been diagnosed with diabetes. He seeks an escape from all this in booze, in opera, but most of all in his job, which Wallander looks to as a way to give both his life and the world around him some meaning.

This means that each of the investigations that Wallander conducts has a deeply personal dimension. But like the work of Sjöwall and Wahlöö, Mankell also uses the cases that Wallander works on to get his readers to think about the complexities of social issues facing Swedish society. For example, in *Faceless Killers*, Wallander investigates a case in which an elderly couple who lived on a farm have been found murdered. Johannes Lovgren was beaten and stabbed to death, while his wife Maria was found hanged. Maria's last word before she dies is "foreigner," which leads not only to a great deal of local speculation about the identity of the killers but also to anti-immigrant sentiments and threats.

Working against this background of community anger and prejudice makes Wallander's investigation even more urgent, and he eventually discovers that Johannes Lovgren was leading a double life that's connected to Sweden's complicity with the Nazis during World War II.

The murderers are revealed to be Czech immigrants who sought political asylum under false pretenses in Sweden because of the country's reputation as a safe and liberal environment with a strong welfare state. What is the reader meant to do with this ending?

On the one hand, in *Faceless Killers*, Mankell addresses the subjects of racism and national identity, as well as the need for Swedes to be aware of the complexities of their country's past. On the other hand, the moral that we're meant to draw from Mankell's examination of these subjects is less clear.

As critic Anna Westerståhl Stenport has commented in relation to *Faceless Killers*, we're led to question whether

> the Swedish welfare state would have been better off as a reclusive entity generously donating aid money to faraway trouble spots without experiencing itself any of the turmoil and social challenges that come with multi-ethnic coexistence.

The point, however, is that neither Mankell nor his novel takes a firm stand on either side of this issue. Just as in Sjöwall and Wahlöö's work, Mankell rejects dogmatism in what is otherwise a highly political work and instead encourages us to make up our own minds.

If we now turn to the work of Stieg Larsson, I'm tempted to say it's that same combination of politics and room for readers to draw their own conclusions that helps to explain the success of the *Millennium* Trilogy. However, a closer examination of Larsson's work suggests some different reasons for the iconic status of the trilogy within 'Nordic Noir.'

It's worth emphasizing just what degree of success we're talking about here. We can do so by taking a quick look at one of my favorite blogs, Better Book Titles, which was started by writer Dan Wilbur several years ago. The purpose of the blog is to give new titles to both classic and new books that reflect more accurately the book's content, themes, meaning, or impact. The blog's better title for *The Girl with the Dragon Tattoo*—the first novel of Larsson's trilogy—is: *The First Book I've Read in Six Years.*

Yes, this new title is a snobbish dig at many of the book's readers, but it also reflects accurately the sense in which *The Girl with the Dragon Tattoo* is an example of the ultimate crossover book. Like J. K. Rowling's *Harry Potter* series or E.L. James' *Fifty Shades of Grey*, Larsson's trilogy was read by millions of people who usually wouldn't read books at all, let alone mysteries.

What was it about Larsson's novels that made them so addictive for so many people? Even though the plots of the novels in the trilogy are quite complicated, it's worth summarizing at least one of them because doing so will help us answer this question.

One of the trilogy's main characters is investigative journalist Mikael Blomkvist, who runs the magazine *Millennium*, which gives the trilogy its title. At the beginning of *The Girl with the Dragon Tattoo*, Blomkvist has been convicted of libeling wealthy businessman Hans-Erik Wennerström. Blomkvist is then hired by another businessman, Henrik Vanger, after Vanger has checked into Blomkvist's background. This background check is conducted by the trilogy's other main character, Lisbeth Salander, a brilliant but socially awkward computer hacker.

Under the cover of writing a history of the Vanger family, Henrik Vanger actually wants Blomkvist to investigate the disappearance of his grandniece, Harriet, who disappeared many years before. In return, Vanger promises to supply Blomkvist with evidence against Wennerström that will convict him and exonerate Blomkvist.

Meanwhile, we learn that Lisbeth Salander was ruled legally incompetent as a child and ever since her affairs have been controlled by a legal guardian. When that guardian, Nils Bjurman, rapes her,

Salander gets her revenge by torturing him until he agrees to let her control her own affairs. Then, for good measure, she tattoos the fact that he is a rapist onto his chest and films the whole encounter so Bjurman can't retaliate against her.

The two plots and the two main characters come together when Blomkvist realizes that he may be on the trail of a prolific and extremely dangerous serial killer. When he requests a research assistant, Vanger's lawyer suggests Salander, and the two of them start working together. After they identify another member of the Vanger family as the killer, that family member imprisons Blomkvist and is about to kill him when Salander shows up at the last moment. She rescues Blomkvist, and the murderer is killed while trying to escape.

We're not done yet. As he promised, Henrik Vanger provides Blomkvist with evidence against Wennerström, but it turns out to be unusable. Using her skills as a hacker, Salander gets evidence against Wennerström that allows Blomkvist to both expose him and write a best-selling book about the case. For good measure, Salander also hacks her way into Wennerström's bank accounts and steals hundreds of millions of dollars from him so that by the end of the novel, she is financially and emotionally independent of everyone except Blomkvist, with whom she seems to have fallen in love.

What have we learned from this summary—a summary that, believe it or not, leaves out a lot of information about the book?! The short answer is that *The Girl with the Dragon Tattoo*, like the other novels in the trilogy, has something for everyone. Larsson writes an extremely hybrid version of mystery and suspense fiction in which we can see elements of the police procedural, the private eye novel, the political thriller, a serial killer narrative, a conspiracy thriller, and even a kind of romance—as we can see in Larsson's focus on the relationship between Blomkvist and Salander.

That last point is worth lingering over for a moment. It's no accident that when Larsson's novels were translated into English, only the second volume in the trilogy, *The Girl Who Played with Fire*, has a title that resembles the original Swedish title. *The Girl with the Dragon Tattoo* was originally titled *Men Who Hate Women*, while *The Air Castle That Was Blown Up* became *The Girl Who Kicked the Hornet's Nest*. By emphasizing the word "girl" in all three translated titles, we can see the importance of both Lisbeth Salander and feminism to the trilogy as a whole.

In the only interview that Larsson ever gave about the *Millennium* Trilogy, he mentioned that one of the inspirations for the character of Lisbeth Salander was Pippi Longstocking, the nine-year-old hero of a very well-known series of children's books by Swedish author Astrid Lindgren that first appeared in 1945. If this seems like a bizarre comparison, consider two facts: first, that Larsson also said that Salander was his version of what Pippi might have been like if she'd grown up, and that Lindgren's Pippi is unconventional, assertive, frequently gets angry, and is enormously strong.

Part of the success of Larsson's trilogy, in other words, derives from the fact that Salander proves to be so successful in responding to the most unusual and dangerous circumstances, so capable of both defending herself and saving others, so committed to defeating evil and seeing justice triumph, that there's more than a little of the comic book superhero about her.

For Larsson's devoted readers, this didn't compromise the real-world political resonances of the books at all. Just as we read Ian Fleming's James Bond novels for their combination of realism and fantasy, the same can be said of the way we read the many adventures of Lisbeth Salander in her crusade against misogyny, corruption, and crime.

I hope I've made it clear that Larsson's success can be explained by how he both adhered to and simultaneously broke with the template established for 'Nordic Noir' fiction by the work of Sjöwall and Wahlöö on the one hand, and Mankell on the other. Although Larsson kept their emphasis on political and social progressivism and the critique of the Swedish state, he added layers of adventure, romance, and intrigue that turned his novels into blockbusters.

Consequently, other writers working in the field at the same time as Larsson now had a wide range of possibilities to choose from when they wrote their own 'Nordic Noir' narratives. In the final part of this lecture, I'd like to demonstrate this point by discussing briefly the work of some of the other most popular authors working today.

Jo Nesbø is a best-selling Norwegian author of crime novels who started out as a stockbroker and musician before beginning his writing career. His series protagonist, Harry Hole—pronounced "Hool-eh," but spelled H-O-L-E—is a troubled and alcoholic homicide detective who works in Oslo.

On the whole, Nesbø eschews Larsson's focus on complex conspiracies involving large numbers of characters. Instead, in a series of novels that began with the publication of *The Bat* in 1997, Nesbø usually has Hole focused on a single complicated case, often involving serial killers, that combines elements of the police procedural and the psychological thriller.

It's interesting to note that, although he's undoubtedly benefitted from the boom in 'Nordic Noir', Nesbø feels somewhat ambivalent about the category. When asked by an interviewer how he felt about Swedish and Norwegian crime novels being lumped in together, Nesbø replied that

> It may not seem this way for outsiders since there are cultural, demographic, and geographical similarities in the stories, but I think the voices are very different. I actually feel more related to the American hard-boiled crime novel than the Scandinavian crime novel, whatever that is.

This question about what exactly is nordic about 'Nordic Noir' comes up again if we look at the work of two female Norwegian crime writers, Karin Fossum and Anne Holt. Both have been described by reviewers as the Queen of Norwegian Crime.

Fossum's successful series featuring police inspector Konrad Sejer is typical of 'Nordic Noir' in the way it's rooted in the mundane details of police procedure. But as Fossum explains, the setting of her work is quite different: "I use the setting of a small rural Norwegian community—the kind of place that I know so intimately. I could never write a novel set in a big city because, frankly, I don't know what it would be like."

As for Holt, who has worked as a lawyer and has even served as the Norwegian Minister of Justice, her series of novels features retired lesbian policewoman Hanne Wilhelmsen. Her books actually owe as much to Agatha Christie as they do to noir conventions.

In *1222*, the first novel in the series, Wilhelmsen finds herself stranded after a train accident, along with 268 other passengers, at a hotel in northern Norway located 1,222 meters above sea level—hence the novel's title. When passengers start to die off, Wilhelmsen has to use her powers of observation—as she's paralyzed from the waist down after being shot in a gunfight—to solve the mystery.

1222 sounds more like a "locked room" mystery in the manner of Christie's *Murder on the Orient Express* than a 'Nordic Noir' in the traditional sense. Perhaps this is why Holt once said, "I write about people, not about Scandinavia. It is never the principal goal for me to describe my own region—it is purely the means to a narrative end."

Despite Holt's remarks, it's clear that the massive success of 'Nordic Noir,' as we've seen in this lecture, comes precisely from the adroit way in which writers in this field are able to combine details of their local cultures with their own variations on the recognized conventions of mystery and suspense fiction. In that sense, Karen Holt's *1222*—like the work of Sjöwall and Wahlöö, Mankell, Larsson, Nesbø, and Fossum—is thoroughly representative of this fascinating subgenre.

JAPANESE AND LATIN AMERICAN MYSTERIES

One of the most exciting and energizing developments in the field of mystery and suspense fiction over the past 20 years has been the genre's continued spread over the entire globe. Today, we're in the middle of a boom in international crime fiction, with classic texts coming back into print in new translations and new writers being published for the first time (some writing in their native languages and some in English). In this lecture, we will examine the work of mystery and suspense fiction writers from outside Anglo-America, Europe, and Scandinavia.

SURREALISM AND FANTASTICAL ELEMENTS

- The first stop on our world tour is Japan, where mystery and suspense fiction has been popular since at least the 1920s. A key figure in Japan is Taro Hirai, who wrote under the pseudonym Edogawa Rampo. Rampo's fondness for the work of Edgar Allan Poe is evident in his pen name: If you pronounce it quickly, it sounds like a Japanese version of "Edgar Allan Poe."

- Rampo began his writing career in 1923, when he published a mystery story entitled "The Two-Sen Copper Coin" in a magazine that had previously published the work of Poe, Sir Arthur Conan Doyle, and G. K. Chesterton. Rampo invents a tale of logical ratiocination that seems to come straight from Poe, but he uses a Japanese example to demonstrate the method of analysis associated with C. Auguste Dupin (in this case, a code based on a Buddhist incantation as well as Japanese-language Braille). "Copper Coin" demonstrates Rampo's inventiveness and his ability to change the inherited tradition of mystery and suspense fiction to suit his own purposes.

- Over the course of a long and productive career, Rampo would prove his ingenuity and creativity again and again in a large number of stories and novels that ran the gamut from puzzle mysteries to locked-room mysteries. He even wrote a series of mysteries called the Boy Detectives Club, featuring a group of young detectives. These books could be considered the Japanese equivalent of the Hardy Boys or Nancy Drew mysteries.

- Even though Rampo had a fondness for the traditional and formal elements of the genre, from the beginning of his career, he combined this traditionalism with unusual, even surreal elements. For example, "The Case of the Murder on D. Hill" deals with sadomasochism, and "The Human Chair" is a story of a man who hides inside a chair to feel the bodies sitting on top of him. This combination of traditional formal devices and surreal or unusual content is one of the hallmarks of Japanese mystery and suspense fiction.

New Traditionalists in Japan

- After World War II, there was something of a reaction against the use of fantastical elements in Japanese mystery and suspense fiction. The work of Seicho Matsumoto is a fine example of this turn toward realism in Japanese crime fiction. In novels such as *Points and Lines*, *Inspector Imanishi Investigates*, and *Pro Bono*, Matsumoto focuses on the ordinary lives of Japanese people and on human psychology. What's more, Matsumoto's work is quite dark, in contrast to the whimsical surrealism of much of Rampo's work.

- In the 1980s, there was a reaction to the social realist school of mystery writing, embodied in the work of writers like Soji Shimada. Known variously as new traditionalist or new orthodox crime writers, authors like Shimada argued for the restoration of the rules that governed the production of classic detective fiction and aimed to produce a kind of mystery writing that was self-consciously artificial and self-reflexive.

- In his 1981 debut novel, *The Tokyo Zodiac Murders*, Soji Shimada begins with a foreword that challenges readers to solve for themselves the mysteries that he is about to describe. Shimada also claims that every reader will have access to all the clues they need to solve the mystery and that none of the characters will have an unfair advantage over the reader.

A DETECTIVE WITHOUT APOLOGY

- In 1998, Scottish writer Alexander McCall Smith published *The No. 1 Ladies' Detective Agency*—and overnight Africa became a prime destination for mystery and suspense fiction. McCall Smith's book, which subsequently grew into an immensely popular series, is set in the town of Gaborone, Botswana, and features Precious Ramotswe as the protagonist. In fact, the book is an African cozy mystery.

- At the start of the first novel in the series, Precious's beloved father has died and left her all his cattle. Defying expectations and tradition, Precious sells the cattle and uses the proceeds to open a detective agency—despite her lack of experience and notwithstanding widespread local skepticism about whether a woman can even be a detective. Over the course of the novel, Precious gradually proves her detractors wrong; by novel's end, although the future of her business is anything but secure, Precious considers herself a detective without apology.

- Precious Ramotswe's closest cousin in mystery and suspense fiction is Agatha Christie's Miss Jane Marple. Like Miss Marple, Precious has no formal training as a detective; she is often underestimated (especially by men); and she knows everyone in her community and uses that knowledge to her advantage. And like Miss Marple, Precious doesn't need specialized training in order to do her work. All she needs is empathy, patience, common sense, and determination—qualities she has in abundance.

■ What's more, *The No. 1 Ladies' Detective Agency* is also cozy in terms of its setting. Gaborone is McCall Smith's version of Christie's St. Mary Mead. It's a small community with very specific local traditions and customs, and Precious is very much at the center of this community.

■ In many respects, crime is not even the primary element in the No. 1 Ladies' Detective Agency series. Most of the cases Precious takes involve relatively minor crimes and often concern issues (such as domestic violence and marital infidelity) that a large number of McCall Smith's readers have likely experienced themselves, which is another reason why the series is so popular.

KWEI QUARTEY AND THE DARKO DAWSON SERIES

■ The continent contains African mystery and suspense fiction writers of every kind, not just those who aspire to write African cozies. Kwei Quartey, for example, is the author of a series of police procedurals set in Ghana that feature protagonist Inspector Darko Dawson. The Darko Dawson series is much closer to hard-boiled crime fiction than McCall Smith's series. Some of its grittiness comes from Quartey's use of the chaotic urban texture of Ghana's capital city, Accra.

■ In Quartey's debut novel, *Wife of the Gods*, the source of conflict is between scientific (that is, Western) medical knowledge and traditional medicinal practices. In *Children of the Street*, Quartey explores the plight of the street children of Accra. Like McCall Smith, Quartey often uses what he perceives as tension between traditional and modern aspects of Africa to energize his plots.

- Writers like Quartey also incorporate familiar elements from mainstream (Western) mystery and suspense fiction to make their work appealing to non-African readers. At the same time, however, they include details that are specific to the African context that those very same readers will find appealing due to their unfamiliarity.

- One African reviewer said of Quartey that he "doesn't really know much about rural life in Ghana" and that he shows "a peculiar interest (almost an obsession) in the Ghana that appeals to the foreign tourist." Clearly, writing mystery and suspense fiction in Africa leaves one open to accusations that one is inauthentic, perhaps because one is seen as importing a foreign genre into an inappropriate context.

LEONARDO PADURA FUENTES

- Because of the chaotic political history of Latin America, mystery and suspense fiction writers from this region often have reason to consider the relation between the violence of the individual and the violence of the state.

- Critic Persephone Braham has written a book entitled *Crimes Against the State, Crimes Against Persons*, which is a comparative study of mystery and suspense fiction in Cuba and Mexico. According to Braham, examples of the genre in both countries are deeply engaged with considering the relationship between crime and the state. Braham analyzes the work of two authors in her case studies: Leonardo Padura Fuentes and Paco Ignacio Taibo II.

- Padura was born in Havana, Cuba, in 1955, and he began his career as an investigative journalist. He is best known to English-speaking readers for his quartet of crime novels published between 1991 and 1998 and translated under the following titles: *Havana Blue, Havana Gold, Havana Red,* and *Havana Black.* Padura's collective name for the quartet is The Four Seasons because the books are set, respectively, in the winter, spring, summer, and autumn of 1989.

- The novels are often described as "morality tales for the post-Soviet era." The series' protagonist is the world-weary police lieutenant Mario Conde. The crimes he investigates allow Padura to show Havana and Cuba as a whole in a state of decay. Collectively, the Havana quartet contains many criticisms of Cuba and the Castro regime.

PACO IGNACIO TAIBO II

- Mexican writer Paco Ignacio Taibo II is best known for his series of idiosyncratic private-eye novels featuring Héctor Belascoarán Shayne. In these novels, Taibo works tirelessly to expose political and economic corruption at the highest levels of Mexican society, but he does so in a manner that combines humor, absurdity, despair, anger, cynicism, and political analysis all at the same time.

- In 2004, Subcomandante Marcos of the Zapatista Army of National Liberation contacted Taibo and asked him if he would collaborate on a novel. The result was an extraordinary piece of work called *The Uncomfortable Dead*, with alternate chapters written by Marcos and Taibo.

> Writers like Quartey also incorporate familiar elements from mainstream (Western) mystery and suspense fiction to make their work appealing to non-African readers.

- In the novel, Belascoarán Shayne teams up with Elias Contreras, an investigator from the Zapatistas, to solve the crimes committed by a mysterious individual named Morales. As the investigation proceeds, the detectives realize that the corruption and crime they're fighting are widespread and systemic—so pervasive, in fact, that there are multiple incarnations of the criminal Morales. Belascoarán Shayne and Contreras decide to each choose their own Morales and punish him appropriately.

■ Belascoarán Shayne finds his Morales. But realizing the futility of turning him over to a corrupt judicial system, Belascoarán Shayne takes matters into his own hands and kills Morales. Absurd, violent, angry, and despairing in equal measure, the solutions that Taibo explores succeed in capturing the reality of a country as violent and seemingly lawless as contemporary Mexico.

QUESTIONS TO CONSIDER
1. Why is mystery and suspense fiction popular in so many different countries?
2. How do writers adapt the genre to suit their own purposes and locales?

SUGGESTED READING
Asong, *Detective Fiction and the African Scene.*

Braham, *Crimes against the State, Crimes against Persons.*

Silver, *Purloined Letters.*

JAPANESE AND LATIN AMERICAN MYSTERIES

I n 2004, Akashic Books, a small independent publishing house based in Brooklyn, New York, published the first volume of what it hoped would become a series. Entitled *Brooklyn Noir*, the volume contained original short mystery and suspense stories that all shared a Brooklyn setting.

Since the publication of that inaugural volume, Akashic's "City Noir" series has gone on to achieve huge success. It now numbers dozens of titles, and forthcoming entries in the series includes volumes set in Rio, Prague, Addis Ababa, Lagos, and Marrakesh. The success of the series confirms the continued primacy of the city as the default setting for mystery and suspense fiction, but for my purposes in this lecture, I want to emphasize the global scope of the series.

One of the most exciting and energizing developments in the field of mystery and suspense fiction over the past 20 years has been the genre's continued spread over the entire globe, and the success of Akashic Books is just one example of that spread. Driven in part by the success of 'Nordic Noir,' particularly Stieg Larsson's Millennium series featuring Lisbeth Salander, publishers are now more willing than ever before to either translate or commission crime fiction from countries that previously would have been considered a bad investment.

Consequently, we're in the middle of a boom in international crime fiction, with classic texts coming back into print in new translations, and new writers being published for the first time, some writing in their native languages and some in English.

The purpose of this lecture is to introduce you to the work of mystery and suspense fiction writers from outside Anglo-America, Europe, and Scandinavia. By looking more closely at work that might not be known to even avid fans of the genre, we'll see not only that the genre once again demonstrates its ability to be endlessly recombined and reinvented to address a dizzying range of issues but also that it's flourishing as never before.

The first stop on our world tour is Japan, where mystery and suspense fiction has been popular since at least the 1920s. The key figure in the genre's early history and subsequent mainstreaming in Japan is Taro Hirai, who wrote under the pseudonym Edogawa Ranpo. His fondness for the work of Edgar Allan Poe can be seen by the fact that if you pronounce his pen name quickly, it is meant to sound like a Japanese version of Poe's full name.

Ranpo began his writing career in 1923 when he published a mystery story entitled "The Two-Sen Copper Coin" in a magazine that had previously published the work of Poe, Sir Arthur Conan Doyle, and G. K. Chesterton. However, this was the first time the magazine had published a piece of mystery fiction by a Japanese writer, making it a landmark in the context of the Japanese version of the genre.

As you might expect from a writer so heavily influenced by Poe and Doyle, Ranpo's first story is a puzzle mystery, but adapted to a Japanese context. Taking a tale of logical ratiocination that seems to come straight from Poe, but using a Japanese example to demonstrate the method of analysis associated with Auguste Dupin in this case, a code based on a Buddhist incantation as well as Japanese-language Braille. This indicates Ranpo's inventiveness and his ability to change the inherited tradition of mystery and suspense fiction to suit his own purposes.

Over the course of a long and productive career, Ranpo would prove his ingenuity and creativity again and again in a large number of stories and novels that ran the gamut from puzzle mysteries to "locked room" mysteries such as 1925's "The Murder on D. Hill." He even wrote a series of mysteries for younger readers featuring a group of young detectives that Ranpo called the "Boy Detectives Club" that is still read by many young people in Japan today. They might be considered the Japanese equivalent of the Hardy Boy or Nancy Drew mysteries.

Ranpo and his work are also important for a couple of other reasons. Being a fan and a student of the genre as a whole, Ranpo took care to establish institutions in Japan that would encourage and support this type of work. In 1946, he helped support the founding of a new journal named Jewels that would feature mystery fiction. And in 1947, he founded the Detective Authors Club, which in 1963 was renamed the Mystery Writers of Japan.

Apart from his interest in homosexuality, another feature of Ranpo's work may come as a surprise if you think of Japan as being a rather straitlaced and repressed culture. Even though Ranpo had a fondness for traditional formal elements of the genre such as the puzzle and "locked room" mysteries, from the beginning of his career, he combined this traditionalism with unusual, even surreal elements.

For example, Ranpo also wrote stories that included sadomasochism "The Case of the Murder on D. Hill" and even a story about a man who hides inside a chair to feel the bodies sitting on top of him "The Human Chair." You could even argue that this combination of traditional formal devices and surreal or unusual content is one of the hallmarks of Japanese mystery and suspense fiction.

After World War II, there was something of a reaction against the use of fantastical elements in Japanese mystery and suspense fiction. Perhaps influenced by a postwar sense of despair and pessimism, the genre moved away from a dependence on traditional formal and puzzle elements and instead embraced a kind of social realism, resulting in stories and novels in which Japanese society as a whole, rather than an individual criminal, was under investigation.

The work of Seicho Matsumoto is a good example of this turn toward the real in Japanese crime fiction. In novels such as *Points and Lines*, *Inspector Imanishi Investigates*, and *Pro Bono*, Matsumoto focuses on the ordinary lives of Japanese people and on human psychology. In addition, his interest in corruption both among the police and among criminals tends to make his work even darker, and very different from the whimsical surrealism of much of Ranpo's work.

Although Japanese mystery fiction today is so varied that it's very difficult to generalize about, it's important to note a couple of other developments before moving on. In the 1980s, a kind of reaction to the social realist school of mystery writing emerged in the work of writers like Soji Shimada. Known variously as new traditionalist or new orthodox crime writers, authors like Shimada argued for the restoration of the rules that governed the production of classical detective fiction. And they aimed to produce a kind of mystery writing that was self-consciously artificial and self-reflective.

In his 1981 debut novel, *The Tokyo Zodiac Murders*, Soji Shimada begins with a foreword that challenges readers to solve for themselves the mysteries that he is about to describe. Shimada also claims that every reader will have access to all the clues they need to solve the mystery and that none of the characters will have an unfair advantage over the reader.

Clearly, we're back on traditional ground in that the novel is set up as an elaborate game or challenge that is played between the reader and the writer. This is very different from the world-weariness of the social realist school of Japanese mystery writing as personified by Matsumoto. But as I said, it's very difficult to generalize about a genre as diverse as Japanese mystery fiction. If some writers were persuaded by Shimada's call for a return to tradition, others definitely were not. Some of the most exciting work being written in the genre today features very dark and extremely violent plots, along with philosophical elements that frequently cause this work to inhabit that blurred line between popular and literary fiction.

Both Natsuo Kirino and Fuminori Nakamura, for example, are writing work that is very challenging. In novels such as *Real World* and *Out*, Kirino pulls no punches as she plumbs the depths of the Japanese underworld and explores how the lives of ordinary people can quickly spin out of control.

Meanwhile, in novels like *Evil and the Mask* and *The Gun*, Nakamura is writing philosophically complex meditations about human evil that apparently owe as much to French existentialism and the work of Friedrich Nietzsche as they do to mystery and suspense conventions. And thanks to the booming market in international crime fiction, the good news is that all of this challenging material is available in translation.

The next stop on our tour is Africa. Until recently, Africa wasn't much of a destination for people interested in the genre. It wasn't that there was no work being produced there, but publishers were unwilling to take a chance on publishing African mystery and suspense fiction until someone could show them that there was a market for it.

The writer who almost single-handedly changed this situation was the Scottish author Alexander McCall Smith. In 1998, he published The *No. 1 Ladies' Detective Agency*. All the novels in what would become an incredibly popular series are set in the town of Gaborone, Botswana, and feature Precious Ramotswe as the protagonist.

At the start of this first novel in the series, Precious's father has died and has left her all his cattle. Going against expectations and tradition, Precious sells the cattle and uses the proceeds to open a detective agency, despite having no experience, and despite widespread local skepticism about whether a woman can even be a detective. Over the course of the novel, Precious gradually proves her detractors wrong, and by novel's end, although the future of her business is anything but secure, Precious thinks of herself as a detective without apology.

What is the secret of this novel's success and how did this success persuade publishers of mystery and suspense fiction that Africa was now fertile territory for the genre? The short answer to this question is that with *The No. 1 Ladies' Detective Agency* McCall Smith succeeded in creating something that many people would have thought of as a contradiction in terms. the African 'cozy mystery.'

So, what exactly is an African 'cozy mystery?' I would argue that Precious Ramotswe's closest analog in mystery and suspense fiction is Agatha Christie's Miss Jane Marple. Like Marple, Precious has no formal training as a detective. Like Marple, Precious is often underestimated by people especially the men around her. Like Marple, Precious knows everything and everybody in her community and uses that knowledge to her advantage. And like Marple, Precious doesn't need specialized training in order to do her work. All she needs is empathy, patience, common sense, and determination, and she has all those qualities in abundance.

Apart from the similarities between Precious and a typical cozy detective, *No. 1 Ladies' Detective Agency* is also cozy in terms of its setting. Gaborone is McCall Smith's version of Christie's St. Mary Mead. It's a small community with very specific local traditions and customs and Precious is very much at the center of this community.

Even though Botswana borders South Africa and McCall Smith often refers to Botswana's neighbor, I think it is crucial that he did not choose South Africa as the primary setting of these books. Why? Because building a cozy mystery series would be much more challenging in the context of the reality and then the legacy of apartheid.

This is not to say that South Africa is an inhospitable environment for mystery and suspense fiction indeed, quite the contrary, but only a variation on the hard-boiled would do. To put it another way, rural Botswana is at least potentially cozy in a way that South Africa very definitely is not.

It's important to mention that, in many respects, crime is not even the primary element in the *No. 1 Ladies' Detective Agency* series. Yes, Precious is a detective, and yes, she does investigate and solve mysteries, but most of the cases she takes involve relatively minor crimes and often concern issues such as domestic violence and marital infidelity that a large number of McCall Smith's readers have likely experienced themselves, which is another reason why the series is so popular.

If crime is only one of the issues that McCall Smith explores in this series, then, what are the others? Precious's own life and the life of her friends, family, and the community around her form the bulk of what gets discussed in any given novel in the series. And as Precious tends to travel quite widely around her community, this gives McCall Smith the perfect opportunity to introduce local color elements into his novels that non-African readers are highly likely to find both interesting and educational.

In fact, the differences between the rural, traditional, and indigenous ways of life on the one hand and the urban, modern, and foreign ways of life on the other often provide the main point of conflict in the series. In the first novel, for example, the main crime under investigation is what looks to be a muti killing, which is when a young person is murdered so that certain parts of their body can be used for witchcraft.

The presence of such a crime gives McCall Smith an opportunity to have Precious consider the tensions between the old ways and realities of living at the turn of the 21st century. It eventually turns out that the boy thought to have been murdered is, in fact, alive and well, and Precious returns him to his family. In this manner, McCall Smith reaffirms his commitment to producing a 'cozy' mystery in an African setting and thus cements his success.

The beneficiaries of McCall Smith's success include African mystery and suspense fiction writers of every kind and not just those who aspire to write African cozies. Kwei Quartey, for example, is the author of a series of police procedurals set in Ghana. These feature protagonist Inspector Darko Dawson, a homicide detective in Accra, Ghana's capital.

Beginning with the publication of *Wife of the Gods* in 2009 the Darko Dawson series is much closer to being hard-boiled than McCall Smith's series. Some of its grittiness comes from Quartey's use of the urban setting of Accra. Whereas McCall Smith capitalizes on the rather old-fashioned assumption that Africa is synonymous with the rural rather than the urban, Quartey makes full use of the chaotic urban texture of the Ghanaian capital city.

In his debut novel, *Wife of the Gods*, the source of conflict is between scientific that is, Western medical knowledge on the one hand and traditional medicinal practices on the other. In *Children of the Street*, the second novel in the series, Quartey explores the plight of the street children of Accra, who are being killed off at an alarming rate in what is either a form of traditional ritual killing or a modern case of serial murder. These plots indicate that, like McCall Smith, Quartey often uses what he perceives as tension between traditional and modern aspects of Africa to energize his plots.

In *Murder at Cape Three Points*, which is set on Ghana's coast, Quartey examines the conflicts that arise when land that has been occupied by a traditional fishing community for hundreds of years is targeted by rapacious real estate and oil companies. Again, the detective occupies that contentious middle ground where the traditional and the modern collide, sometimes with explosively violent results.

In *Wife of the Gods*, while investigating the murder of a medical student who was disseminating information about AIDS prevention in rural Ghana, Darko Dawson finds himself fighting with the local witch doctor about his trokosi. These are young women betrothed to this traditional healer both as a form of tribute and in order to protect the women's families' from harm. Although Quartey technically presents both sides of the trokosi issue, it's clear from Dawson's antipathy toward the traditional healer where his sympathies really lie.

Like McCall Smith, writers like Quartey walk a fine line between including enough familiar elements from mainstream Western mystery and suspense fiction to make their work appealing to non-African readers, while also including details that are specific to the African context that those very same readers will find appealing due to their unfamiliarity.

Judging from Quartey's success, he's managed to strike that balance. But it's interesting to note that some African critics and reviewers have not been so impressed. Noting that Quartey has spent much of his life in the U.S. after being born in Ghana—his mother is African-American—one African reviewer said of Quartey that he "doesn't really know much about rural life in Ghana" and that he shows "a peculiar interest almost an obsession in the Ghana that appeals to the foreign tourist." Clearly, writing mystery and suspense fiction in Africa leaves one open to accusations that one is inauthentic, perhaps because one is seen as importing a foreign genre into an inappropriate context.

Before moving on to our last stop, I want to mention briefly a final example of African crime fiction that makes a virtue out of the potential for inauthenticity, and that's *Nairobi Heat*, a novel by Mukoma wa Ngugi, the son of internationally renowned African writer Ngugi wa Thiong'o.

Born in the U S., raised in Kenya, and now living in the U.S., Mukoma draws on his ambiguity about his own identity in his novel. His protagonist, Ishmael, is an African-American homicide detective from Madison, Wisconsin, who travels to Nairobi in his attempt to solve the murder of a famous African peace activist. Once in Kenya, Ishmael has to confront the complicated history of the relationship between Africans and African-Americans while also working under the shadow of the Rwandan genocide as he searches for the truth about a single murder.

Nairobi Heat is an impressive novel that works on a number of different levels simultaneously. But the one I'd like to emphasize is what Mukoma implies by bringing together the Rwandan genocide and a homicide investigation into a single murder. What is the meaning or the importance, Mukoma encourages us to ask, of an individual death in the context of the death of hundreds of thousands of people?

Obviously, there's no simple answer to that question, but I give Mukoma credit for asking it because it requires us to think about the purpose of mystery and suspense fiction as a whole. If it dignifies a single death by investigating it and then finding and punishing the perpetrator, does the genre also risk overlooking death when it happens en masse rather than on the individual level?

This is a good question to keep in mind as we move on to the final stop in our tour, Latin America. Due to the political history of this part of the world, mystery and suspense fiction writers from this region often have reason to consider the relation between the violence of the individual and state violence.

With this point in mind, I'd like to recommend a wonderful book by critic Persephone Braham entitled *Crimes Against the State, Crimes Against Persons*, which is a comparative study of mystery and suspense fiction in Cuba and Mexico. According to Braham, examples of the genre in both countries are deeply engaged with considering the relationship between crime and the state. But what exactly counts as both crime and the state in these two countries is complicated.

In closing this lecture, therefore, and with appropriate acknowledgment of the influence of Braham's work on my own reading, I'd like to look more closely at the work of two authors she draws on in her case studies. Leonardo Padura Fuentes and Paco Ignacio Taibo II.

Padura was born in Havana, Cuba, in 1955, where he still lives. He began his career as an investigative journalist, and some of that same muckraking impulse survives in his crime fiction. Although his first novel is a love story, he is best-known to English-speaking readers for his quartet of crime novels published between 1991 and 1998 and translated under the following titles, *Havana Blue*, *Havana Gold*, *Havana Red*, and *Havana Black*. Padura's collective name for the quartet is The Four Seasons because the books are set respectively in the winter, spring, summer, and autumn of 1989.

The year is important because 1989 marked the beginning of what became known as the "Special Period" in Cuba that was triggered by the dissolution of the Soviet Union in the same year. The economic impact of this dissolution on Cuba was severe and lasted for most of the 1990s. During this period, Cubans had to come to terms with the consequences of living in the post-Soviet era, and that is why Padura's quartet of novels is often described as morality tales for the post-Soviet era.

The series' protagonist is the world-weary Police Lieutenant Mario Conde. The crimes he investigates allow Padura to show Havana, and Cuba as a whole, in a state of decay. The streets are dangerous and shabby, violence and corruption are always lurking just beneath the surface, and the only dependable people in Conde's life are his immediate family and those he has known since his childhood.

Collectively, the Havana quartet contains many criticisms of Cuba and the Castro regime, but the criticisms are all implied and could only have been made during the "Special Period," when the state of decay could be blamed on the withdrawal of Soviet support.

By contrast, there's nothing implicit about the social criticism contained in Mexican writer Paco Ignacio Taibo II's work. Ever since the late 1960s, when he was a leading figure in student protests again state violence and corruption, Taibo has been a thorn in the side of successive Mexican political administrations, not least because his books are tremendously popular.

Although he has written a number of nonfiction works, including a huge biography of Che Guevara, Taibo is best known for his series of idiosyncratic private eye novels featuring Héctor Belascoarán Shayne. In these novels, Taibo works tirelessly to expose political and economic corruption at the highest levels of Mexican society, but he does so in a manner that combines humor, absurdity, despair, anger, cynicism, and political analysis all at the same time.

Though they offer no concrete or practical solutions to the problems that he identifies, it is impossible to come away from a Taibo book without feeling energized and hopeful. A closer examination of one of his books will give you a better idea of why this is so.

In 2004, Subcomandante Marcos of the Zapatista Army of National Liberation contacted Taibo and asked him if he would like to collaborate on a novel. The result was an extraordinary piece of work called *The Uncomfortable Dead*, with alternate chapters written by Marcos and Taibo.

In the novel, Belascoarán Shayne teams up with Elias Contreras, an investigator from the Zapatistas, to try and solve the crimes committed by a mysterious individual named Morales. As the investigation proceeds, the detectives realize that the corruption and crimes they're fighting are so widespread and so systemic they include globalization, privatization, and even capitalism itself that they are looking for multiple Morales. Once they reach this point of the investigation, Belascoarán Shayne and Contreras decide to each choose their own Morales and punish him appropriately.

The Zapatista investigator takes his Morales back to Chiapas in southern Mexico, the home of the Zapatistas. After a trial, Morales is sentenced to 10 years community service. This might seem like an absurdly inappropriate sentence, and in a sense it is. But the fact that Morales absolutely loathes the idea of doing anything to help the Zapatistas actually makes this sentence the perfect example of poetic justice.

Belascoarán Shayne, meanwhile, finds his Morales. But realizing his futility of turning him over to a judicial system that is just as corrupt as Morales, Shayne takes matters into his own hands and kills Morales by throwing him down a stairwell. Absurd, violent, angry, and despairing in equal measure, the "solutions" that Taibo explores succeed in capturing the reality of a country as violent and seemingly lawless as contemporary Mexico. In *The Uncomfortable Dead*, Taibo not only makes a valuable contribution to analyses of the current situation but also demonstrates the flexibility and power of mystery and suspense fiction to address the world around it.

By both engaging with the details of their specific cultures and then connecting these details to issues of interest to people around the world, mystery and suspense fiction from Japan, Africa, and Latin America makes a valuable contribution to the genre.

Precursors to True Crime

M odern true crime focuses largely on celebrity cases, historical cases, cold cases, and serial killers. The foundational elements of true crime go back hundreds of years, however. These elements consist of fact-based narratives with crime at their center, narratives that claim to be factual but actually use a variety of fictional techniques, and narratives that are designed to instruct and entertain their audience. In this lecture, we'll construct a prehistory for true crime by examining such materials as Puritan execution sermons, rogues' biographies, and newspaper coverage. What's more, we will examine how true-crime narratives draw on elements of mystery and suspense fiction.

A Pedagogic Dimension

- Puritan-era America was just as obsessed by the acts, trials, and executions of criminals as we are today. Public hangings aroused tremendous popular interest, and the audiences for executions reportedly constituted some of the largest public gatherings in the Puritan era. Not surprisingly, Puritan ministers seized the opportunity to instruct the crowds attending these events about the proper way to view the criminal's demise.

- For example, in 1675, the influential Puritan minister Increase Mather preached an execution sermon in Boston entitled "The Wicked Man's Portion" that is very representative of the genre. The message to be drawn from the execution of the criminal is spelled out very clearly in the sermon's subtitle: "Wherein is shewed that excess in wickedness doth bring untimely death." Biblical passages accompanying the sermon drive the message home even more firmly.

- The use of biblical passages to underline the message of the execution sermon is typical of the pedagogic dimension of these sermons—a dimension that can also be found in contemporary examples of true crime. Some of the lessons are explicit (this is what will happen to you if you commit this crime), and some are implicit (our community is defined by certain values, and this is what we do to those who violate those values).

- In her book entitled *Murder Most Foul*, historian Karen Halttunen has argued that the doctrine of original sin played a significant role in determining Puritan attitudes toward the criminal, and the influence of this doctrine can be detected in execution sermons. She writes: "The effect of the execution sermon's treatment of criminal causality was to establish a strong moral identification between the assembled congregation and the condemned murderer. For the doctrine that the root of crime was innate depravity undercut any notion of the murderer's moral peculiarity, with all humankind bound in that original sin committed by the first parents of the race."

EMPHASIS ON ENTERTAINMENT
- The best-known collections of execution sermons and other early true-crime narratives appear in the middle of the 18th century. *The Newgate Calendar*, a monthly bulletin of executions at the Newgate Prison in London, first appeared in England in the 1740s. This format proved to be so popular that it was reprinted and revamped dozens of times, all the way through to the 20th century.

- Its American equivalent was *The American Bloody Register*, first published in 1784. You'll look in vain for any biblical references on the title page of the *Bloody Register*, but you'll learn that it contains "A true and complete history of the loves, last words, and dying confessions of three of the most noted criminals that have ever made their exit from a stage in America."

- The phrasing here suggests that the focus of the narrative is on the fame (or notoriety) of these criminals. Moreover, the reference to a stage (the scaffold) implies a full awareness of the public execution as a spectacle—a spectacle whose primary purpose is now to entertain rather than to instruct.

In 1675, the influential Puritan minister Increase Mather preached an execution sermon in Boston entitled "The Wicked Man's Portion" that is very representative of the genre.

- There is a significant difference between the earlier execution sermons and the later execution narratives. The new element is an interest in the lives of the criminals themselves and an emphasis on the exceptional nature of the criminal—exceptional not only in the sense of being uniquely wicked or evil but also in the sense of being distinctly entertaining, dashing, even admirable.

THE CLEVER ROGUE

- As Puritan influence over American society began to weaken in the late 17th century, other forms of true-crime narrative began to appear that gave criminals the opportunity to present their side of the story in their own voice. What's more, these criminal narratives also became increasingly secular.

- A kind of celebrity culture organized around the criminal that culminated in what became known as rogues' biographies, where criminality was seen almost as an admirable expression of an unbridled personality. The tone of these rogues' biographies is quite different from that of the Puritans' execution sermons.

They're more sensational, and they also tend to characterize the murderers as monsters.

- Critic Daniel Williams has noted that these changes in crime narratives were influenced by the development of Enlightenment concepts of freedom—concepts that gradually replaced the doctrine of original sin. According to Williams, self-determination, self-reliance, and self-initiative all become socially dominant ideals in the 18th century.

- Williams explains: "After the Revolution, after the country had itself defied authority, descriptions of deviant and defiant individuals became especially popular in American literature, and the criminal, the clever rogue in particular, became both hero and antihero, both epitome and parody of the American character. As a literary figure, the criminal moved from Puritan condemnation to post-Revolutionary celebration."

MURDERER AS MONSTER

- Historian Karen Halttunen has argued that Americans struggled to come up with an explanation for criminality that was as intellectually satisfying as the concept of original sin. This problem, she says, was especially acute where the concepts of environmental influence, motive, or uncontrolled passion as reasons for crime just didn't seem to explain the circumstances of the crime.

- Halttunen explains: "[A] significant number of murder narratives printed between 1750 and 1820 demonstrated the inadequacy of all these attempts to explain the crime, as some men and women murdered against character, or from an inexplicable compulsion to kill, or in cold-blooded insensibility. These crimes challenged the prevailing rational view of human nature."

- The answer to the dilemma posed by these inexplicable crimes was to make a virtue out of necessity and heighten the air of mystery surrounding them by using the language of gothic fiction. In particular, the notion of monstrosity assumed a prominent role in crime narratives. As Halttunen explains, the "image of the murderer as monster expressed the incomprehensibility of murder within the rational Enlightenment social order."

USE OF FICTIONAL ELEMENTS

- There was more sensationalism and a greater emphasis on monstrosity in true-crime narratives beginning in the 18th century. However, there was also a greater use of fictional elements. Unlike the original execution sermons, which were fairly accurate, later examples of true-crime narrative were more creative with the facts. After all, they were distributed over a

wider geographical area to people who hadn't witnessed the actual execution.

■ Fictional elements assumed a greater importance because these later narratives placed more emphasis on entertaining rather than instructing, on thrilling readers rather than sending them to consult specific passages in the Bible. What we start to see in the 18th and 19th centuries are true-crime narratives that more explicitly combine entertainment and moral precepts.

■ Although this combination of moral lesson and thrilling entertainment might seem paradoxical, it demonstrates that 19th-century true-crime narratives aimed to reach quite a diverse audience, including the old and the young, traditionalists and freethinkers alike.

THE PENNY PRESS

■ Beginning in the 19th century, we see a rise in newspaper reporting about murder. Although, as we have seen, there are many examples of American true-crime narratives dating all the way back to Colonial times, journalistic coverage of crime was a fairly late arrival on the scene.

■ Newspapers had traditionally paid very little attention to crime, not only because they didn't want to waste precious space but also because they were constrained by what they considered a sense of delicacy and civic responsibility. This all changed with the explosion of the penny press in the mid-1830s.

■ The most famous penny newspaper of the day was *The New York Herald*, published by James Gordon Bennett. Bennett, a shrewd businessman, knew that nothing sold more newspapers than hideous crimes. As he once put it, American readers "were more ready to seek six columns of the details of a brutal murder...

than the same amount of words poured forth by the genius of the noblest author of our times."

- From the mid-1830s onward, crime news became a staple of newspaper coverage. It was easy and cheap to gather, it was already familiar to readers who were avid consumers of other forms of true-crime narrative, and it gave newspapers the opportunity to argue that they were performing a civic duty—namely, warning their readers about the dangers of the rapidly expanding American cities. (There again we see the pedagogic dimension of true crime.)

- Of course, the popular press, then as now, was criticized for being excessively sensational. But like it or not, the popular press—or yellow press, as it came to be known—was here to stay. It was the great-grandparent, as it were, of the tabloid newspapers and reality television shows of today.

MARY ROGERS TO MARIE ROGÊT

- In this market, certain criminal cases quickly became causes célèbres. Consider the case of the murder of shopgirl Mary Rogers, which was the inspiration for Edgar Allan Poe's story "The Mystery of Marie Rogêt." The Rogers case took place in 1841, the same year Poe published "The Murders in the Rue Morgue." In her book *The Mysterious Death of Mary Rogers*, historian Amy Gilman Srebnick comments that were it not for the newly developed concept of public news and the recent emergence of a reading public craving sensation from the penny press, the story and the mystery of Mary Rogers would probably have gone almost unnoticed.

- Srebnick argues that the murder of Mary Rogers not only became an "emblematic crime" in the way it linked female death, sexuality, and a peculiarly urban sense of mystery, but it also ensured that crime reporting became a major aspect of popular journalism in America.

■ Srebnick's remarks indicate precisely how early examples of true crime overlap with the genre of mystery and suspense fiction. Depending on the writer and the intended audience, the same sensational crime could provide the raw material for a newspaper article, a true-crime narrative that combined facts with gothic fictional elements, or Edgar Allan Poe's "The Mystery of Marie Rogêt."

QUESTIONS TO CONSIDER
1. What are the similarities and differences between early true-crime texts and mystery and suspense fiction?

2. Why was it so important for early examples of true crime to claim that they possessed some kind of social utility?

SUGGESTED READING
Halttunen, *Murder Most Foul.*

Tucher, *Froth and Scum.*

PRECURSORS TO TRUE CRIME

I f you ask people when what we call true crime began, most of them would say the 20th century. If they know of Truman Capote's landmark book *In Cold Blood*, published in 1966, they might date the beginning of the genre more precisely. But even if they don't know of Capote, my sense is that most people would think of true crime as a distinctly modern phenomenon. Are they right?

Well, yes and no. If by true crime we mean a genre that markets itself under that name, that exists as a category recognized and promoted by publishing houses, and that focuses largely on celebrity cases, famous historical cases, cold cases, and serial killers, then yes, true crime is more or less a modern phenomenon.

But if by true crime we are referring to fact-based narratives with crime at their center, narratives that claim to be factual but actually use a variety of fictional techniques, and narratives that are designed to instruct and entertain their audience, well, that type of true crime goes back hundreds of years.

In this lecture, we'll discuss the precursors to the modern version of true crime. By examining such materials as Puritan execution sermons, rogues' biographies, and newspaper coverage of crime from this standpoint, we'll be able to construct a prehistory for true crime. But we'll also see how this genre draws on elements of mystery and suspense fiction while distinguishing itself by emphasizing its factual, objective status.

Our story begins in Puritan New England, and I'm well aware that this seems like a counterintuitive starting point. Surely the Puritans had their minds fixed too firmly on what it took to get to heaven to be concerned with crime here on earth? In fact, Puritan-era America was just as obsessed by the acts, trials, and executions of criminals as we are today. It's just that their interest necessarily took different forms. And one of these forms was not only reading about crimes but also attending executions.

Public hangings aroused tremendous popular interest, and the audiences for executions reportedly constituted some of the largest public gatherings in the Puritan era. Not surprisingly, Puritan ministers seized the opportunity to instruct the crowds attending these events about the proper way to view the criminal's demise.

Clergymen typically delivered sermons on capital cases on the Sunday before the sentence was to be carried out, or very often on the day of the execution itself. By all accounts, these sermons were often as well attended as the executions themselves, and the fact of their subsequent publication and distribution made them extremely influential and well-known documents, documents that obviously had a strong religious flavor.

For example, in 1675, an influential Puritan minister by the name of Increase Mather preached an execution sermon in Boston entitled "The Wicked Man's Portion" that is very representative of the genre. The message to be drawn from the execution of the criminal is spelled out very clearly in the sermon's subtitle, "Wherein is shewed that excesse in wickedness doth bring untimely death."

Below this subtitle appear biblical passages that drive the message home even more firmly. In this case, Mather chose Proverbs 10:27, "The fear of the Lord prolongeth days, but the years of the wicked shall be shortened" and Ephesians 6:2-3, "Honour thy father and mother; which is the first commandment with promise; that it may be well with thee, and thou mayest live long on the earth."

This use of biblical passages to underline the message of the execution sermon is typical of what I would call the pedagogic dimension of these sermons, a dimension that can also be found in contemporary examples of true crime. Some of the lessons are explicit, this is what will happen to you if you commit this crime, and some are implicit, our community is defined by certain values, and this is what we do to those who violate those values.

The Bible passages also enabled the sermon's reader to later use it at home as a kind of study guide. Considering that the Bible was very likely the only book in many Puritan homes, the references to Bible verses on both the front page and in the margins of these sermons made them a very useful resource for parents to educate, and perhaps frighten, their children.

In a wonderful book entitled *Murder Most Foul*, historian Karen Halttunen has argued that the doctrine of original sin played a profoundly important role in determining Puritan attitudes toward the criminal, and the influence of this doctrine can be detected in execution sermons. She writes,

> The effect of the execution sermon's treatment of criminal causality was to establish a strong moral identification between the assembled congregation and the condemned murderer. For the doctrine that the root of crime was innate depravity undercut any notion of the murderer's moral peculiarity, with all humankind bound in that original sin committed by the first parents of the race.

Unlike many contemporary examples of true crime, execution sermons did not present the criminal as some type as monstrous outsider. Rather, in the sermons the criminal is seen as a representative member of the community, precisely because he or she has sinned. In fact, one could argue that criminals were model citizens of the Puritan community because by sinning, confessing that sin, and then asking for God's forgiveness, they dramatized the process of conversion and redemption.

Thanks to the efforts of the Puritan ministers, execution sermons were enormously popular. We know this partly because their publishers used them to advertise their other products because they knew that these sermons reached a large and diverse audience. Products advertised included another publication from Increase Mather entitled "The Folly of Sinning" and a history of King Philip's War, which took place between 1675 and 1676. The ad notes that the latter is "Sold by Samuel Philips at the Brick Shop near the Town House in Boston."

Another index of the popularity of execution sermons is that collections of these sermons and other narratives started to be published, making up a sort of greatest hits of the genre, as it were. *Pillars of Salt*, published in 1699, is an early example of this type of collection and was written by Cotton Mather, who was even more influential than his famous father, Increase Mather.

Like the earlier sermons, the subtitle of *Pillars of Salt* gives a very descriptive summary of the volume's contents, so the customer knows exactly what he is getting for his hard-earned money, "An History of Some Criminals Executed in this Land for Capital Crimes. With Some of their Dying Speeches; Collected and Published for the Warning of Such that Live in Destructive Courses of Ungodliness." Note that this subtitle also indicates the spirit in which this volume is meant to be read. Even in these very early days, it seems, it was important to provide the reader with a justification for reading true crime.

The best-known collections of execution sermons and other early true-crime narratives appear a little later, in the middle of the 18th century. The first was called *The Newgate Calendar*. It first appeared in England in the 1740s and was originally a monthly bulletin of executions that took place at the Newgate prison in London.

Thanks to the popularity of this bulletin, the title was taken up and used by a number of publishers. These later versions included true that is, highly embellished accounts of the lives of famous criminals such as the highwayman Dick Turpin and the pickpocket and fence Moll Cutpurse. This format proved to be so popular that it was reprinted and revamped dozens of times, all the way through to the 20th century.

Its American equivalent was *The American Bloody Register*, first published in 1784. It was enormously popular, mainly because it stuck to the tried and tested format introduced by *The Newgate Calendar*. You'll look in vain for any biblical references on the title page of the *Bloody Register*, but you'll learn that it contains, "A true and complete history of the loves, last words, and dying confessions of three of the most noted criminals that have ever made their exit from a stage in America."

The phrasing here is fascinating because it suggests that the focus of the narrative is on the fame or notoriety if you prefer of these criminals. Moreover, the reference to a stage by which they mean the scaffold implies a full awareness of the public execution as a spectacle, and a spectacle whose primary purpose is now to entertain rather than instruct.

These collections demonstrate that the criminal was an object of sympathy and compassion as well as revulsion and punishment. By emphasizing the dangerously thin line that separated the criminal from the spectator, Puritan ministers used execution sermons to reassert their cultural, spiritual, and political authority.

And by arguing that every member of the community was subject to the withdrawal of God's grace at a moment's notice, clergymen had a powerful argument for why their congregations should let themselves be guided by the Puritan ministerial elite. This control turned out to be inherently unstable, however, precisely because it required generating a certain amount of public sympathy for the criminal.

It could be argued that there's something intrinsic in true crime narratives that generates sympathy for the criminal. There's certainly a very obvious sense in which such narratives are always about the criminal rather than the victim. Up to a point, this feature of crime narratives served the purposes of the Puritans well because a certain degree of identification with the criminal was necessary for the ideological message of the execution sermons to be effective. But even when Puritan control of crime narratives seemed absolute, there was concern about an inappropriate kind or degree of public sympathy.

This concern turned out to be justified because there is a significant difference between the later narratives and the earlier execution sermons. The new element is an interest in the lives of the criminals themselves, an interest that goes beyond the earlier Puritan emphasis on these individuals as representatives. Instead, this new emphasis is on the exceptional nature of the criminal. They are exceptional not only in the sense of being uniquely wicked or evil but also in the sense of being uniquely entertaining, dashing, even admirable.

This shift indicates that our attitudes toward criminals are never simply condemnation or revulsion but also fascination and even sympathy. As long as the Puritans maintained strict control over the production of these narratives, the dangers of sympathy for the criminal could be contained. But the effects of the sermons are unpredictable. While it's entirely possible that the audience for sermons did indeed tremble at the thought of being sinners in the hands of an angry God, it's also possible they identified with the criminal in a way that ministers would have found most troubling.

As Puritan influence over American society began to weaken in the late 17th century, other forms of true crime narrative began to appear that both exemplified and intensified that weakening. Significantly, these new forms of crime narrative all gave criminals the opportunity to present their side of the story, in their own voice. As the social and religious background of criminals changed, and it became less and less likely for them to have been born and raised as Puritans, these criminal narratives also became increasingly secular.

Whereas information about the criminals had once constituted a fairly minor part of execution sermons, now more and more lives, dying speeches, and final warnings were published as separate documents, having been liberated, as it were, from their sermonic context. And as the decline in Puritan authority accelerated, more and more crime narratives were written in a realistic style, including detailed attention to the events leading up to the murder, and information about the private lives of the protagonists.

These changes contributed to the development of a celebrity culture organized around the criminal that culminated in what became known as rogue's biographies, where criminality was seen almost as an admirable expression of unbridled personality. The tone of these biographies is quite different from that of the execution sermons. They're more sensational, and they also tend to characterize the murderers as monsters.

Critic Daniel Williams has noted that these changes in crime narratives were influenced by the development of enlightenment concepts of freedom, concepts that gradually replaced the doctrine of original sin. According to Williams, self-determination, self-reliance, and self-initiative all become socially dominant ideals in the 18th century. As he explains,

> After the Revolution, after the country had itself defied authority, descriptions of deviant and defiant individuals became especially popular in American literature, and the criminal, the clever rogue in particular, became both hero and anti-hero, both epitome and parody of the American character. As a literary figure, the criminal moved from Puritan condemnation to post-Revolutionary celebration.

But although these new understandings of the relation between self and community impacted the content and character of 18th crime narratives, I don't want to give the impression that these new types of criminal narrative celebrated criminality. If there was any celebration of criminality at all, it still had very definite limits. With the declining influence of the doctrine of original sin, it suddenly became much more difficult to explain the actions of criminals, especially when they seemed to violate what the Enlightenment saw as the innate goodness and rationality of humans.

Karen Halttunen has argued that Americans struggled to come up with an explanation for criminality that was as intellectually satisfying as the concept of original sin. This problem, she says, was especially acute when considering those types of crime where the concepts of environmental influence, motive, or uncontrolled passion as reasons for crime just didn't seem to explain the circumstances of the crime. As Halttunen explains,

> A significant number of murder narratives printed between 1750 and 1820 demonstrated the inadequacy of all these attempts to explain the crime, as some men and women murdered against character, or from an inexplicable compulsion to kill, or in cold-blooded insensibility. These crimes challenged the prevailing rational view of human nature.

The answer to the dilemma posed by these inexplicable crimes was to make a virtue out of necessity and heighten the air of mystery surrounding them by using the language of Gothic fiction. In particular, the notion of monstrosity assumed a prominent role in crime narratives. As Halttunen explains, "The image of the murderer as monster expressed the incomprehensibility of murder within the rational Enlightenment social order."

So this is why these new types of true crime narratives are not only more sensational but also tend to characterize the criminals as monsters, placed explicitly outside of society by the crimes they've committed. Whereas Puritans made great efforts to keep criminals integrated into Puritan society, these later sources see criminals as social misfits and outsiders, partly because they lacked a compelling explanatory framework that would help them to make sense of the worst of these criminals.

I want to emphasize, however, that the concept of monstrosity didn't simply replace the concept of representativeness as an explanation of criminality. Rather, monstrosity and representativeness continue to coexist as a way of addressing the public ambivalence about criminals, an ambivalence that comes from our sense that criminals like murderers are in an obvious sense so very different from ordinary people and yet in another sense they seem disturbingly like us. It's worth emphasizing that you can see examples of this ambivalence in contemporary examples of true crime. Think, for example, of true crime books about serial killers, in which the killers are often presented simultaneously as monsters and as neighbors you'd never suspect, and you'll see what I mean.

Representations of violence in true crime narratives, both early and contemporary, consistently try to make sense of this duality at the heart of our feelings about violent criminals by changing and adapting as our society as a whole changes. This is a key reason for the enduring popularity of these narratives, and it's also why true crime provides us with such a great window into what makes American society tick.

So, there was more sensationalism and a greater emphasis on monstrosity in true crime narratives beginning in the 18th century. But, as my earlier reference to Gothic fiction suggested, there was also a greater use of fictional elements, and this change took place for a couple of reasons.

First, unlike the original execution sermons, which were pretty much only read by the people who had seen the actual execution, and which therefore had to be fairly accurate, later examples of true crime narrative could afford to be more creative and twist the facts a little bit. After all, they were distributed over a wider geographical area, to people who hadn't witnessed the actual execution.

But also, and this is the second point, the later narratives *needed* to be more creative. Fictional elements assumed a greater importance because these later narratives placed a greater emphasis on entertaining rather than instructing, on thrilling readers, rather than sending them to specific passages in the Bible. What we start to see in the 18th and 19th centuries, then, are true crime narratives that are much more upfront about explicitly combining entertainment and moral precepts.

But this not to say that it was necessarily easy to manage the combination. For example, the Preface to a bound collection of crime narratives published in 1812 under the title *The Criminal Recorder or, An Awful Beacon to the Rising Generation of Both Sexes*, illustrates the sorts of contradictions or tensions this combination could bring about.

The preface begins by recommending the narratives as suitably cautionary tales of guilt and punishment, adding that adults would find them useful in steering their children away from crime. However, perhaps concerned that this impeccably moral reason for purchasing the collection made it sound too dull, the preface then goes on to say, "Let it not be hastily supposed by the gay and youthful, that this volume is a dull or canting lecture upon religion and morals."

Although this combining of moral lesson and thrilling entertainment might seem almost paradoxical, it shows that 19th-century true crime narratives aimed to reach quite a diverse audience, including the old and the young, traditionalists and freethinkers. So they needed to present themselves in a variety of ways.

I also want to emphasize that this ability of true crime to adapt itself to the needs and desires of a large number of different audiences is another reason for its success. Like mystery and suspense fiction as a whole, true crime from its earliest stages has been very sensitive to the need for niche marketing.

We can see this same combination of variety, sensation, and marketing in the rise of newspaper reporting about murder, which started to emerge in the 19th century. Although, as we have seen, there are many examples of American true crime narratives dating all the way back to colonial times, it might surprise you to know that journalistic coverage of crime was a fairly late arrival on the scene.

There had been some early attempts to bring the American public coverage of homicides, along with other strange and shocking occurrences, as with *The American Magazine of Wonders* of 1809. But these were more almanacs than examples of journalism. Their range was very broad as we can see by the fact that they carried reports about sea monsters, exotic customs from foreign lands, and animal deformities and the murders they covered had usually taken place a number of years before, and usually outside of the United States.

Newspapers had traditionally paid very little attention to crime, not only because they didn't want to waste precious space reporting on events they thought people would already have heard about through other publications, but also because they were constrained by a sense of delicacy and civic responsibility. This all changed with the explosion of the penny press in the mid-1830s.

The most famous penny newspaper of the day was *The New York Herald*, published by James Gordon Bennett. Bennett was a shrewd businessman, and he knew that nothing sold more newspapers than hideous crimes. As he once put it, American readers "were more ready to seek six columns of the details of a brutal murder... than the same amount of words poured forth by the genius of the noblest author of our times." Bennett was more than happy to give the public what they wanted, providing detailed and extremely graphic coverage of the most infamous murders of the time.

From the mid-1830s onward, crime news became a staple of newspaper coverage. It was easy and cheap to gather, it was already familiar to readers who were avid consumers of the other forms of true crime narrative that we've been looking at, and it was easy for newspapers to argue they were performing a civic duty—namely, warning their readers about the dangers of the rapidly expanding American cities. There again we see the pedagogic dimension of true crime that I mentioned earlier.

During this period, newspaper coverage of murder took off thanks to the occurrence of highly marketable crimes such as the murders of prostitute Helen Jewett in 1836 and of shop girl Mary Rogers in 1841 the inspiration for Edgar Allan Poe's story "The Mystery of Marie Rogêt." Of course, the popular press, then as now, also came in for a lot of criticism for being excessively sensational. But like it or not, the popular press—or yellow press, as it came to be known—was here to stay. It was the great-grandparent, as it were, of the tabloid newspapers and television shows of today.

The success of the popular press came partly from the fact that it was able to satisfy the desires of its consumers so well. But it was also the result of such factors as rapidly growing urban populations, rising literacy rates, and increasingly efficient networks of production and distribution for printed materials. All of these factors created a new and very large market for burgeoning forms of popular culture that all had their fingers on the pulse of public demand.

In this market, certain criminal cases quickly became *causes célèbres*. The case I'd like to focus on is the murder of Mary Rogers because it was one that fascinated Poe. The Rogers case took place in 1841, the same year Poe published "The Murders in the Rue Morgue." In her book, *The Mysterious Death of Mary Rogers*, historian Amy Gilman Srebnick comments that were it not for the newly-developed concept of public news, and the recent emergence of a reading public craving sensation from the penny press, the story and the mystery of Mary Rogers would probably have gone almost unnoticed.

But, according to Srebnick,

Rogers's life and death occurred at the very moment that a new urban and commercial written culture was taking shape. The newspaper, the dime novel, the sensational pamphlet, and the magazine with its serialized stories were the places where the Rogers story was both created and popularized.

As a result, Srebnick argues, the murder of Mary Rogers not only became an emblematic crime in the way it linked female death, sexuality, and a peculiarly urban sense of mystery but also ensured that crime reporting became a major aspect of popular journalism in America.

Srebnick's remarks are fascinating because they indicate precisely how the early examples of true crime narratives that we've been looking at in this lecture overlap with the genre of mystery and suspense fiction. Depending on the writer and the intended audience, the same sensational crime could provide the raw material for a newspaper article, a true crime narrative that combined a factual basis with fictional elements drawn from the Gothic, or Edgar Allan Poe's "The Mystery of Marie Rogêt."

There could be no better example of why it's so important to study these early forms of true crime narrative. They give us a sense of the context out of which contemporary true crime emerged while also suggesting that the traffic between fact and fiction in mystery and suspense fiction has always traveled in both directions.

TRUE CRIME IN THE 20ᵀᴴ CENTURY

T rue crime is a nonfiction genre in which the author uses an actual crime and real people as a point of departure. Modern true crime is integrally related to mystery and suspense fiction. Both genres draw on fiction and nonfiction techniques to achieve their effects; both are centrally concerned with crime; and critics have disparaged both as trivial and even detrimental to their readers. Examining modern true-crime texts reminds us of the importance of formula in the success of mystery and suspense fiction.

EDMUND PEARSON

- Edmund Pearson is primarily responsible for moving the true-crime genre into the modern period. In fact, beginning in the 1920s, Edmund Pearson succeeded in raising true-crime narrative to the level of literary art.

- A librarian by trade, Pearson was editor of publications at the New York Public Library from 1914 to 1927. The shift in Pearson's career where we see his interest in crime emerge can be located quite precisely in his 1923 volume *Books in Black or Red*. The final chapter is entitled "With Acknowledgments to Thomas De Quincey." De Quincey was an English author who had written the noted essay "On Murder Considered as One of the Fine Arts."

- Pearson saw in De Quincey a way to have a legitimate interest in crime. Using the blueprint established by De Quincey, Pearson published a series of hugely successful true-crime books, beginning with *Studies in Murder* in 1924 and concluding with *More Studies in Murder* in 1936. Pearson made it possible for true crime to come out into the open and take its place with other legitimate genres.

THE "PURE MURDER"

■ Edmund Pearson presented himself as a connoisseur of crime, only interested in the "pure murder." Pearson wanted to make crime narratives safe for respectable members of society, and that meant rejecting the sensational, including serial killers. In fact, the mixture of antiquarianism and contemporaneity that defines Pearson's true-crime writing is probably the single most significant reason for his success.

■ Pearson forces his readers to face the uncomfortable fact that the difference between them and the criminal is one of degree rather than kind. He insists on this point not to exonerate the criminal but rather to encourage a clear-eyed attitude toward society's responsibility to punish the criminal. In this respect, the Puritans can be said to have had as much influence on Pearson as Thomas De Quincey, and it's this peculiar mixture of Puritanism and aestheticism that gives Pearson's work its distinctive flavor.

IN COLD BLOOD

■ A sea change for true crime took place in the 1950s, in the form of Truman Capote's *In Cold Blood*. For a book that would have such a huge impact, *In Cold Blood* had modest beginnings. It was inspired by a 300-word article on page 19 of the *New York Times*. The story described the unexplained murder of the Clutter family in rural Holcomb, Kansas. Fascinated by this brief news item, Capote traveled to Holcomb to visit the scene of the massacre.

■ Over the course of the next few years, Capote became acquainted with everyone involved in the investigation and most of the residents of the small town. Rather than taking notes during interviews, Capote committed conversations to memory and immediately wrote down quotations as soon as an interview ended. Capote spent years working on the book, which was published in 1966, and it turned out to be a huge international success.

- The most controversial aspect of *In Cold Blood* was Capote's claim that his study of the murder of the Clutter family constituted a new genre: the nonfiction novel. Capote maintained he had written a completely objective account of the case by scrupulously removing every trace of his presence from the text.

- Even though Capote spent nearly six years researching the case, he appears nowhere in the book, and the word "I" is never used. Some reviewers complained about his apparent absence, claiming that it damaged the book. Far more serious, however, were repeated accusations that there was a good deal more fiction in Capote's book than fact.

- In the midst of the avalanche of success enjoyed by *In Cold Blood*, no one seemed to notice that while Capote boasted about how scrupulous he had been to keep himself out of his account, he was more than happy to ride the tidal wave of publicity generated by the book. This bizarre combination of invisibility and relentless self-publicizing is probably *In Cold Blood*'s most profound influence on contemporary true-crime narratives. Capote showed true-crime writers how to participate in the culture of celebrity that had grown up around criminals.

ANN RULE
- No contemporary true-crime writer is more celebrated than Ann Rule. Rule began trying to sell true-crime work in 1963, but she didn't get her break until 1968, when *True Detective* offered her a stringer position. The editor liked Rule's work but told her to use a male pseudonym because readers wouldn't believe a

woman knew anything about murder. This is when she started using the pseudonym Andy Stack.

- Rule came to prominence in 1980 with her first book, *The Stranger Beside Me*, about serial killer Ted Bundy. Over the course of a long and productive career, she published more than 20 books and 1,400 articles. Despite Rule's illustrious career, *The Stranger Beside Me* remains her most significant book because it took both her career and the genre of true crime to a new level.

- Ann Rule's attitude toward murder and her degree of empathic involvement in the case is completely different from Edmund Pearson's. Part of this difference can be explained by her role model in the genre: What Thomas De Quincey is to Pearson, Truman Capote is to Rule.

- Unlike Pearson, who tends to treat murder as an intriguing puzzle, Rule views murder as a dramatic family tragedy. Whereas Pearson is completely uninterested in the murderer as a person, Rule is obsessed with getting inside the head of the murderer.

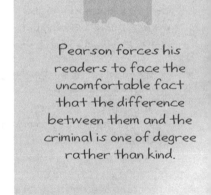

Pearson forces his readers to face the uncomfortable fact that the difference between them and the criminal is one of degree rather than kind.

- Rule's interest in the personal histories of the murderers implies the weight she gives to environmental explanations of crime. Pearson, on the other hand, was a particularly harsh critic of the view that one's social environment produced criminality. Concerned by what he interpreted as attacks on the principle of individual responsibility, he refused to believe that people could be swayed by outside forces.

THE CRIMINAL AS "OTHER"

- In short, for Edmund Pearson, responsibility for the murder begins and ends with the killer. For Ann Rule, each killer is also in some sense a victim.

- What's more, Rule relies far more on the belief that, although the criminal may look like us, he or she is somehow irreducibly different. Her work aims to convince us that, despite the appearance of similarities between the life of the murderer and our own, the murderer is completely "other"—that is, alien and abnormal. Rule implies that we can be reassured about our own normality and be absolved of any guilt we may feel for reading true crime in the first place.

- Our guilt is the source of a major difference between the work of Pearson and Rule—and the final sign of how much the genre of true crime has changed over the course of time. When Pearson was writing, most people believed that violence took place in a minority of the population and that they were not implicated.

- By the 1970s and 1980s, however, this feeling of not being implicated was no longer tenable. Society's greatest truism was that violent crime was out of control, and the emergence of the figure of the serial killer at this time confirmed the public perception that anyone could be victimized, anytime, anywhere.

THE MASK OF SANITY

- True-crime writers like Ann Rule present serial killers as monsters. The monstrosity of murderers in contemporary examples of the genre also dictates some more specific features of true-crime narratives, many of which are driven by a desire to explain (or disavow) the killer's apparent ordinariness.

- One of the most common images in true-crime narratives about serial killers is the "mask of sanity." The term is taken from a 1941

Ann Rule relies far more on the belief that, although the criminal may look like us, he or she is somehow irreducibly different.

book called *The Mask of Sanity*, which was written by psychiatrist Hervey Cleckley and describes Cleckley's clinical interviews with adult male incarcerated psychopaths. It's considered a seminal work and the most influential clinical description of psychopathy in the 20th century. The title refers to the normal mask that conceals the mental disorder of the psychopathic person in Cleckley's conceptualization.

■ The mask of sanity turns the killer's apparent ordinariness into the most compelling sign of his evil by depicting that ordinariness as a facade hiding the truth of his identity. According to popular perception, one of the most frightening characteristics of the serial killer is that the figure usually presents to the public the image of the all-American boy or the shy, quiet neighbor. The mask of sanity concept reassures us that the killer's apparent normality is false and that underneath his benevolent appearance is a driven killer who stalks his prey with determined cunning.

ORIGINS OF DEVIANCE

- The mask of sanity as a diagnosis and sign of monstrosity is bolstered by a second common feature of true-crime narratives about serial killers: the search for the origins of deviance.

- The search for the origins of deviance is a distinctively recent innovation in true crime. Ann Rule's work on Bundy contains this feature, but then so does the vast majority of true-crime work on serial killers. The search for origins often involves going back to seemingly innocuous childhood incidents and reinterpreting them in light of later events.

- The most sustained example of the "had I but known" school of true-crime narratives is *A Father's Story*, Lionel Dahmer's memoir about his infamous son, American serial killer Jeffrey Dahmer. The book is filled with examples of the ordinary turned into the ominous. For example, when Lionel Dahmer recounts a fishing trip with the young Jeffrey, he recalls his son's fascination with the fish's internal organs and asks whether this was a sign of things to come.

- All such questions are rhetorical. In the world of the true-crime narrative, the lives of serial killers are bound by an inexorable logic that leads them to their crimes. We take great comfort in the deterministic logic that binds these people to their evil fate from their very earliest days. No matter how absurd this determinism may be, it has the advantage of making that apparently ordinary life as deviant as possible from its very beginning.

Questions to Consider

1. How did true crime change and evolve over the course of the 20th century?

2. Why is Truman Capote's *In Cold Blood* such a seminal text in the history of true crime?

Suggested Reading

Biressi, *Crime, Fear and the Law in True Crime Stories.*

Murley, *The Rise of True Crime.*

TRUE CRIME IN THE 20TH CENTURY

A s we saw in another lecture in this series, although most people tend to think of true crime as a 20th-century phenomenon, in fact, the roots of the genre stretch all the way back to the execution sermons of the Puritan era.

In this lecture, we'll focus on modern forms of true crime, which are integrally related to mystery and suspense fiction because both genres draw upon fictional and nonfiction techniques to achieve their effects. The two genres are also related in more obvious ways, they are both centrally concerned with crime, and critics have disparaged both of them as trivial and even damaging to their readers.

With these points in mind, looking at modern true crime texts gives us an opportunity to remind ourselves of the importance of formula in the success of mystery and suspense fiction, along with the influence of the frequently blurred line between fact and fiction in these narratives.

But what exactly is true crime? Let's begin with a simple definition. True crime is a non-fiction genre in which the author uses an actual crime and real people as a point of departure. The crimes almost always include murder. They can be fairly factual or highly speculative and heavily fictionalized depending on the writer. Some works are instant books produced quickly to capitalize on popular demand while others may reflect years of thoughtful research and inquiry. Still, others revisit historic crimes or alleged crimes and propose solutions, such as books examining political assassinations, well-known unsolved murders, or deaths of celebrities.

Almost every part of this definition could be and has been contested, but it's a useful starting point, not least because it indicates that a wide variety of materials could be classified, albeit loosely, as true crime. All of these materials claim to be factual accounts of crimes and their perpetrators, and all of them use various fictional techniques to embellish or enhance the effect of the stories they tell. From the very beginning of the genre, then, the question of what is 'true' about 'true crime'? has been very relevant.

Even though modern forms of true crime draw in various ways on earlier materials, Edmund Pearson is the person primarily responsible for moving the true crime genre into the modern period. Beginning in the 1920s, Edmund Pearson seemed to succeed almost single-handedly in raising true crime narratives to the level of literary art. How did he do it?

Edmund Pearson came to true crime as a bibliophile and aesthete. A librarian by trade, Pearson's early publications were mostly about books and book collecting, an interest that was facilitated by his position as editor of publications at the New York Public Library from 1914 to 1927. The shift in Pearson's career where we see his interest in crime emerge can be located quite precisely in the final chapter of his 1923 book, *Books in Black or Red*, entitled, With Acknowledgments to Thomas De Quincey. De Quincey was an English author and essayist who had written a very famous essay in 1827 entitled "On Murder Considered as One of the Fine Arts."

Pearson saw in De Quincey a way to have a legitimate interest in crime. Using the blueprint established by De Quincey, Pearson published a series of hugely successful true crime books beginning with *Studies in Murder* in 1924 and concluding with *More Studies in Murder* in 1936.

The success of Pearson's work gave true crime narratives a status they'd never before enjoyed. Rather than being associated with the penny press or cheap forms of street literature, Pearson's true crime narratives typically appeared in high-class magazines such as "The Forum," "Liberty," "The New Yorker," and "Vanity Fair" before being published in book form. Pearson made it possible for true crime to come out into the open and take its place with other legitimate genres.

Pearson presented himself as a connoisseur of crime, only interested in what he called in his 1923 essay on De Quincey, the pure murder. Pearson wanted to make crime narratives safe for respectable members of society, and that meant rejecting the sensational, including serial killers.

Given all the crimes Pearson excludes, what is left to constitute a pure murder? He addresses this issue in an essay called "What Makes a Good Murder?" when he lauds the old-fashioned murders of the 19th century over the crude and garish spectacle of gang killings.

Pearson was publishing his true crime narratives during the era of Prohibition when mobsters such as Al Capone came to dominate the criminal landscape of America. With his aesthetic sensibilities offended by the brutality of what he called the Chicago school of murderers, Pearson's crime narratives turn back eagerly to the more civilized age of 19th-century crimes. The philosophical and aesthetic questions raised by murder are of much more interest to Pearson than a gruesome account of the murders themselves.

Pearson's determined refusal to engage with the crimes that dominated his own time may suggest that he wanted to elevate the genre of true crime out of history altogether by turning it into a disinterested object of aesthetic contemplation. But unlike De Quincey, Pearson engaged vigorously with contemporaneous debates about criminal responsibility, the insanity defense, the death penalty, and the causes of crime.

The mixture of antiquarianism and contemporaneity that defines Pearson's true crime writing was probably the single most important reason for his success. His habit of concentrating on old cases helped to give true-crime writing an air of respectability, while his involvement in the hot-button legal issues of the day gave true-crime work a social utility that made reading it almost a civic duty, rather than evidence of the reader's prurience.

It also helped, of course, that Pearson's views on law and order were quite conservative. Writing against a background of widespread police corruption and mobster lawlessness, as well as the popularization of the insanity defense, as used in the high-profile case of Leopold and Loeb in 1924 the year Pearson's first true crime book appeared, Pearson was a determined reactionary on the subject of criminal responsibility.

He believed the appropriate fate for a convicted murderer was execution. At first, we might assume Pearson's defense of the death penalty and his attacks on the insanity defense are based on the belief that criminals are set definitively outside the community of law-abiding citizens. In fact, Pearson's support of the concept of criminal responsibility is dictated by his determination not to view criminals as monsters, separate from ordinary people.

Pearson forces his readers to face the uncomfortable fact that the difference between them and the criminal is one of degree, rather than kind. He insists on this point not to exonerate the criminal, but rather to encourage a clear-eyed attitude toward society's responsibility to punish the criminal. In this respect, the Puritans can be said to have as much influence on Pearson as Thomas De Quincey, and it's this peculiar mixture of Puritanism and aestheticism that gives Pearson's work its distinctive flavor.

By the end of Pearson's career in the 1930s, however, the industry of true crime writing had simply become too large to need the veneer of respectability. Instead, it was quite content to churn out gory and sensationalistic narratives for an eager public. However, another sea change for true crime was to take place, as we'll see if we now move on to the 1950s.

For a book that would turn out to have such a huge impact, Truman Capote's *In Cold Blood* had modest beginnings. It was inspired by a 300-word article that ran on page 19 of the New York Times on Monday, November 16, 1959. The story described the unexplained murder of the Clutter family in rural Holcomb, Kansas. Fascinated by this brief news item, Capote traveled with his friend Harper Lee to Holcomb and visited the scene of the massacre.

Over the course of the next few years, he became acquainted with everyone involved in the investigation and most of the residents of the small town. Rather than taking notes during interviews, Capote committed conversations to memory and immediately wrote quotes as soon as an interview ended. He claimed his memory retention for verbatim conversations had been tested at 94 percent.

Capote spent years working on the book, which was published in 1966, and it turned out to be worth the effort. *In Cold Blood* was a huge international success, and it bought Capote a level of fame he had never enjoyed before. A writer of Capote's stature had never written true crime before, and it completely transformed the true crime genre.

But the most controversial aspect of *In Cold Blood* was Capote's claim that his study of the murder of the Clutter family constituted a new genre, the nonfiction novel. This claim provoked heated debate among a wide range of critics and was largely responsible for the book's huge sales and the enormous amount of publicity that surrounded its publication.

What exactly was new, if anything, about Capote's text, compared to earlier true crime narratives? For one thing, Capote was much more engaged with the subjects of his narrative than any other writer of true crime up to that point. He developed a warm friendship with the two convicted murderers, Richard Hickock and Perry Smith, even accompanying them to the scaffold, weeping over their deaths, and paying for their grave markers.

Although Capote spoke at length about his relationship with Smith and Hickock in interviews, the formal structure of In Cold Blood itself hides this engagement. By inventing the nonfiction novel, Capote claimed to have written a completely objective account of the case by scrupulously removing every trace of his presence from the text.

Even though Capote spent nearly six years gathering information, researching, and living with the case, he appears nowhere in the book and the word I is never used. Some reviewers complained about his apparent absence, claiming that it damaged the book. Far more serious, however, were the repeated accusations about the supposed factuality of In Cold Blood. Critics pointed to numerous examples of dialogue between characters that Capote couldn't possibility have known about to argue that there was a good deal more fiction in Capote's book than he admitted.

In the midst of the avalanche of success enjoyed by In Cold Blood, no one seemed to notice the absurdity of Capote boasting, on the one hand, about how scrupulous he had been about keeping himself out of his account and yet, on the other hand, being more than happy to ride the tidal wave of publicity generated by the book. Rather than an inconsistency, however, this bizarre combination of invisibility and relentless self-publicizing is probably In Cold Blood's most profound influence on contemporary true crime narratives.

Capote showed true crime writers how to participate in the culture of celebrity that had grown up around criminals. Indeed, in many ways, Capote set the stage for writers of true crime narratives to become even more famous than their subjects.

No contemporary true crime writer is more popular and famous than Ann Rule, whose work exemplifies two very important features of contemporary true crime, first, the genre's recent and very successful preoccupation with serial killers, and second, the ways in which contemporary true crime shows the influence of earlier forms of the genre.

Rule began trying to sell true crime work in 1963, but she didn't get her break until 1968 when True Detective offered her the position of Northwest stringer for the magazine. A stringer is a part-time contributor or correspondent. The editor liked Rule's work but told her she'd have to use a male pseudonym because readers wouldn't believe a woman knew anything about murder.

This is when she started using the pseudonym Andy Stack. After proving her ability in several magazines, Rule was invited to start writing under her own name but decided to keep the pen name at that time in the interest of protecting herself and her family from her subjects.

She came to prominence in 1980 with her first book, *The Stranger Beside Me*, about serial killer Ted Bundy. And over the course of a long and productive career until her death in 2015, she published over 20 books and 1,400 articles. Although some of her cases were high-profile, such as the Bundy case, later in her career she preferred to write about what are known as sleeper cases, about which there hasn't been much media coverage, because she didn't want the reader to know the ending before picking up the book. She also tried to keep in touch with the families of the victims and sometimes added updates to a later edition of a book to include new information.

Despite her long and illustrious career, *The Stranger Beside Me* remains her most significant book because it took both her career and the genre of true crime to a new level. To understand exactly why it's so significant, we have to understand how Rule's work compares to that of Pearson and Capote.

Despite the many differences between Pearson and Rule, they do have certain things in common. They both write narratives about murder that, like true crime writing, in general, can be said to have a therapeutic purpose. Although their methods are very different, Pearson and Rule share the constant aim of true crime writing, to make sense of murder by explaining how and why it happens.

Despite these similarities, there are also some major differences. Rule's attitude toward murder, the degree of her empathic involvement in the cases she writes about, is completely different from Pearson's, and part of this difference can be explained by her role model in the genre. What Thomas De Quincey is to Pearson; Truman Capote is to Rule.

As I mentioned earlier, when Capote published *In Cold Blood* the rules for true crime changed forever. First, with his concept of the nonfiction novel, Capote provided a way for writers to justify fictional enhancement of the facts of any case. Second, by providing an exhaustive account of the murderers' psychological and family histories, Capote provided both a compelling cause-and-effect narrative with which to structure true crime accounts and a way for the author to empathically portray the plight of the murderer as well as the victim.

Unlike Pearson, who tends to treat murder as an intriguing puzzle, Rule customarily views murder as a dramatic family tragedy. Whereas Pearson is completely uninterested in the murderer as a person, Rule is obsessed with getting inside the head of the murderer and dissecting their personal histories. Pearson and Rule thus have very different approaches to dramatizing the issues that concern them about murder, and this difference of approach leads to a number of other equally significant differences between them.

Rule's interest in the personal histories of the murderers she discusses implies the weight she gives to environmental explanations of crime. Just as Capote believed that Hickock and Smith's family histories influenced their murder of the Clutter family, Rule believes her highly charged recreations of her killers' childhoods provide the answer to the question of why they killed.

Pearson, on the other hand, was a particularly harsh critic of the view that one's social environment produced criminality. Concerned by what he interpreted as attacks on the principle of individual responsibility, he refused to believe that people could be swayed by outside forces and criticized the tendency to rely on such forces for an explanation of crime.

Although Rule doesn't pay much attention to the murderer's broader social environment, for example, the influence of pornography or violence in the media are rarely mentioned in her work, she does give great weight to the killer's family history. Pearson would have rejected this idea out of hand, but Rule sees her murderers as bound by an iron fate set in early childhood. From puberty on, her killers are just acting out a script written by somebody else, usually their parents.

In short, for Pearson, responsibility for the murder begins and ends with the killer. For Rule, each killer is also in some sense a victim, so that their fate indicts a wider system of familial relations. It might seem, then, that Rule's true crime narratives are simply empathic, perhaps even sympathetic, accounts of murderers, and that this is why they're so popular. However, this is not the whole story.

It's true that Rule, unlike Pearson, uses true crime to provide a window on today's world, rather than seeking refuge in an earlier time. However, the view she provides has to be carefully controlled in order to earn her reader's praise. Although the killer may in some sense be a sympathetic figure, Rule can't let the implied identity between killer and reader go too far, because it's too disturbing. The killer must be both like us and completely different from us. We must be able both to recognize him and to recognize our distance from him.

This is the source of another significant difference between Pearson and Rule. Although Pearson was an anomalous figure in the 1920s and 1930s in his harsh criticism of environmental explanations of crime, he was up-to-date with a vengeance in his refusal to recognize an intrinsic physical or psychological difference between the criminal and non-criminal.

Rule, on the other hand, relies far more on the belief that, although the criminal may look like us, he's somehow irreducibly different. Her work aims to convince us that, despite the appearance of similarities between the life of the murderer and our own, that murderer is completely other, alien, abnormal. Therefore, Rule implies that we can be reassured about our own normality, and be absolved of any guilt we may feel for reading true crime in the first place.

Our guilt is the source of the last major difference between Pearson and Rule, and the final sign of how much the genre of true crime has changed over the course of time. When Pearson was writing, it wasn't considered inappropriate for him to appraise different murders according to aesthetic standards, or to enjoy murders as one might a fine wine. Although there was widespread concern in the 1920s about the rising tide of crime, most people were able to convince themselves that the violence took place amongst a minority of the population and that they were not implicated.

By the 1970s and 1980s, this feeling of not being implicated was no longer tenable. Society's greatest truism was that violent crime was out of control, and the emergence of the figure of the serial killer at this time seemed to confirm the public perception that anyone could be victimized, anytime, anywhere.

Ann Rule rode the wave of this public paranoia about serial murder in particular and violence in general with The Stranger Beside Me. But she also had to find a way to channel this wave by making people feel that reading her books was a positive contribution to stopping crime, rather than a prurient participation in it.

Rule addressed this problem by making her books implicit exercises in public policy. She argues that she writes about currently incarcerated serial killers to make sure they never get paroled. It was no longer enough, as it was in Pearson's time, to write about murder simply out of aesthetic interest. Rule tries to persuade her reader that true crime has an important role to play in fighting crime by telling the reader both about the severity of the problem and why law enforcement personnel should be adequately supported in their attempts to solve it. The fact that Rule feels it necessary to do this, and that her readers responded so positively, speaks volumes about the changes in the true crime genre between the time of Edmund Pearson and that of Ann Rule.

Let's return for a moment to how true crime writers like Rule present serial killers as monsters. The monstrosity of murderers in contemporary examples of the genre also dictates some more specific features of true crime narratives, many of which are driven by a desire to explain or disavow the killer's apparent ordinariness.

One of the most common images in true crime narratives about serial killers is *the Mask of Sanity*. First published in 1941, *The Mask of Sanity* is a book written by Hervey Cleckley, M.D., describing Cleckley's clinical interviews with adult male incarcerated psychopaths. It's considered a seminal work and the most influential clinical description of psychopathy in the 20th century. The title refers to the normal mask that conceals the mental disorder of the psychopathic person in Cleckley's conceptualization.

The mask of sanity turns the killer's apparent ordinariness into the most compelling sign of his evil by depicting that ordinariness as a facade hiding the truth of his identity. According to popular perception, one of the most frightening characteristics of the serial killer is that he usually presents to the public the image of the all-American boy or the shy, quiet neighbor. The mask of sanity concept reassures us that the killer's apparent normality is false and that underneath his benevolent appearance is a driven killer who stalks his prey with determined cunning.

Although the presumption of monstrosity in true crime narratives is necessary in order to distance serial killers from ordinary men, it immediately creates a dilemma. How do we tell the difference between the mask of sanity and a real face? If serial killers appear to be ordinary men, how can we distinguish between apparently ordinary men who are actually serial killers and really ordinary men?

These questions suggest that the mask of sanity as a diagnosis and sign of monstrosity is never enough. It always has to be bolstered by a second common feature of true crime narratives about serial killers, the search for the origins of deviance.

This search is a distinctively recent innovation in true crime. Ann Rule's work on Bundy contains this feature, but then so does the vast majority of true crime work on serial killers. The search for origins often involves going back to seemingly innocuous childhood incidents and reinterpreting them in the light of later events.

The most sustained example of what I call the Had I but known school of true crime narratives is *A Father's Story*, Lionel Dahmer's memoir about his infamous son Jeffrey Dahmer, which is filled with examples of the ordinary turned into the ominous. For example, when Lionel Dahmer recounts a fishing trip with the young Jeffrey, he recalls his son's fascination with the fish's internal organs and asks whether this was a sign of things to come.

All such questions are meant to be rhetorical. In the world of the true crime narrative, the lives of serial killers are bound by an inexorable logic that leads them to their crimes. We take great comfort in the deterministic logic that binds these children to their evil fate from their very earliest days. No matter how absurd this determinism may be, it has the advantage of making that apparently ordinary life as deviant as possible from its very beginning. To suggest any other possibility would risk having the ordinary be simply, well, ordinary.

In some ways, the stakes of true crime narratives are higher than mystery and suspense fiction. Although both types of narrative address public anxiety and fascination with violence and crime, the true status of true crime makes those anxieties particularly intense. Yet these two genres also have many things in common, and the growth and continued popularity of true crime can shed light on why mystery and suspense fiction has also been able to maintain its appeal with so many readers.

HISTORICAL MYSTERIES

H istorical mystery and suspense fiction is a flourishing part of the genre. Historical-fiction writers take the foundational elements of mystery and suspense fiction and move them to earlier periods in human history as a way of exploring both continuities and changes between yesterday and today. In this lecture, we'll look at two types of historical mysteries: single novels by authors of literary fiction who draw on the conventions of mystery and suspense fiction when revisiting periods in the past and mystery series that feature a single series protagonist who experiences a variety of adventures.

THE ALIENIST

- Caleb Carr began his career as a military historian but then combined his interest in history with writing fiction. The result was *The Alienist*, which was published in 1994. Set in New York City in 1896, *The Alienist* contains historical figures, such as New York City police commissioner (and later president) Theodore Roosevelt and the journalist Jacob Riis.

- Carr combines real-life personages with fictional characters to tell the story of the search for a serial killer who murders and mutilates young male prostitutes. The novel's protagonist is the psychologist Dr. Laszlo Kreizler, the alienist of the book's title, who creates what amounts to a psychological profile of the killer. Such a profile would have been an historical anomaly during the 1890s, and Carr is well aware of that fact. What is entertaining about the prospect is how a concept and a figure familiar to readers of contemporary psychological thrillers is exported to a very different historical context.

- *The Alienist* was a huge hit, and its popularity suggests one key to success in historical mystery fiction. The author needs to strike a balance between historical anomaly (such as moving a psychological profiler into the 1890s) and historical accuracy (using painstaking historical research).

- The importance of this balance suggests that readers enjoy historical mysteries both for the mystery elements and for the successful and convincing re-creation of historical detail. However, critic Stephen Dobyns in the *New York Times Book Review* argued that Carr's meticulous and detailed historical research was "both a curse and a blessing, for although the novel's ostensible subject is who-is-killing-these-children, the real subject is New York City in the 1890s."

- Dobyns's observation demonstrates that historical mysteries can easily become overwhelmed by too much historical detail, in which case the mystery elements becomes subordinated to such an extent that the reader might lose interest. It might seem like an obvious point, but readers of historical mysteries want to have their cake and eat it, too. They want to be transported to another historical setting and be simultaneously entertained by a good mystery yarn. When one of these elements dominates the other, the novel flirts with failure.

THE INTERPRETATION OF MURDER

- In his 2006 novel, *The Interpretation of Murder*, Jed Rubenfeld combines the use of real-life historical figures and the re-creation of a historical place in an unusual and thought-provoking manner. Rubenfeld is a professor of law and has written books on constitutional law. When he turned his hand to writing fiction, he was drawn to a particular incident in psychoanalyst Sigmund Freud's life that is itself something of a mystery.

The readers of historical mysteries want to be transported to another historical setting and be simultaneously entertained by a good mystery yarn.

- Freud visited the United States only once in his life, in 1909, and apparently the visit was nothing short of a disaster. When Freud was later asked what he thought of America, he replied that it was a "colossal mistake." Inspired by this comment, in *The Interpretation of Murder*, Rubenfeld writes a speculative reconstruction of Freud's visit to the United States to find out what went wrong.

- Rubenfeld's creative answer is that Freud, along with real-life colleagues Carl Jung and Sándor Ferenczi and the fictional American psychoanalyst Stratham Younger, all become involved in a murder investigation that takes place among the elite of New York City's wealthiest citizens. What makes the novel work is that Rubenfeld develops the full implications of the similarities that exist between the figures of the detective and the psychoanalyst.

■ Rubenfeld's title *The Interpretation of Murder* is, of course, an allusion to Freud's famous 1899 book *The Interpretation of Dreams*. Just as Freud is able to successfully decode and interpret details in dreams in order to build a larger narrative that resolves the patient's neurosis, so in Rubenfeld's novel we see the founder of psychoanalysis and his colleagues work to interpret clues (some physical, but mostly psychological) to solve a mystery. It is an ingenious parallel, and Rubenfeld develops it very successfully.

THE NAME OF THE ROSE

■ Any given example of the historical mystery will likely be more successful if the reader already has some preexisting knowledge of the period and with the conventions of the mystery and suspense fiction genre. That way, the reader can appreciate how the author is both drawing on and reworking aspects of those generic conventions in clever and creative ways.

■ This is particularly true of *The Name of the Rose*, a celebrated novel published in 1980 by the Italian literary theorist Umberto Eco. *The Name of the Rose* has at least as much, if not more, to say about the generic foundations of mystery and suspense fiction as it does about its historical period.

■ *The Name of the Rose* is a murder mystery set in a monastery in northern Italy in 1327. That bare summary only scratches the surface of what Eco's novel really is about, however. Apart from its historical mystery elements, *The Name of the Rose* is filled with literary, philosophical, theological, and historical references, some of which are quite obscure. What's more, the novel also contains many passages in Latin and other languages.

- In short, this isn't a book you'd normally expect to be a best seller, and yet, that's exactly what it became. It sold more than a million copies in Italy, and when it was translated into English in 1983, the hardcover version sold another million copies in the United States. A film adaptation starring Sean Connery was released in 1986, and the success of that film further confirmed *The Name of the Rose*'s status as a publishing phenomenon.

A History of the Genre Itself

- *The Name of the Rose* is filled with allusions—some obvious, some obscure—to various forms of mystery and suspense. In fact, Eco's novel is a historical mystery in the sense that it's a history of the genre itself. It's filled with clues about the lurking presence of the genre's key figures and conventions that are there for the attentive and knowledgeable reader to note and contemplate.

- For example, Eco's protagonist is an older Franciscan monk named William of Baskerville. Fans of mystery and suspense fiction will of course immediately recognize "Baskerville" as a nod to Sir Arthur Conan Doyle's 1902 novel *The Hound of the Baskervilles*. If we then suspect that William is meant to be modeled after Sherlock Holmes, we find much evidence to confirm that suspicion.

- Even though William is a monk and is therefore a man of faith (unlike Holmes), in many ways he's also conspicuously modern in comparison to his medieval background. He places little confidence in biblical prophecies and is impatient with overly dogmatic thinking and nitpicking theological disputation. Instead, William relies on what passes for cutting-edge science in 1327. In this respect, he anticipates the Renaissance and the Enlightenment as much as he personifies medieval times.

- Some of the references to mystery and suspense fiction in *The Name of the Rose* are very subtle. William's main antagonist in the novel—the Professor Moriarty to his Holmes, if you will—is an elderly Spanish monk named Jorge of Burgos. Jorge controls access to the secrets of the monastery's labyrinthine library, wherein lies a book that is the key to the mystery.

- As Eco points out in his postscript to the novel, "library plus blind man can only equal Borges." In other words, Jorge of Burgos is a reference to Jorge Luis Borges, an Argentinean writer whose work often dealt with libraries and labyrinths and who wrote hugely influential experimental mystery narratives.

- In *The Name of the Rose*, therefore, we have a highly self-conscious and artificial form of the historical mystery that works on a variety of levels simultaneously. It's a compelling and satisfying murder narrative, a detailed and evocative historical mystery, and a thought-provoking reflection on some of the genre's foundational conventions.

THE CADFAEL CHRONICLES

- No discussion of the historical mystery would be complete without acknowledging the importance of the novel series. When we consider the novel series, one name immediately rises above all others: Ellis Peters. Ellis Peters is one of the pen names used by Edith Pargeter, who was born in England in 1913.

- Over the course of her career, Peters published two series of mystery novels. The first was a series of police procedurals featuring Detective Sergeant George Felse that has a contemporary setting. After publishing 13 novels in the series, however, Peters set herself a new challenge by writing historical mysteries. The result was a 20-book series of historical crime stories set in 12th-century Shrewsbury and featuring Brother Cadfael, a monk and amateur detective.

- According to critics Gina Macdonald and Michele Theriot, in the Brother Cadfael series, Peters "discovered the perfect fit for her varied interests, values, and inclinations—a forum for history, war, romance, religion, and mystery, all amid familiar landscapes, and for the exploration of universal concerns and esoteric medieval lore." While this description is a useful summary of the defining characteristics of the series, let's look more closely at the reasons for its success.

  > The first successful element is Brother Cadfael himself. Although Cadfael is a monk, religion is not a major emphasis in the series. One reason is that Peters wants to use Cadfael to examine secular aspects of medieval society. Also, Cadfael is a somewhat unusual monk. Although he now lives a cloistered life, he was previously a Crusader and a sailor, and Peters draws on Cadfael's varied life experiences to help us understand how a monk can be such an effective amateur detective.

  > Second, the setting of the series is extremely significant. By choosing the border region between England and Wales, which was the site of much conflict and turbulence during the medieval period, Peters is able to explore not only conflicts between cultures but also conflicts both between and within families.

  > Third, the fact that Cadfael appears in a series of novels means that we have ample opportunity to become thoroughly familiar with both Cadfael and the vividly described fictional world he inhabits over a long period of time.

QUESTIONS TO CONSIDER
1. What is the appeal of historical mystery fiction for its legions of fans?

2. How and why do historical mystery texts adapt the foundational aspects of the genre for their own ends?

SUGGESTED READING

Browne and Kreiser Jr., eds., *The Detective as Historian*.

Emerson, *How to Write Killer Historical Mysteries*.

HISTORICAL MYSTERIES

W e're used to thinking of mystery and suspense fiction as moving through space. Examples of the genre explore a variety of settings, including everything from the locked room to the country house, the suburb to the city, and even countries spanning the globe. But can mystery and suspense fiction move through time?

This is a more complicated question than it might at first appear because many of us tend to associate the genre with modernity. Why? Partly because of the genre-founding work of Edgar Allan Poe, which appeared in the 1840s. Consider how Poe's mystery tales can be set against issues like the growth of cities in the United States and the anxieties that growth caused and the rise of organized police forces which, as we've seen in another lecture in this course, Poe was deeply skeptical about. Mystery and suspense fiction has always been popular partly because it addresses contemporary issues.

We can also see evidence of this fact in the Sherlock Holmes stories of Sir Arthur Conan Doyle. Remember that we first meet Holmes at the same time Dr. John Watson does, at the beginning of the novel *A Study in Scarlet*. Because Holmes is busy conducting experiments in a laboratory when this meeting takes place, we get a sense of the way in which Doyle presents Holmes as a man of his times, modern and up-to-date with respect to the kinds of knowledge he possesses and is able to use in his cases.

And finally, the modernity of the private eye figure speaks for itself. From the moment this figure began to appear in the American pulp magazines of the 1920s, he was presented to readers as up-to-date with a vengeance. There was supposedly no shred of the Victorian gentleman amateur detective left about him. Instead, he moved through streets that his readers moved through and spoke in a way that his readers spoke. directly and without pretension.

Given these examples, the concept of historical mystery and suspense fiction might seem like something of a contradiction, and yet it is, in fact, a flourishing part of the genre. As we will see in this lecture, many writers take the foundational elements of the genre and move them to earlier periods in human history as a way of exploring both continuities and changes between today and yesterday.

Using mystery and suspense fiction conventions can also be a great way of translating aspects of earlier historical periods into terms that the modern reader can identify with. In doing so, historical mysteries expand the scope and popularity of the genre while also educating as well as entertaining their readers.

We've discussed examples of historical mysteries in other lectures in this course, but for various reasons we didn't consider them primarily in terms of their being historical mysteries. When we discussed Walter Mosley's Easy Rawlins mysteries in our lecture on black mystery fiction, for example, we focused on how Mosley's work was in dialogue with both classic hard-boiled writers like Raymond Chandler and other black mystery writers like Chester Himes. We spent more time discussing Mosley's representation of the city and the figure of the detective than we did discuss the fact that the Easy Rawlins novels, which began appearing in the 1990s, are set between the 1940s and the 1960s.

In a similar vein, when we looked at Mardi Oakley Medawar's Tay-Bodal mystery series in our lecture on Native American mysteries, which are set in the second half of the 19th century, we focused mainly on how Medawar's work compares to that of other writers of Native American mystery and suspense narratives such as Tony Hillerman and Linda Hogan, rather than considering how and why Medawar uses her historical setting.

Our focus in this lecture will be very different. We'll look at two types of historical mysteries. The first are single novels by authors known primarily for writing literary fiction who draw upon the conventions of mystery and suspense fiction to achieve their goals when revisiting periods in the past. We'll examine both what these goals are and why these writers believe that the combination of the mystery genre and a historical setting is so effective.

The second type of historical mystery fiction we'll discuss is mystery series that feature a single series protagonist who experiences a variety of adventures. By considering some of the similarities and differences between these two types, we'll focus on why historical mysteries are so popular among their legions of fans.

The first author I'd like to discuss is Caleb Carr. For the first part of his career, Carr was known as a military historian, thanks to books such as *America Invulnerable: The Quest for Absolute Security from 1812 to Star Wars* and *The Devil Soldier: The Story of Frederick Townsend Ward*, which were well-reviewed but only sold modestly. Incidentally, his father, Lucien Carr, was close friends with many of the Beat writers, including Jack Kerouac and Allen Ginsberg, as a young man in the 1950s.

Everything changed once Carr began to combine his interest in history with writing fiction. The result was *The Alienist*, which was published in 1994. This was not Carr's first novel that was *Casing the Promised Land*, which had come out in 1980 and then basically disappeared without a trace—but it was his first historical mystery.

The Alienist is set in New York City in 1896. Some of the novel's characters are historical figures, such as then-New York City police commissioner and later president Theodore Roosevelt and the journalist Jacob Riis, author of the trailblazing book of investigative photojournalism, *How the Other Half Lives*, which was published in 1890 and documented the desperate lives of New York City slum dwellers from all races and ethnicities.

Carr combines these real-life personages with fictional characters in *The Alienist* in order to tell a story involving the search for a serial killer who murders and mutilates young male prostitutes. The novel's protagonist is the psychologist Dr. Laszlo Kreizler, the alienist of the book's title, who creates what amounts to a psychological profile of the killer. Such a profile would have been a historical anomaly during the 1890s, and Carr is well aware of that fact. What's entertaining about the prospect, as well as the book as a whole, however, is how a concept and a figure familiar to readers of contemporary psychological thrillers is imported into a very different historical context.

By collecting and studying what appear to be minor clues, Kreizler and the other members of his investigative team theorize that the killer experienced sexual abuse as a child and had a very religious upbringing. Carr generates additional suspense by having Kreizler, and his colleagues hunted not only by the killer himself but also by various members of the establishment, who all have their own reasons for wanting to see the investigation fail.

I was a big hit, and its success suggests several factors that contribute to the success of historical mystery fiction as a whole. First, the author needs to strike a balance between historical anomaly such as moving a psychological profiler into the 1890s and historical accuracy such as the scrupulous attention, based on painstaking historical research, that Carr pays to re-creating the sights, smells, and other characteristics of the metropolis of New York City at the end of the 19th century.

The importance of this balance suggests that readers read historical mysteries both for the mystery elements and for the successful and convincing re-creation of historical detail. Consequently, historical mysteries, like other forms of mystery and suspense fiction, tend to be judged according to whether or not they are realistic. But in this case, realism means accuracy with regard to historical re-creation rather than, say, with regard to characterization, although that can also be a factor.

Reviews of *The Alienist* indicate that the second type of balance that often determines the fate of a historical mystery novel has to do with successfully combining historical research with a compelling mystery. Although most reviewers felt that Carr managed to pull this off, Stephen Dobyns in the New York Times Book Review argued that Carr's meticulous and detailed historical research was "both a curse and a blessing, for although the novel's ostensible subject is who-is-killing-these-children, the real subject is New York City in the 1890s."

Dobyns' remark indicates that historical mysteries can easily become overwhelmed by too much historical detail, in which case the mystery elements becomes subordinated to an extent that the reader might lose interest. It might seem like an obvious point, but readers of historical mysteries want to have their cake and eat it, too. They want to be transported to another historical setting and be simultaneously entertained by a good mystery yarn. When one of these elements dominates over the other, the novel flirts with failure.

It's interesting to note that Carr went on to write another type of historical mystery narrative that tends to be judged by different standards. In 2005, he published *The Italian Secretary: A Further Sherlock Holmes Adventure*, in which Holmes and Watson investigate the murder of workers at Queen Victoria's castle in Scotland. This type of historical mystery, which adapts a classic figure in the genre and attempts to add to that figure's reputation, tends to be judged in terms of fidelity to the original, a very specific kind of accuracy. I'm going to be kind to Carr and not say anything more about The Italian Secretary. As Carr himself wisely pointed out, "Only Conan Doyle can write real Sherlock Holmes."

In his 2006 novel, *The Interpretation of Murder*, Jed Rubenfeld combines the use of real historical figures and the recreation of a historical place in an unusual and thought-provoking manner.

Rubenfeld is a professor of law and began his career by writing highly-regarded books on constitutional law, such as *Freedom and Time: A Theory of Constitutional Self-Government*, which was published in 2001. When he turned his hand to writing fiction, he was drawn to a particular incident in psychoanalyst Sigmund Freud's life that is itself something of a mystery.

Freud only visited the United States once in his life, in 1909, and apparently, the visit was nothing short of a disaster. When Freud was later asked what he thought of America, he replied that it was a colossal mistake. Inspired by this comment, in *The Interpretation of Murder*, Rubenfeld writes a speculative reconstruction of Freud's visit to the United States to find out what went wrong.

Rubenfeld's creative answer is that Freud, along with real-life colleagues Carl Jung and Sándor Ferenczi, and the fictional American psychoanalyst Stratham Younger, all become involved in a murder investigation that takes place among the elite of New York City's wealthiest citizens.

There are a number of factors that make *The Interpretation of Murder* a successful historical mystery, and some of them we've already seen in our discussion of Carr. Rubenfeld's attention to historical detail is meticulous, and his re-creation of the sights and sounds of New York City in the first decade of the 20th century is creative and convincing.

What really makes the novel work, however, is that just as Carr gets a lot of mileage from transporting the figure of the psychological profiler back to the 19th century, so Rubenfeld develops the full implications of the similarities that exist between the figures of the detective and the psychoanalyst. These similarities have been noted before by a number of writers, including the famed Slovenian cultural critic Slavoj Žižek.

Among other things, they consist in a resemblance between the clue on the one hand and the symptom or the dream on the other.

Rubenfeld's title *The Interpretation of Murder* is, of course, an allusion to Freud's famous 1899 book *The Interpretation of Dreams*. Just as Freud is able to successfully decode and interpret details in dreams in order to build a larger narrative that resolves the patient's neurosis, so in Rubenfeld's novel we see the founder of psychoanalysis and his colleagues working to interpret clues some physical, but mostly psychological to solve a mystery. It is an ingenious parallel, and Rubenfeld develops it very successfully.

What *The Interpretation of Murder* also suggests is that at least to some extent, the success of a historical mystery depends on what a reader brings to it. Historical mysteries are probably the most pedagogical examples of the mystery and suspense fiction genre, in the sense that an intrinsic part of their appeal lies in the expectation that readers will learn things about a historical period that they didn't know before.

With this said, any given example of the historical mystery will likely work better and be more successful if the reader already has a little preexisting knowledge of the period the novel's set in, and it certainly helps if the reader is familiar with the conventions of the mystery and suspense fiction genre. That way, the reader can appreciate how the author is both drawing upon and reworking aspects of those generic conventions in clever and creative ways.

This is particularly true of *The Name of the Rose*, a famous novel published in 1980 by the Italian literary theorist Umberto Eco, which has at least as much, if not more, to say about the generic foundations of mystery and suspense fiction as it does about the historical period in which it's set.

The Name of the Rose has been described as a medieval murder mystery. It's set in a monastery in Northern Italy in the year 1327, and the plot revolves around an investigation into several murders that take place at the monastery. But this bald summary only scratches the surface of what Eco's novel really is.

Apart from the historical mystery elements, *The Name of the Rose* is filled with literary, philosophical, theological, and historical references, mostly having to do with obscure medieval religious disputes such as whether Jesus Christ owned the clothes he wore, and if he didn't, what are the consequences of this fact for the wealth of the Catholic Church. In addition, the novel also contains many passages in Latin and other languages.

In short, this isn't a book you'd normally expect to be a bestseller, and yet that's exactly what it became. It sold more than a million copies in Italy, and when it was translated into English in 1983, the hardcover version sold another million copies in the United States. The paperback rights sold for over half a million dollars, which was reportedly the largest sum of money ever paid for a paperback translation. A film adaptation directed by Jean-Jacques Annaud and starring Sean Connery was released in 1986, and the success of that film further confirmed *The Name of the Rose*'s status as a publishing phenomenon.

What can explain the extraordinary success of Eco's novel? I'd like to say it's his attention to historical detail, as befits a historical mystery novel, and to some extent that's true. But it's not the whole story. As I've indicated, Eco's reader does receive a large amount of information about historical events during the medieval period that were taking place outside the walls of the monastery, but much of that information is detailed rather than vivid.

As for the world of the monastery itself, its daily habits and routines are re-created meticulously, but there's no getting around the fact that it's a spatially limited fictional world filled with a numerically limited number of characters, very different from the teeming metropolis of New York City that we find in both Carr and Rubenfeld's work. In this regard, *The Name of the Rose* is closer to being a country house mystery in the Agatha Christie mold than it is a historical mystery in the more conventional sense.

And perhaps this is the key to the novel's success. *The Name of the Rose* is filled with allusions, some obvious, some not so obvious, to various forms of mystery and suspense. Quite apart from being a historical mystery just because it's set in an earlier time period, Eco's novel is also a historical mystery in the sense that it's a history of the genre itself. It's filled with clues about the lurking presence of the genre's key figures and conventions that are there for the attentive and knowledgeable reader to note and contemplate.

Let me give you a few examples of what I mean. Eco's protagonist is an older Franciscan monk named William of Baskerville. The fan of mystery and suspense fiction will of course immediately recognize Baskerville as a nod to Sir Arthur Conan Doyle's 1902 novel *The Hound of the Baskervilles*. If we then suspect that William is meant to be modeled after Sherlock Holmes, we find much evidence to confirm that suspicion.

Even though William is a monk and is, therefore, a man of faith, unlike Holmes, in many ways he's also conspicuously modern in comparison to his medieval background. He places little confidence in biblical prophecies and is impatient with overly dogmatic thinking and nitpicking theological disputation. Instead, William relies on what passes for cutting edge science in 1327. In this respect, he anticipates the Renaissance and the Enlightenment as much as he personifies medieval times.

And to seal the deal, William is accompanied by a young novice named Adso of Melk, whose training William is in charge of. The fact that Adso is constantly learning from his mentor and that he chronicles William's sayings and deeds makes the comparison between Adso and Dr. John Watson very obvious.

But as I said earlier, some of the references to mystery and suspense fiction in *The Name of the Rose* are much more subtle. William's main antagonist in the novel—the Professor Moriarty to his Holmes, if you will—is an elderly Spanish monk named Jorge of Burgos. Jorge controls access to the secrets of the monastery's labyrinthine library, in which lies a book that William desperately wants access to because it is the key to the mystery.

As Eco points out in his postscript to the novel, Library plus blind man can only equal Borges. In other words, as some but not all readers of Eco's novel will realize, Jorge of Burgos is a reference to Jorge Luis Borges whose work we'll discuss in another lecture in this series. Borges was a blind Argentinean writer whose work often dealt with libraries and labyrinths, and who wrote hugely influential experimental mystery narratives.

In *The Name of the Rose*, therefore, we have a highly self-conscious and artificial form of the historical mystery that works on a variety of levels simultaneously. It's a compelling and satisfying murder mystery, a detailed and evocative historical mystery, and a thought-provoking reflection upon both the strengths and weaknesses of some of the genre's foundational conventions. When looked at from this perspective, a final question is raised. How could this novel not have been a best-seller?

Up to this point of the lecture, I've focused on stand-alone historical mysteries that help illuminate some of the defining characteristics of this type of mystery and suspense fiction as a whole. But no discussion of the historical mystery would be complete without acknowledging and examining the importance of series of novels to the historical mystery. When we consider this aspect of the genre, one name immediately rises above all others. Ellis Peters, the author of what is, in my view, the best and most successful historical mystery series in the genre's history.

Ellis Peters is one of the pen names used by Edith Pargeter, who was born in Horsehay, England in 1913. Under her own name, Pargeter wrote a large number of historical non-mystery novels, beginning with *Hortensius, Friend of Nero,* which was published in 1936. She published her first crime novel, *Fallen into the Pit,* under her own name in 1951. But beginning with her second crime novel, 1959's *Death Mask*, she began using the pseudonym Ellis Peters for all her subsequent mystery fiction.

Over the course of her career, Peters published two series of mystery novels. The first was a series of police procedurals featuring Detective Sergeant George Felse that has a contemporary setting. After publishing 13 novels in the series, however, Peters reportedly felt ready to set herself a new challenge by writing historical mysteries that would allow her to combine her training and interest in history with the region in which she grew up, the border region between England and Wales.

The result was a series of historical crime stories set in 12th-century Shrewsbury featuring Brother Cadfael, a monk and amateur detective. The first novel in the series, *A Morbid Taste for Bones: A Mediaeval Whodunnit* was published in 1977, and Peters went on to write a grand total of 20 novels in the series, concluding with *Brother Cadfael's Penance. The Twentieth Chronicle of Brother Cadfael*, which was published in 1994, the year before Peters died.

According to the critics Gina Macdonald and Michele Theriot, in the Brother Cadfael series, Peters "discovered the perfect fit for her varied interests, values, and inclinations—a forum for history, war, romance, religion, and mystery, all amid familiar landscapes, and for the exploration of universal concerns and esoteric medieval lore." This description is a useful summary of the defining characteristics of the series, but let's look more closely at the reason for its success.

First, there's Brother Cadfael himself. Not unlike Eco's William of Baskerville, although Cadfael is a monk, he doesn't have much to say about religion, and it's not a major emphasis in the series. This is partly because Peters wants to use Cadfael to examine other aspects of medieval society, but also because Cadfael is a somewhat unusual monk. Although he now lives a cloistered life, he was previously a crusader and sailor, and Peters draws on Cadfael's varied life experiences throughout the series in order to help us understand how a monk can be such an effective amateur detective.

Second, the setting of the series is extremely important. By choosing the border region between England and Wales, which was the site of much conflict and turbulence during the medieval period, Peters is able to explore not only conflicts between cultures but also conflicts both between and within families. Combine this setting with the fact that each novel in the series is usually based on an actual historical event such as the siege of Shrewsbury in 1138, which forms the backdrop for the 1979 novel *One Corpse Too Many*, and the series has the degree of historical verisimilitude that discerning readers are looking for.

And finally, there's the fact that Cadfael appears in a series of novels. This means that we have ample opportunity to become thoroughly familiar with both Cadfael and the vividly described fictional world he inhabits over a long period of time.

Peters once commented that "Many perfectly good historical novels somehow set their characters at a terrible distance from us, as though they're not the same species." This is emphatically not the case with Peters' Brother Cadfael novels. In them, she is able to bridge the gap between past and present by recreating a detailed and evocative fictional world peopled with characters that are both very different from us but who, in all their imperfections and even vices, resemble us more than we might care to admit. Perhaps this is the secret to the success of not only Ellis Peters's work but also of historical mystery fiction as a whole.

SPIES, THRILLERS, AND CONSPIRACIES

S py and conspiracy narratives are a fascinating and varied part of the mystery and suspense fiction genre. In this lecture, we'll understand that what constitutes realism for suspense narratives can be very different from the realism of mystery narratives. The reason is that suspense fiction works very differently from much of mystery fiction. Arguably more sensitive to geopolitical and global concerns than traditional mysteries, suspense narratives featuring spies and conspiracies explore a wide range of concerns rarely touched on by most mystery writers.

RUDYARD KIPLING'S *KIM*

- Rudyard Kipling's 1901 novel *Kim* contains many elements characteristic of spy and conspiracy fiction. *Kim* tells the story of Kimball O'Hara, an orphan boy who was born in India to Irish parents. Because he grew up living by his wits on the streets of Lahore, Kim becomes so tanned that he looks like an Indian boy, and in fact he believes himself to be Indian.

- At one point in the novel, Kim meets and befriends Mahbub Ali, a horse trader who works for the British secret service, although Kim

Rudyard Kipling

doesn't know this at the time they meet. When he's not at school, Kim travels with Mahbub Ali, who trains Kim to play what he calls the Great Game, or espionage.

■ Kipling's *Kim* reveals several important aspects about espionage narratives as a whole.

  › First, just as much of the popularity of *Kim* has been attributed to Kipling's success in re-creating the sights and sounds of colonial-era India, so many subsequent espionage narratives will be evaluated by a standard of realism that emphasizes verisimilitude.

  › Second, the reference to the Great Game demonstrates that spy novels describe extremely ritualized forms of interaction between two opposing sides that share a highly politicized view of the world. In this regard, there's an interesting similarity between spy novels, which are often taken to be the last word in realism, and the highly artificial form of the puzzle mystery. Both are bound by rules, some implicit and some explicit, that govern their plot structure and outcomes.

  › Third, the use of the phrase "Great Game" suggests that even though the stakes of the games played in espionage fiction are very high, they also have a playful dimension. Not only are they ritualistic, but often all the players are known to each other. In other words, being a spy often means belonging to an elite club. Part of the pleasure readers derive from spy fiction is the feeling that by learning the rules of the game and seeing it played out, they're also part of this club, albeit at one remove.

  › Finally, the conclusion of *Kim* suggests that while allegiance is a key element of spy narratives, it is not always clear where allegiances lie. Many of these narratives contain double and even triple agents. In spy narratives, loyalty can either be a simple decision or a highly complex one.

JOHN BUCHAN'S *THE THIRTY-NINE STEPS*

- John Buchan, born in Scotland in 1875, is considered by many to be the father of the spy novel. What came to be known as the "Buchan touch" refers to the hallmarks of his work: characters that are romantic but not melodramatic, detailed and evocative descriptions of landscape and setting, and plots that move swiftly to a satisfying conclusion.

- Buchan is known for his emphasis that beneath the apparently calm and placid surface of civilization lie tangled conspiracies that threaten chaos if not controlled. As he puts it in his 1915 novel *The Thirty-Nine Steps*: "Away behind all Governments and Armies there was a big subterranean movement going on, engineered by very dangerous people."

- *The Thirty-Nine Steps* tells the story of Richard Hannay, a young Scotsman visiting England. Hannay meets an American man named Scudder, who drops some hints about secrets that are of great interest to England. After Scudder is murdered in Hannay's flat, Hannay is hunted down by two groups: Scudder's enemies and the police, who believe Hannay is guilty of the murder.

- From this point on, the novel becomes a series of cliff-hanging episodes, with a race against time thrown in to heighten the suspense still further. Although the payoff of the narrative may be the foiling of the conspiracy, the center of the novel is Hannay's desperate situation. He's an innocent man who finds himself in extraordinary circumstances and must use his wits and initiative to survive the situation.

- One other feature of *The Thirty-Nine Steps* that makes it very significant to the spy and conspiracy genre is the identity of the villain. Rather than being a member of the underworld, Buchan's master spy is in fact the very epitome of respectability. Indeed, this is what makes him so dangerous.

IAN FLEMING'S JAMES BOND

- Later examples of the spy and conspiracy genre would make Buchan's focus on a single spy look somewhat quaint. In the work of Ian Fleming and his novels featuring secret agent James Bond, organizations—principally governments and the countries that they represent—are the real source of the threat.

- Ian Fleming was born into a wealthy family in London in 1908. For the first part of his career, he worked predominantly as a journalist, but with the publication of his first novel, *Casino Royale*, in 1953, he started to become synonymous with his famous fictional creation. Partly because of Fleming's vivid imagination and love of the dramatic, James Bond arguably became more of a caricature than a character.

- Fleming starts with the real world but then moves away from it rapidly to write adventure tales in which a single, almost-superhuman individual is capable of overcoming anything that criminal organizations and the Soviet bloc can throw at him.

- And this, of course, is exactly why Bond was not only incredibly popular when he first appeared but is still flourishing in the form of the film franchise that began back in 1962 with the release of *Dr. No*. In fact, Fleming's novels and their film adaptations were immensely popular not in spite of—but precisely because of—their lack of realism. They gave the audience the realities of the Cold War in a form that was palatable and easy to consume.

- The emphasis on individualism that we've seen in many examples of mystery and suspense fiction survives and thrives in the spy novel. Readers find the conflict between mega-organizations (with all their assets and bizarre gadgetry) and the resourceful individual to be irresistible.

Ian Fleming starts with the real world but then moves away from it rapidly to write adventure tales in which a single, almost-superhuman individual is capable of overcoming anything that criminal organizations and the Soviet bloc can throw at him.

JOHN LE CARRÉ'S *THE SPY WHO CAME IN FROM THE COLD*

- A writer whose work could not be more different from that of Ian Fleming is John le Carré. John le Carré is the pen name of David Cornwell, who was born in Poole, England, in 1931. Just as Dashiell Hammett's work for the Pinkerton Detective Agency gave his hard-boiled crime fiction an unparalleled degree of realism, the same can be said of le Carré's career in the British intelligence service before he became a full-time writer.

- For much of his career as an intelligence operative, le Carré felt intense ambivalence about his work. Based on his experiences, he once commented, "There is no victory and no virtue in the Cold

War, only a condition of human illness and a political misery." As you can imagine, this ambivalence not only finds its way into le Carré's work but in some ways is the structuring principle of that work.

■ After the 1963 publication of *The Spy Who Came in from the Cold*, le Carré's work began to attract attention as a significant contribution to the espionage genre. The novel tells the story of Alec Leamas, a British intelligence agent who wants to retire from active duty—that is, "come in from the cold." His superiors convince him to take on one last assignment before he retires. The plot quickly thickens when Leamas starts to understand the real nature of his mission and the fact that he's been set up by his superiors.

■ The subsequent novels le Carré produced were highly praised for their decidedly unromantic, even mundane approach to espionage work. The novelist Anthony Burgess has noted, "Le Carré's contribution to the fiction of espionage has its roots in the truth of how a spy system works…. The people who run Intelligence totally lack glamour, their service is short of money, they are up against the crassness of politicians. Their men in the field are frightened, make blunders, grow sick of a trade in which the opposed sides too often seem to interpenetrate and wear the same face."

The people who run Intelligence totally lack glamour, their service is short of money, they are up against the crassness of politicians.

■ If James Bond is meant to personify the ability of the individual to resist and defeat the collective power of large organizations, even entire countries, le Carré's novels allow for no such comforting fantasies.

DAN BROWN'S *THE DA VINCI CODE*

- While there's always been a significant amount of overlap between the espionage novel and conspiracy fiction, Dan Brown's career indicates that there's a huge market for what we might call the pure conspiracy narrative (that is, a narrative freed from any association with either professional spies or contemporary geopolitics).

- Dan Brown's fourth novel, *The Da Vinci Code*, which was published in 2003, became a worldwide best seller. Although the novel's protagonist, Harvard symbologist Robert Langdon, had been introduced in Brown's 2000 novel *Angels & Demons*, it was the combination of the character of Langdon and *The Da Vinci Code*'s plot that took Brown's career to the next level.

- *The Da Vinci Code* begins with the murder of the chief curator of the Louvre Museum in Paris. When a mysterious riddle is discovered near the body, French authorities call on Langdon to help them investigate the mystery. A complex trail of clues leads Langdon to the paintings of Leonardo Da Vinci and eventually takes him on a long and dangerous quest for the Holy Grail. By the end of the novel, both Langdon and the reader have learned a great deal about a centuries-old conspiracy involving the Catholic Church.

- The key to the immense popularity of *The Da Vinci Code* has to do with how the novel helps the whole world make sense. This is what Marxist critic Fredric Jameson has described as the way in which conspiracy narratives give their readers a vision of the social totality. In a world that seems more and more confusing, overwhelming, and incomprehensible, espionage and conspiracy narratives give us the feeling that we can make sense of the world around us and perhaps even change it for the better.

QUESTIONS TO CONSIDER

1. What differentiates espionage and conspiracy texts from other types of mystery and suspense fiction?

2. Why is the James Bond franchise still alive and well in the 21st century?

SUGGESTED READING

Palmer, *Thrillers*.

Wark, ed., *Spy Fiction, Spy Films and Real Intelligence*.

SPIES, THRILLERS, AND CONSPIRACIES

I n a number of lectures in this course, we've discussed the realism of mystery and suspense fiction. Although we've found that realism can be a very slippery term and that it can mean different things in different contexts, it's also true to say we can make some generalizations about it.

In this lecture, we'll see that what constitutes realism for suspense narratives can be very different from the realism of many types of mystery narrative. Why is this? Mostly because suspense fiction works very differently from much mystery fiction. Arguably more sensitive to geopolitical and global concerns than traditional mysteries, suspense narratives featuring spies and conspiracies explore a wide range of concerns rarely touched upon by most mystery subgenres.

For instance, espionage and conspiracy narratives frequently contain a race against time element that adds suspense to the narrative. In addition, the protagonists of these narratives are often mavericks, although this emphasis on individualism is often combined with a focus on relationships between large organizations and countries. Spy and conspiracy narratives are a fascinating and various part of the mystery and suspense fiction genre, and they have proved themselves to be enduringly popular among readers.

Rudyard Kipling might seem like an unlikely place to begin a lecture about espionage and conspiracy fiction, but a discussion of his 1901 novel *Kim* reveals a number of useful things that will help orient our analysis of this subgenre.

Kim tells the story of Kimball O'Hara, who was born in India to Irish parents but who became an orphan when he was still young. Because he grew up living by his wits on the streets of Lahore, Kim becomes so tanned that he looks like an Indian boy, and in fact, he believes himself to be Indian.

At one point in the novel, Kim meets and befriends Mahbub Ali, a horse trader who works for the British secret service, although Kim doesn't know this at the time they meet. When Kim's true background is discovered, he's sent to school at St. Xavier's, a school for British colonials. Although Kim misses the street life, he proves to be a good student. When he's not at school, he travels with Mahbub Ali, who, along with other members of the secret service, trains Kim to play what he calls the Great Game, or espionage.

After completing his training, Kim again assumes the identity of a street boy, but this time, it's a disguise that enables him to achieve his true goal, which is to uncover the existence of Russian spies in the north of India for the British. The novel unfolds more as a military-themed adventure story than a quest for a secret piece of information, but by the time the novel ends, Kim is assured that he has played the Great Game well. The problem is that the reader is left unsure about what exactly this means. Why? Partly because we are not sure who has won, and partly because Kim still feels somewhat divided in his allegiances between being Indian and being British.

I've summarized the plot of Kipling's *Kim* at some length because I think it reveals several important points about espionage narratives as a whole. First, just as much of the success of Kim has been attributed to Kipling's success in recreating the sights and sounds of colonial-era India, so many subsequent espionage narratives will be evaluated by a standard of realism that emphasizes verisimilitude. Many readers of spy fictions want to feel that the author possesses insider knowledge of one kind or another and is sharing that knowledge with readers, who then become part of the in-group, as it were.

Second, the reference to the Great Game indicates that spy novels are a highly ritualized form of literature that describe highly ritualized forms of interaction between two opposing sides that share a paranoid, or at least a highly politicized, view of the world. In this regard, there's an interesting similarity between spy novels, which are often taken to be the last word in realism, and the highly artificial form of the puzzle mystery. Both are bound by rules, some implicit and some explicit, that govern their plot structure and outcomes.

Third, the use of the phrase Great Game suggests that even though the stakes of the games played in espionage fiction are very high in many novels they even determine the fate of the free world, they also have a playful dimension. Not only are they ritualistic, but often all the players are known to each other. In other words, being a spy often means belonging to an elite club as we see when Kim is trained in spycraft. Part of the pleasure readers derive from spy fiction is the feeling that, by learning the rules of the game and seeing it played out, they're also part of this club, albeit at one remove.

And finally, the conclusion of Kim suggests not only that allegiance is a key element of spy narratives, but also that the question of which side one belongs to isn't always as straightforward as it might appear. At first glance, this last claim seems to contradict common sense about spy narratives. Surely this subgenre is all about belonging to one side or another?

Well, yes, that's true. But just think how many of these narratives contain characters who move from one side to the other and then back again, or double and even triple agents who are working for both sides at once or perhaps even for themselves while pretending to swear allegiance to just one side. It quickly becomes clear that the notion of belonging in spy narratives is quite complex. Indeed, it may even be that one way of distinguishing between more or less realistic spy narratives is the degree to which they depict the question of loyalty as either simple or complex.

Let's see how some of these questions play out in the work of John Buchan, who many people regard as the father of the spy novel. Born in Perth, Scotland, in 1875, Buchan would go on to have a rich and productive career during which he worked in a variety of genres. Nevertheless, he's most famous for his thrillers. What came to be known as the Buchan touch refers to the hallmarks of his work, characters that are romantic but not melodramatic, detailed and evocative descriptions of landscape and setting, and plots that move swiftly on their way to a satisfying conclusion.

With regard to the spy novel, in particular, Buchan is best-known for his emphasis on the fact that, beneath the apparently calm and placid surface of civilization lie tangled conspiracies that constantly threaten chaos if not controlled and resolved. As he puts it in his 1915 novel *The Thirty-Nine Steps*, "Away behind all Governments and Armies, there was a big subterranean movement going on, engineered by very dangerous people." A closer look at his most famous novel will illustrate the key features of Buchan's work.

The Thirty-Nine Steps tells the story of Richard Hannay, a young Scotsman who's visiting England after thirty years in South Africa. Hannay meets an American man named Scudder, who drops some hints about secrets that are of great interest to England. After Scudder is murdered in Hannay's flat, Hannay is hunted down by two groups, Scudder's enemies, and the police, who believe Hannay is guilty of the murder.

From this point on, the novel becomes a series of one cliff-hanging episode after another, with a race against time element thrown in for good measure to heighten the suspense still further. Hannay possesses Scudder's notebook, which contains vital information, but the question is, can Hannay remain free long enough to deliver the information to the proper authorities and avert disaster? Eventually, Hannay succeeds and in doing so not only foils the plot of a secret spy organization but also reveals the meaning of the novel's title.

The fame of Buchan's novel would be enhanced still further by Alfred Hitchcock's 1935 film adaptation of *The 39 Steps*. I think Hitchcock was on to something when he realized that the apparent center of Buchan's plot—namely, the secret in Scudder's notebook—was what Hitch famously called a maguffin. What's a maguffin? The thing the narrative appears to be about, but which in fact is merely a way of introducing the real subject of the narrative.

So what's the real subject of Buchan's *The Thirty-Nine Steps*? Although the payoff of the narrative may be the foiling of the conspiracy, the center of the novel is Hannay's desperate situation. He's an innocent man who finds himself in extraordinary circumstances and must use his wits and initiative to survive the situation in any way that he can. If Rudyard Kipling's *Kim* was trained to play the Great Game, then we can say that Hannay is simply thrown into it without any of the game's rules being explained to him. Can he survive? The answer to that question is what engages the reader.

Before leaving Buchan, there's one other feature of *The Thirty-Nine Steps* that makes it very significant, and that's the identity of his villain. Rather than being a member of the underworld, Buchan's master spy is, in fact, the very epitome of respectability. Indeed, this is one of the things that makes him so dangerous.

In this way, Buchan not only illustrates the extent to which paranoia is intrinsic to many spy narratives but also suggests that respectability may be the ultimate conspiracy. The more respectable someone appears to be, the more suspicious they are, because, in espionage and conspiracy fiction, it's the powerful rather than the powerless that you have to keep your eye on.

If we follow this logic to its inevitable conclusion, it should come as no surprise that later examples of the genre would make Buchan's focus on a single spy look somewhat quaint. In the work of Ian Fleming and his novels featuring secret agent James Bond, it is organizations, principally governments and the countries that they represent, that are the real source of the threat. Against power of this magnitude, what can a single individual hope to do? Answering that question will help us explain the enduring popularity of the character of James Bond.

Ian Fleming was born into a wealthy family in London, England, in 1908. Because his mother controlled the family's wealth, however, Fleming wasn't able to access any of that wealth and instead had to work for a living, which reportedly he resented quite intensely. For the first part of his career he worked predominantly as a journalist, but with the publication of his first novel, *Casino Royale*, in 1953, he started to become synonymous with his famous fictional creation.

Ironically, given Bond's later reputation, Fleming chose such an undistinguished name for his protagonist because he was a great admirer of the work of Graham Greene and Eric Ambler. He originally aspired to write realistic espionage fiction using a rather featureless protagonist in the manner of the writers he admired. During the war, Fleming had worked for Naval Intelligence, and he certainly had a fund of experience he could have drawn upon in his novels.

Obviously, things turned out very differently. Partly because of Fleming's vivid imagination and love of the dramatic, and partly because of the pressure he imposed on himself to produce a new Bond novel every year, James Bond arguably became more of a caricature than a character. And yet the novels' lack of realism didn't make them any less successful. Quite the opposite, as one review of *Moonraker*, Fleming's third Bond novel, suggests, "A fantastic piece of nonsense. I didn't believe a word of it. But I couldn't put the book down until it was finished."

I argued earlier that verisimilitude was key to the success of espionage and conspiracy fiction, yet now I seem to be arguing the opposite. How can this be? Bear in mind the fact that Fleming's James Bond novels appeared as the Cold War was rapidly heating up. It might seem as if his audience would have wanted realistic spy novels during this period, novels suffused with a sense of real politics that would help them understand and process what was going on so that they could understand the story behind the headlines.

Some might argue that Fleming did, at least to some extent, provide this kind of service in the Bond novels. *From Russia with Love* and *On Her Majesty's Secret Service*, for example, do draw upon contemporary geopolitics in their plots. It's obviously much more accurate, however, to argue that Fleming starts with the real world but then moves away from it rapidly to write adventure tales in which a single almost superhuman individual is capable of overcoming anything that criminal organizations and/or the Soviet bloc can throw at him.

And this, of course, is exactly why Bond was not only incredibly popular when he first appeared, but is still alive and kicking today in the form of the film franchise that began all the way back in 1962, with the release of *Dr. No*. Not in spite of but precisely because of their lack of realism, Fleming's novels and their film adaptations were popular. They gave the audience the realities of the Cold War in a form that was palatable and easy to consume.

How was it palatable? In the sense that, no matter how serious the situation gets, Bond always has everything under control. The emphasis on individualism that we've seen in many other examples of mystery and suspense fiction think of Poe and Doyle's genius amateur detectives, or the private eyes of Hammett and Chandler turns out to survive in the spy novel. Why? Because readers find the conflict between organizations with all their resources, including bizarre gadgets and the individual who has the ability to use those resources effectively to be irresistible.

When Fleming once described the goal of his writing as getting intelligent, uninhibited adolescents of all ages, in trains, airplanes, and beds, to turn over the page, he may have been selling himself short. It might be more accurate to say that the spy novels featuring James

Bond performed a valuable social function—namely, alleviating Cold War anxieties about the state of the world and entertaining people in the process.

With this said, espionage and conspiracy fiction is such a varied subgenre that there is obviously no one correct way to write it. The best way to illustrate this point is to now turn to a writer whose work could not be more different from that of Ian Fleming, but who's still had an enormous influence on the form.

I'm referring to John le Carré, who was born David Cornwell in Poole, England, in 1931. Just as Dashiell Hammett's work for the Pinkerton Detective Agency gave his hard-boiled crime fiction an unparalleled degree of realism, the same can be said of le Carré's career before he became a full-time writer. From around the late 1940s to the early 1960s, le Carré worked off and on for the British intelligence services in a variety of places and in a variety of capacities.

Why was his work off and on? Mostly because, for much of his career as an intelligence operative, le Carré felt intense ambivalence about the work he was doing. Based on his experiences, he once commented that "There is no victory and no virtue in the Cold War, only a condition of human illness and a political misery." If the espionage novel is apparently predicated on a clear dividing line between good and evil, the West and the East, from le Carré's point of view both sides are equally imperfect and at fault. In his words, "We are in the process of doing things in defense of our society which may very well produce a society which is not worth defending."

As you can imagine, this ambivalence not only finds its way into le Carré's work but in some ways is the structuring principle of that work. His first two spy novels, *Call for the Dead* in 1961 and *A Murder of Quality* in 1962, were written while he was working for the British Foreign Office, which is why he had to publish them using a pseudonym. It was not until his third novel, *The Spy Who Came in from the Cold*, was published in 1963, however, that le Carré's work really began to attract attention as making a significant contribution to the espionage genre.

The novel tells the story of Alec Leamas, a British intelligence agent who wants to retire from active duty or come in from the cold. His superiors convince him to take on one last assignment before he retires, an assignment that involves Leamas pretending to defect in order to give false information to the East Germans that implicates one of their officers as a British agent. The plot quickly thickens when Leamas starts to understand what his real mission is, and the fact that he's been set up by his bosses.

The Spy Who Came in from the Cold was so successful that it finally enabled le Carré to retire from the intelligence services and to devote himself to writing full-time. The subsequent novels he produced, like Spy, were highly praised for their decidedly unromantic, even mundane approach to espionage work.

As the novelist, Anthony Burgess once commented when discussing le Carré's work as a whole,

> Le Carré's contribution to the fiction of espionage has its roots in the truth of how a spy system works... The people who run Intelligence totally lack glamour, their service is short of money, they are up against the crassness of politicians. Their men in the field are frightened, make blunders, grow sick of a trade in which the opposed sides too often seem to interpenetrate and wear the same face...

Burgess not only comments perceptively about le Carré's work but also gets at the heart of what makes that work radical and what differentiates it from the James Bond novels of Ian Fleming. If James Bond is meant to personify the power of the individual to resist and defeat the collective power of large organizations, even entire countries, le Carré's novels allow for no such comforting fantasies.

In fact, it would be going too far to say that, in a sense, there are no individuals in le Carré's work. Instead, there are only faceless, colorless, and impersonal representatives of two political systems that are meant to be antithetical but which again and again prove themselves to be disturbingly similar.

In this context, although le Carré's most famous fictional creation is probably the spymaster George Smiley, who appears in a number of his novels, it feels a little inaccurate to describe Smiley as a series protagonist. Why? Because, if Smiley distinguishes himself at all, it is by his studied anonymity, which allows him to do his job effectively, despite the frequent misgivings he has about that job.

While Smiley and his colleagues are very different from the archetypal secret agent personified by James Bond, they do have one very obvious thing in common. Like the protagonists of the other novels we've looked at in this lecture, they're all men. Even more than some other varieties of mystery and suspense fiction, it seems that the espionage and conspiracy subgenre is something of a boys' club.

Fortunately, that situation is starting to change. And interestingly, that change is being spearheaded by another former representative of the British Intelligence Services, Stella Rimington, the first woman ever to head MI5 and the first leader of the British Security Service whose name was made public.

After retiring from the Intelligence Service, Rimington fulfilled a long-held ambition to become a novelist. This has resulted in a series of novels, beginning with the publication of *At Risk* in 2005, that feature female MI5 agent Liz Carlyle. Rimington has used the series not only to analyze recent political issues such as drone warfare and the Arab Spring but also to examine what the security services look like from the perspective of a female operative. In doing so, Rimington has added a valuable new dimension to this subgenre.

Although Rimington's novels have sold well, they are dwarfed by the success of Dan Brown as indeed are most of the other writers I've discussed in this lecture, with the possible exception of Ian Fleming. While there's always been a significant amount of overlap between the espionage novel and conspiracy fiction, Dan Brown's career indicates that there's a huge market for what we might call the pure conspiracy narrative that is, a narrative freed from any association with either professional spies or contemporary geopolitics . The popularity of this kind of narrative, I want to suggest, is both related to but also different from the demand for spy fiction.

Brown's success as an author is largely a function of the way in which his fourth novel, *The Da Vinci Code*, which was published in 2003, became a worldwide bestseller. Although the novel's protagonist, Harvard symbologist Robert Langdon, had been introduced in Brown's 2000 novel *Angels & Demons*, it was the combination of Langdon and *The Da Vinci Code*'s plot that took Brown's career to the next level.

That book begins with the murder of the chief curator of the Louvre Museum in Paris. When a mysterious riddle is discovered near the body, French authorities call upon Langdon to help them investigate the mystery. Following a complex trail of clues leads Langdon to the paintings of Leonardo Da Vinci and eventually takes him on a long and dangerous quest for the Holy Grail. By the end of the novel, both Langdon and the reader have learned a great deal about a centuries-old conspiracy involving the Catholic Church.

What was it about The Da Vinci Code that made it so successful? I'm going to go out on a limb here and say that it was definitely not the quality of the writing. In fact, in my view, Dan Brown is one of the worst writers we discuss in this entire course. I think it has more to do with how the novel helps the whole world make sense.

Let me explain what I mean by taking a brief detour. In a fascinating book entitled *Combined and Uneven Apocalypse*, critic Evan Calder

Williams discusses John Carpenter's classic 1988 science fiction/horror film *They Live*, in which the protagonist learns that the world is being controlled by aliens. The ostensible meaning of the film is Oh no. The world is being run by aliens. However, according to Williams, the real meaning of the film is Oh good. The world is being run by aliens.

Why is an alien invasion a good thing? Because now we know that the world is being run by others—whether it be aliens or Dan Brown's secret society, suddenly everything is comprehensible. Everything is coherent and organized, even if only in the sense that we can now identify a clear enemy.

This is what Marxist critic Fredric Jameson has described as the way in which conspiracy narratives give their readers a vision of the social totality. In a world that seems more and more confusing, overwhelming, and incomprehensible, the success of the espionage and conspiracy narratives we've discussed in this lecture is related to the way they give us a comforting sense that we can make sense of the world around us, and perhaps even change it for the better.

We might even argue that the spy becomes a kind of private eye, but instead of knowing the city, he unravels a conspiracy about which we may be ignorant, even though it threatens us. In doing so, the spy, like other heroes in mystery and suspense fiction, attracts our admiration both because of his competence and because, at least in theory, he makes the world a safer place.

FEMALE-CENTERED MYSTERY AND SUSPENSE

I n the vast majority of mystery and suspense narratives, female characters tend to appear in one of three roles: victim, femme fatale, or detective. While this group of roles is not necessarily restrictive, it is, however, incomplete. In this lecture, we'll see how the genre's representation of the female experience has become much more complex and nuanced. For example, writers are more likely to use strong women protagonists who don't have to seduce men, or they feel free to create female characters who are the killers rather than the victims. Moreover, some examples of the genre focus on relationships among women characters; in these cases, male characters play a secondary, rather than a primary role.

NEW ROLES FOR WOMEN

- The middle decades of the 20th century saw the publication of a wide variety of popular fiction written by women that contained many different types of female characters. This era in some ways represents the high point of diversity in terms of women's roles in mystery and suspense fiction.

- Dorothy Hughes is one writer who imagined new roles for women. It's significant that much of Hughes's work appeared in the 1940s, a time when gender roles in America were being redefined rapidly. Since so many American men were abroad fighting in World War II, the war years saw unprecedented numbers of women entering the paid labor force for the first time.

- Hughes's 1947 novel *In a Lonely Place* is a sharp and explicit criticism of the usual roles for women in mystery and suspense fiction. The novel is set in post–World War II Los Angeles and features protagonist Dix Steele, a veteran fighter pilot and a serial killer of young women. Although Brub Nicolai, the police officer in charge of the murder investigation, is both conscientious and committed, his friendship with Steele renders him unable to see that the murderer is standing (literally) right in front of him.

- By contrast, the two main female characters in the novel have no illusions about Steele. Sylvia, Brub's wife, realizes that there's something wrong with Steele from the first time she meets him. Laurel, Steele's girlfriend, takes a little longer to come around to Sylvia's point of view. Eventually, the two women set a trap for Steele that leads to his capture by the police.

- While not detectives in the professional sense of the term, Sylvia and Laurel prove to have the intelligence and courage to capture a serial killer, and in doing so, they extend the roles that women play in the genre.

"In Gun We Trust"

- Other female writers of mystery and suspense fiction during this period take a different tack by exploring the potential of women to commit acts of violence in their own right. In the extraordinary 1957 novel entitled *Bunny Lake Is Missing*, written by pulp author Merriam Modell using the pen name Evelyn Piper, the novel's protagonist, Blanche Lake, finds herself in a situation where she's willing to do almost anything, including murder, to achieve her goal.

- Blanche's daughter has gone missing. What's worse, no one at the school even remembers seeing her, and even though the police investigate the disappearance, it's clear that they think Blanche is insane and doesn't even have a daughter.

- Although she begins the novel as an insecure and vulnerable young woman, as events unfold, Blanche not only turns out to have hidden reserves of strength and determination, but she also discovers a potential for violence that she's willing and able to use in order to get her daughter back. For example, having armed herself, at one point Blanche utters the immortal line: "In gun we trust."

SUBVERTING GENRE CONVENTIONS

- Like Hughes and Piper, Vera Caspary once enjoyed considerable commercial and critical success, but her work has since been neglected. The exception to this rule, of course, is her 1942 novel *Laura*. The classic film noir adaptation of *Laura*, directed by Otto Preminger and with Gene Tierney in the title role, seemingly cemented the novel's reputation.

Some female-centered mystery and suspense narratives suggest that a woman's violence can be a product of violent struggle within femininity itself.

- Unfortunately, Caspary was unhappy with the film adaptation because it makes Laura look more like a garden-variety femme fatale than she is in the novel. In fact, the novel works as a subtle commentary on the woman as an object of desire in mystery and suspense narratives—a figure on which various male characters project their needs and fantasies. This emphasis demonstrates not only Caspary's familiarity with genre conventions but also her desire to subvert them.

THE VIOLENCE WITHIN

- Some female-centered mystery and suspense narratives suggest that a woman's violence can be a product of violent struggle within femininity itself. The work of Margaret Millar is particularly instructive in this regard. Millar began her career in the early 1940s by publishing three novels, beginning with *The Invisible Worm* in 1941, which featured Paul Prye, a psychiatrist detective. Millar's oeuvre also includes a series of police procedurals featuring Inspector Sands and a series of legal thrillers whose protagonist is Latino attorney Tom Aragon.

- Many of Millar's novels use variations of what has been characterized by critic Jake Hinson as the classic tale of a woman in distress. Millar puts her female protagonist in a difficult situation at the start of the novel and then keeps raising the pressure relentlessly until the explosive twist ending.

- This is a perfect description of one of Millar's best novels, *Beast In View*, which was published in 1955 and won an Edgar from the Mystery Writers of America for Best Mystery Novel. It tells the story of Helen Clarvoe, a reclusive heiress who receives an unwelcome phone call from an old friend by the name of Evelyn Merrick. The phone calls become more frequent and threatening, and so Clarvoe asks her family lawyer, Paul Blackshear, for help.

- The strength of the book lies not only in its characterization but also in the fact that Millar devotes equal time to both Helen and Evelyn, who in a sense become the shared protagonist of the book. Just how true this is becomes clear in the twist ending of the novel, when we learn that although Evelyn Merrick does indeed exist, she's entirely innocent of stalking Helen. Instead, it transpires that the "Evelyn" we've grown to fear over the course of the novel is Helen's alter ego, the more sexually aggressive and independent part of herself that she's split off and externalized into another personality.

> Many of Millar's novels use variations of what has been characterized by critic Jake Hinson as the classic tale of a woman in distress.

- Even more shocking and unexpected is the fact that it is Evelyn who eventually wins the struggle between her and Helen. When Evelyn/Helen kills herself, she becomes both murderer and victim simultaneously. In *Beast In View*, Millar writes a novel that possesses both great psychological complexity and keen insight into the struggles between desire and respectability that women can internalize—struggles that in this case turn out to be literally fatal.

ALTERNATIVE REALITIES

- It may seem odd to include Patricia Highsmith in a discussion about female-centered mystery and suspense narratives, as the vast majority of her work features male rather than female protagonists. Moreover, as critic Diana Cooper-Clark once observed to Highsmith, "I find that in a number of your novels the women seem despicable in trivial ways."

- But consider Highsmith's 1977 novel *Edith's Diary*, which stands out in the context of Highsmith's oeuvre as a whole by virtue of having a complex, sympathetic, and three-dimensional female protagonist. The novel tells the story of Edith Howland, a freelance writer and housewife, who tries to organize and analyze her life by keeping a diary. But as Edith's personal life collapses around her, her diary starts to play a different role.

- Specifically, in her diary entries, Edith starts to create an alternative reality in which she is happy and successful and her son is an accomplished and prosperous engineer with a beautiful wife and two adorable children. While there is no crime in *Edith's Diary*, nevertheless, it's a tremendously suspenseful, even heartbreaking novel—as we're forced to witness the gradual but inexorable process through which Edith comes to inhabit fantasy rather than reality.

WOMEN'S CAPACITY FOR RAGE

- One of the most popular female writers working in the genre today is Gillian Flynn. In just three novels—*Sharp Objects*, *Dark Places*, and *Gone Girl*—Flynn has reshaped the landscape of contemporary mystery and suspense fiction. A key part of her success has been her ability to build on the achievements of her predecessors by offering a range of ways in which women can appear in the genre and by placing women at the center of her narratives.

- Her debut novel, *Sharp Objects*, published in 2006, tells the story of Camille Preaker, a reporter who returns to Wind Gap, Missouri, the small town where she was raised, in order to investigate a series of child murders. Ensuing events illustrate the fact that her return is as much an exploration of and coming to terms with her own past as it is an investigation of the murders.

- *Dark Places*, published in 2009, is set in Kansas and features protagonist Libby Day, who as a seven-year-old, witnessed the murder of her mother and two sisters. Libby testified against her brother Ben, who was convicted of the crimes. Now a penniless and directionless adult, Libby comes across the Kill Club, a group of enthusiasts who revisit and discuss notorious murder cases. As Libby gets to know them, she finds out that most of them believe her brother to be innocent. This forces Libby to revisit the past and the events of that night, with shattering consequences.

- Although her first two novels both sold well, *Gone Girl*, published in 2012, took Flynn's career to a different level. Nick and Amy Dunne appear on the surface to be the perfect married couple, but the truth is very different. When Amy finds out that Nick is cheating on her, she fakes her own death in order to frame Nick for the murder. Using a combination of Amy's diary entries and an account of Nick's actions, Flynn shows just how toxic and violent a decaying marriage can be.

- Each of Flynn's novels explores women's capacity for rage and the varying consequences of the rage. What's more, in every one of Flynn's novels, women in all of their contradictory complexity are at the center of the narrative. Like the other writers we have discussed in this lecture, Flynn refuses to let her female characters be limited to a single role. Instead, her work demonstrates the fact that when women are allowed to dominate mystery and suspense narratives, extraordinary things can happen.

1. What roles are available for women in the genre—other than being victims, femmes fatales, or detectives?

2. In what ways do female-centered mystery and suspense narratives encourage readers to examine the situation of women in society as a whole?

SUGGESTED READING

Klein, ed., *Diversity and Detective Fiction.*

Plain, *Twentieth Century Crime Fiction.*

FEMALE-CENTERED MYSTERY AND SUSPENSE

I n the vast majority of mystery and suspense narratives that we've examined in this course, female characters tend to appear in one of three roles: victim, femme fatale, or detective. Of course, there are enormous differences between these three roles and I don't want to imply that this group of roles is necessarily restrictive. But it is incomplete.

We'll see in this lecture that as the genre continues to develop, female characters appear in mystery and suspense fiction as three-dimensional, rounded characters that don't obey the logic of being either dead, seductive, or crime-solvers. This development makes the genre's representation of female characters much more complex and nuanced while also enabling the genre to reflect and comment on changes taking place in the societies around it.

For example, strong women characters can influence mystery and suspense plots as protagonists without seducing male characters or solving crimes. This includes narratives in which women are the killers rather than the victims. Moreover, some examples of the genre focus on relationships among women characters; in these cases, male characters play a secondary, rather than primary role.

Mystery and suspense fiction narratives have always distinguished themselves by their sensitivity to their social context. The changing roles that women play is a great example of the ways in which the genre continues to evolve and flourish in the 21st century. In 2003, the Feminist Press of the City University of New York launched a series entitled Femmes Fatales: Women Write Pulp that was designed to bring American pulp fiction written by women between the 1930s and the 1960s back into print. Despite the title of the series, which implies that it was only designed to publish mystery and suspense fiction, in fact, it included titles from a wide variety of genres, including lesbian romances, science fiction, melodrama, as well as hard-boiled noir.

I begin with this detail to emphasize the fact that the middle decades of the 20th century saw the publication of a wide variety of popular fiction written by women that contained many different types of female characters. Thanks to the Feminist Press, as well as the author and critic Sarah Weinman, who has edited an anthology of short stories entitled *Troubled Daughters, Twisted Wives: Stories from the Trailblazers of Domestic Suspense*, and a boxed set of novels with the collective title *Women Crime Writers: Eight Suspense Novels of the 1940s & 50s* for the Library of America, this work is much better-known than it used to be.

However, I want to focus on material from the middle of the 20th century for the first part of this lecture not only because it's still understudied and underappreciated, but also because this era in some ways represents the highpoint of diversity in terms of women's roles in mystery and suspense fiction.

A good example of a writer that the Feminist Press' Femmes Fatales series succeeded in bringing readers' attention to is Dorothy Hughes. Hughes was born in Kansas City, Missouri, and over the course of her career, she published 14 crime novels and one nonfiction crime book. Although her work was highly regarded during her lifetime— she received the Grand Master Award from the Mystery Writers of America in 1978 for both her fiction and her mystery criticism—today much of her work is out of print.

The critic Nancy C. Joyner has described much of Hughes' fiction as "domestic thrillers in which the accomplished and upper-class protagonist becomes innocently involved in a situation of evil intrigue, finally resolved through the hero's cunning, character, and sheer luck."

What is domestic about Hughes' work? Partly the fact that she put a lot of effort into imagining new roles for women at a time when American society as a whole was being forced to consider the same subject. It's significant that much of Hughes' work appeared in the 1940s, at a time when gender roles in America were being redefined rapidly.

Since so many American men were abroad fighting in World War II, the war years saw unprecedented numbers of women entering the paid labor force for the first time. When the war ended, and the men returned home, it seemed that women were expected to return quietly to the kitchen, and many women were not happy about that situation.

Two of Hughes' novels, in particular, explore the way the war disrupted what were previously considered to be unshakeable gender relations. In *The Blackbirder*, which was published in 1943, we learn about the dangerous situation in which Julie Guille, a 22-year-old refugee from occupied France, finds herself in after entering the U.S. illegally via Cuba. After a friend of hers from Paris is murdered in New York City, Julie is convinced she'll be next, and so she escapes to New Mexico in search of the Blackbirder, a human trafficker, who Julie hopes will be able to get her out of the country.

Julie is eventually saved not by depending on the Blackbirder but by her own bravery, intelligence, and belief in herself. What distinguishes Julie from so many other female characters in mystery and suspense fiction is not only the fact that she's the protagonist, but also her determination not to become a victim, the status reserved for so many other women in the genre before her.

Hughes' 1947 novel, *In a Lonely Place*, shares with *The Blackbirder* a fictional universe influenced by war but is even sharper and more explicit in its criticism of the usual roles for women in mystery and suspense fiction. The novel is set in post–World War II Los Angeles and features protagonist Dix Steele, a veteran fighter pilot and a serial killer of young women. The fact that Steele also aspires to write a crime novel is Hughes' sly commentary on the centrality of violence against women to the genre.

Although Brub Nicolai, the police officer in charge of the murder investigation, is both conscientious and committed, his friendship with Steele, and in particular their bonding over memories of their wartime camaraderie, renders Brub unable to see that the murderer is standing literally right in front of him.

By contrast, the two main female characters in the novel have no illusions about Steele. Sylvia, Brub's wife, realizes that there's something wrong with Steele from the first time she meets him. Laurel, Steele's girlfriend, takes a little longer to come around to Sylvia's point of view, but eventually, by working together, it is these two women, rather than Brub, who set a trap for Steele that leads to his capture by the police. While not detectives in the professional sense of the term, Sylvia and Laurel prove to have the intelligence and courage to capture a serial killer, and in doing so, they extend the roles that women play in the genre.

If Hughes's work often explores the ability of female characters to both resist and defeat a violence that is frequently coded as male, then other female writers of mystery and suspense fiction during this period take a different tack by exploring either the potential or the reality of women to commit acts of violence in their own right.

In an absolutely extraordinary 1957 novel entitled *Bunny Lake is Missing*, written by pulp author Merriam Modell using the pen name Evelyn Piper, the novel's protagonist, Blanche Lake finds herself in a situation where she's willing to do almost anything, including murder, to achieve her goal.

Imagine this scenario: you're a young mother who has just moved to a new city and started a new job, and at the end of the day you go to collect your young daughter from her first day at daycare. The problem is your daughter's gone missing. What's worse, no one at the school even remembers seeing her, and even though the police investigate the disappearance, it's clear that they think you're insane and that you don't even have a daughter.

This is the nightmarish situation into which Piper plunges Blanche Lake, who is in a race against time to not only find her daughter but also to prove her very existence to those who think she's hallucinating. Piper does a brilliant job of suffusing her fictional scenario with a steadily and relentlessly increasing amount of dread, but the real triumph of the novel is its characterization of Blanche Lake.

Although she begins the novel as an insecure and vulnerable young woman, as events unfold, Blanche not only turns out to have reserves of strength and determination that neither she nor the reader could have dreamed of, but she also discovers a potential for violence that she's willing and able to use in order to get her daughter back. For example, having armed herself, at one point Blanche utters the immortal line: "In gun we trust." In this simple sentence, Piper captures both the centrality of violence to American identity and the potential of a violent woman to extend and even upend the conventions of mystery and suspense fiction.

Like Hughes and Piper, Vera Caspary is another writer who once enjoyed considerable commercial and critical success but whose work has since become somewhat neglected. The exception to this rule, of course, is her 1942 novel *Laura*, which actually began as a play before Caspary adapted it into a novel. After a long and complicated process, which involved making changes Caspary didn't agree with, the classic film noir adaptation of *Laura*, directed by Otto Preminger and with Gene Tierney in the title role, seemingly cemented the novel's reputation.

Unfortunately, Caspary had good reason to be unhappy with the film adaptation, no matter how successful it was, because it makes Laura look more like a garden variety femme fatale than she is in Caspary's novel. In fact, the novel works as a subtle commentary on the woman as an object of desire in mystery and suspense narratives, a figure upon which various male characters project their needs and fantasies. Although some of this emphasis survives in the film version, it's much more pronounced in Caspary's novel, which indicates not only her familiarity with genre conventions but also her desire to subvert them.

The same is true, if not more so, of Caspary's 1945 novel, *Bedelia*, which also features a strong and charismatic female protagonist. While Laura had a contemporary setting, Caspary chose to set Bedelia in 1913. Why? Because this gave her an effective way of stressing the limitations placed on women who yearned to be independent in a period that was even more restrictive than the 1940s.

The novel tells the story of Charlie Horst and his wife, Bedelia, who on the surface appear to be blissfully happy newlyweds. As the novel progresses, however, Charlie realizes just how little he knows about his wife's past. He gradually becomes convinced that Bedelia is not only a criminal but also a serial killer of her previous husbands by means of poison and that he may be the next victim.

What's striking about Caspary's treatment of this subject is not so much that Charlie's suspicions turn out to be correct but that Caspary spends very little time exploring Bedelia's motives for her homicidal actions. When she's trying to persuade Charlie not to turn her over to the authorities, Bedelia attempts to explain or exonerate herself by saying, "I'm your wife, you know, and I'm sick. I'm a very sick woman, your wife. I've never told you, dear, how sick I am." Although Bedelia is referring to her physical health, given what we know about her at this stage of the novel, this seems as much a psychological as a physical diagnosis.

Bedelia's fate is also instructive. She dies, technically by her own hand, but in reality because, like a dutiful wife, she obeyed her husband's instructions to take her own poison. In this way, Caspary suggests that there's no room for a character like Bedelia to live, either in America in 1913, or in mystery and suspense fiction in the 1940s.

If Bedelia's violence is directed outward, other female-centered mystery and suspense narratives suggest that a woman's violence can also be a product of violent struggle within femininity itself. The work of Margaret Millar is particularly instructive in this regard. She is yet another example of a female mystery and suspense writer who was once very highly regarded—she received the Mystery Writers of America's Grand Master Award in 1983—but whose work is now unfairly neglected.

Millar was born Margaret Sturm in Kitchener, Ontario, in 1915 and married her high school sweetheart Kenneth Millar, who would later go on to great fame as a mystery writer publishing under the name of Ross Macdonald. In fact, Macdonald chose to use a pseudonym so that his work wouldn't be confused with that of his wife, who was already an established author when Macdonald began his career. According to Macdonald, he was inspired by his wife's work to become a writer: "By going on ahead and breaking trail she helped to make it possible for me to become a novelist."

Millar began her career in the early 1940s by publishing three novels, beginning with *The Invisible Worm* in 1941, which featured Paul Prye, a psychiatrist-detective. Apart from writing a number of stand-alone mystery novels, Millar's oeuvre also includes two other series, one police procedurals featuring Inspector Sands, and the other legal thrillers whose protagonist is a Latino lawyer by the name of Tom Aragon.

As this brief summary suggests, Millar's work was very diverse, but many of her novels use variations of what has been characterized by critic Jake Hinson as a woman in distress plot. Millar puts her female protagonist in a difficult situation at the start of the novel and then keeps raising the pressure relentlessly until the explosive twist ending.

This is a perfect description of one of Millar's best novels, *Beast in View*, which was published in 1955 and won an Edgar from the Mystery Writers of America for Best Mystery Novel. It tells the story of Helen Clarvoe, a reclusive heiress who receives an unwelcome phone call from an old friend by the name of Evelyn Merrick. The phone calls become more frequent and threatening, and so Clarvoe asks her family lawyer, Paul Blackshear, for help.

The strength of the book lies not only its characterization but also in the fact that Millar devotes equal time to both Helen and Evelyn, who in a sense become the shared protagonist of the book. Just how true this is becomes clear in the twist ending of the novel, when we learn that although Evelyn Merrick does indeed exist, she's entirely innocent of stalking Helen. Instead, it transpires that the Evelyn we've grown to fear over the course of the novel is Helen's alter-ego, the more sexually aggressive and independent part of herself that she's split off and externalized into another personality.

Even more shocking and unexpected is the fact that it is Evelyn who eventually wins the struggle between her and Helen, as we learn from the closing words of the novel, which are told from Evelyn's point of view: "She pressed the knife into the soft hollow of her throat. She felt no pain, only a little surprise at how pretty the blood looked, like bright and endless ribbons that would never again be tied."

When Evelyn/Helen kills herself, she becomes both murderer and victim simultaneously. In *Beast In View*, Millar writes a novel that possesses both great psychological complexity and keen insight into the struggles between desire and respectability that women can internalize, struggles that in this case turn out to be literally fatal.

At first glance, it might seem eccentric to now add Patricia Highsmith to a lecture about female-centered mystery and suspense narratives.

Why would this be eccentric? Partly because the vast majority of Highsmith's work, and in particular her novels as opposed to her short fiction, features male rather than female protagonists. Moreover, as critic Diana Cooper-Clark once pointed out to Highsmith, most of her female characters are portrayed rather negatively: "I find that in a number of your novels the women seem despicable in trivial ways. They are often cheats, Melinda in *Deep Water*, Hazel in *The Glass Cell*, Alicia in *Suspension of Mercy*, Miriam in *Strangers on a Train*."

Highsmith responds to this observation by saying that "the whole picture looks as if I suspect that women have narrow characters, which is not really true. It is not my personal feeling at all." In fact, she adds, "I have quite an esteem for women's strength."

Was Highsmith telling the truth? Well, consider the fact that in some cases she seems to have encouraged the view of herself as being hostile to women, as when she published the deliberately provocative short fiction collection entitled Little Tales of Misogyny, which includes stories like "The Coquette," "The Fully Licensed Whore, or, The Wife"—that's all one title—"The Breeder," "The Mobile Bed-Object," and "The Perfect Little Lady." Given these titles, even though they may be tongue-in-cheek, Highsmith's response in the interview seems quite disingenuous.

But then consider her 1977 novel *Edith's Diary*, which stands out in the context of Highsmith's oeuvre as a whole by virtue of having a complex, sympathetic, and three-dimensional female protagonist. The novel tells the story of Edith Howland, a freelance writer, and housewife, who tries to organize and analyze her life by keeping a diary. But as Edith's life collapses around her, with her husband leaving her for a younger woman, her being left to care for her ex-husband's invalid uncle, and her son Cliffie turning out to be a complete waste of space, her diary starts to play a different role.

Specifically, in her diary entries, Edith starts to create an alternative reality in which she is happy and successful, and her son is an accomplished and prosperous engineer with a beautiful wife and two adorable children. There is no crime in Edith's Diary unless you count Cliffie administering a fatal overdose of codeine to the bedridden uncle, which he may or may not have done deliberately. Nevertheless, it's a tremendously suspenseful, even heartbreaking novel, as we're forced to witness the gradual but inexorable process through which Edith comes to inhabit fantasy rather than reality.

When Edith accidentally slips on the stairs and falls to her death at the end of the novel, the last thing she experiences is a great sense of personal injustice. This indicates the extent to which Edith's Diary can be thought of as a crime novel. But what exactly the crime is, and who the criminal might be, remain unclear. Thankfully, Highsmith clarifies neither of these points, which leaves us free to admire how creatively she repurposes the suspense novel to achieve her particular ends.

The writers I've discussed so far in this lecture make it clear what a rich legacy these women left for subsequent writers in the genre who wished to rethink and extend the representation of female characters in mystery and suspense fiction. What did later writers do with this legacy? I'd like to close out this lecture by answering this question through a discussion of the work of one of the most popular female writers working in the genre today: Gillian Flynn.

In just three novels, Sharp Objects, published in 2006, Dark Places, published in 2009, and Gone Girl, published in 2012, Flynn has reshaped the landscape of contemporary mystery and suspense fiction. How has she done it? There are various answers to that question, of course, but I believe a key part of her success has been her ability to build upon the achievements of her predecessors by offering a range of ways in which women can appear in the genre by placing women at the center of her narratives.

Her debut novel, Sharp Objects, tells the story of Camille Preaker, a reporter who returns to Wind Gap, Missouri, the small town where she was raised, in order to investigate a series of child murders. Ensuing events illustrate the fact that her return is as much an exploration of and coming to terms with her own past as it is an investigation of the murders, and indeed the two things turn out to be connected. I can't say any more than that because I don't want to give away the ending!

Dark Places is set in Kansas and features protagonist Libby Day, who as a seven-year-old witnessed the murder of her mother and two sisters. Libby testified against her brother Ben, who was convicted of the crimes. Now a penniless and directionless adult, Libby comes across "The Kill Club," a group of enthusiasts who revisit and discuss notorious murder cases. Libby sells family memorabilia to the members of the club as a way of making some money, but as she gets to know them, she finds out that most of them believe her brother to be innocent. This forces Libby to revisit the past and the events of that night, with shattering consequences for both her and others.

Although her first two novels both sold well, *Gone Girl* took Flynn's career to a different level. Nick and Amy Dunne appear on the surface to be the perfect married couple, a kind of reflection of the idyllic suburb they live in, but the truth is very different. When Amy finds out that Nick's cheating on her, she fakes her own death in order to frame Nick for the murder. Using a combination of Amy's diary entries and an account of Nick's actions, Flynn shows just how toxic and violent a decaying marriage can be.

What do these three novels have in common? A clue comes in the form of an interview Flynn gave after the publication of Gone Girl, in which she says of herself:

> I am on the surface an incredibly even-keeled, laid-back Midwestern type, but in my mind, I occasionally indulge in wonderful dreamscapes of revenge and become quite a drama queen. And the fact is, I don't say the things that I would in my grand Bette Davis-on-her-fifth-vodka sort of speeches, but I certainly identify with that moment of pure rage.

I'm not suggesting that Flynn's novels are psycho-biographies. Rather, what I'm arguing is that each of her novels explores women's capacity for rage and the varying consequences of the rage.

Sometimes, those consequences are played out on the body of Flynn's protagonist, as with Camille in Sharp Objects, who self-harms to such an extent that her body is covered with scars, making her visibly as well as emotionally damaged. And sometimes those consequences are directed outward, as with Amy's elaborate revenge plot against her cheating husband.

In every one of Flynn's novels, however, women in all of their contradictory complexity are at the center of the narrative. Like the other writers we have discussed in this lecture, Flynn refuses to let her female characters be limited to a single role. Instead, her work demonstrates the fact that when women are allowed to dominate mystery and suspense narratives, extraordinary things can happen.

POETIC JUSTICE

M any mystery and suspense tales are uninterested in the legal system. Some narratives end with the arrest or death of the guilty party. In other stories, the outcomes are inconsistent with the standards of the legal system—for example, criminals may escape or be let off by the detective. Yet in the vast majority of these narratives, the reader still feels that justice has been done. The reason is that although the type of justice meted out may not always match the technical or legal definition of justice, it still falls under the heading of poetic justice.

THE WAY THE WORLD SHOULD BE

- Consider what Edgar Allan Poe's foundational mystery tales have to say about justice. In "The Murders in the Rue Morgue," C. Auguste Dupin successfully identifies the parties responsible for the murders, but they are not brought to justice. In "The Mystery of Marie Rogêt," Dupin predicts how the police might go about finding the perpetrator, and Poe confirms in a footnote that Dupin's prediction was correct. But we never see justice done.

- And finally, in "The Purloined Letter," we come closest to the traditional understanding of justice. The stolen letter is recovered, and Dupin sets up a situation that will eventually lead to the minister's ruin. But we never see that ruin unfold.

- The reason: Poe is not interested in justice. Instead, his points of focus are analysis and the character of the detective Dupin. From Poe's point of view, it's enough for the reader to see Dupin at work and for him to conclude each of his cases successfully. Justice in the legal sense of the word is beside the point.

- The absence of legal justice doesn't take anything away from mystery and suspense fiction, however. Indeed, poetic justice can often be more satisfying than legal justice because it speaks to our sense of the way the world should be, rather than the way it is.

"A SCANDAL IN BOHEMIA"

- Sir Arthur Conan Doyle's Sherlock Holmes stories have a much higher percentage of outcomes where the perpetrator is taken into police custody. These outcomes reflect Conan Doyle's belief that the detective works hand in hand with the legal system. However, Conan Doyle is completely uninterested in what happens to the criminal after he's led away by the police. Conan Doyle's brand of mystery story ends with the detective's victory.

- An interesting example of poetic justice in the Sherlock Holmes mysteries can be found in "A Scandal in Bohemia." Although Conan Doyle has depicted Holmes as an apparently infallible detective, he does something extraordinary in this story: He not only has Holmes lose the case but also has him defeated by a woman.

- Holmes is hired by the King of Bohemia to recover a compromising photograph of the king and Irene Adler. Not only does Holmes fail to recover the photograph, but he's also outwitted by Adler, who escapes to Europe with the photograph.

> The absence of legal justice doesn't take anything away from mystery and suspense fiction. Indeed, poetic justice can often be more satisfying than legal justice

- Poetic justice is driven home by the closing episode, in which the king laments that if Adler had been his social equal, he would have married her and made her his queen. Holmes's only response to this is to comment acidly, "From what I have seen of the lady she seems indeed to be on a very different level to your Majesty." The king, of course, does not get the point. But the reader sees that justice has been done because Irene Adler is free of the king, who was unworthy of her.

A SELF-REFERENTIAL MOMENT

- Given the fact that so many of Agatha Christie's novels finish with a grand climax where the detective reveals the identity of the murderer, it should come as no surprise that much of her work contains a more conventional sense of justice. But even though most of her criminals are safely in the hands of the law by the end of the story, Christie shares her predecessors' disinterest in the legal process after the arrest. Once again, the detective's supremacy over the criminal is the ultimate payoff.

- And yet, because Christie understood the importance of balancing formula and innovation, there are some notable examples of poetic justice in her work.

- For example, in *The Murder of Roger Ackroyd*, a novel that is noted for its disrespect toward generic convention, Hercule Poirot not only allows Dr. Sheppard to take his own life rather than be arrested by the police, but he also gives Sheppard the time to finish his record of the case before killing himself.

- This is a strikingly self-referential moment in Christie's work, where completing the record of the case so that we may have access to the truth about what happened takes precedence over justice in the narrow sense of the word.

HARD-BOILED JUSTICE

- According to hard-boiled justice, many criminals wind up dead rather than under arrest. In the pioneering stories of Carroll John Daly, for example, featuring his archetypal private eye Race Williams, it often seems that the only acceptable form of closure is a room filled with dead bodies.

- To take one example among many others, "I'll Tell the World" tells the story of Race Williams's investigation into a complex scheme organized by a lawyer, a doctor, and a United States senator. These three individuals conspire to institutionalize a man because they want control over his money. At the climax of the story, having already committed his usual quota of violent acts, Williams shoots and kills the doctor and the senator but not before being shot three times and nearly dying himself.

- Needless to say, Williams survives the gunfight. Given the obvious affinities between Race Williams and the heroes of westerns and dime novels, the reader sets the story aside with the comforting sense that a frontier-style form of justice has been carried out.

- It's also worth noting the characteristics of the villains in Daly's story. They aren't lowlife members of the underworld but instead are respectable and even powerful members of mainstream society. One reason for the prevalence of poetic justice in hard-boiled mysteries is that the official law enforcement and justice systems are frequently seen as either corrupt or inefficient. In other words, in a society where official justice is not to be trusted, poetic justice is the best possible form of justice.

LIMITS OF POETIC JUSTICE

- Writers such as Dashiell Hammett and Raymond Chandler, noted for their realism, understand the limits of poetic justice.

- For example, at the end of Dashiell Hammett's *The Maltese Falcon*, Sam Spade has to make one of his most difficult decisions: turn Brigid O'Shaughnessy over to the police. It's an extremely difficult decision for him, partly because he's in love with Brigid. But the bottom line is that Sam is a realist. Once he realizes that Brigid murdered his partner Miles Archer, Sam can't save Brigid even if he wanted to. It's his duty as a private eye to see that his slain partner is avenged.

- But Spade is also a realist in another sense. Remember that his role as private eye is not a hobby or an avocation; he is a professional. He runs a business, and so he needs to have a working relationship with the cops in San Francisco. Spade has to turn Brigid over to the police if he wants to continue working as a private eye. Poetic justice might dictate that Sam find a way to spare Brigid. However, poetic justice in the world of *The Maltese Falcon* is simply not an option.

- We see another example of the limits of poetic justice in Raymond Chandler's *The Big Sleep*. By the end of the novel, Philip Marlowe has solved both mysteries presented to him by the Sternwood family: who was blackmailing the general and who killed Rusty Regan, Vivian Sternwood's husband. Even though Marlowe realizes that Regan was shot and killed by Carmen, Vivian's sister, and that Vivian helped to cover up her husband's murder, the novel ends with Carmen being sent to a sanatorium for treatment and with Vivian going unpunished.

- The reason Marlowe doesn't have the Sternwood sisters arrested is that he has already demonstrated earlier in the novel that his ultimate loyalty is to his client, General Sternwood. Faced with a choice between punishing the guilty and sparing the general from the knowledge of his rotten family, Marlowe chooses to let the general die in blissful ignorance.

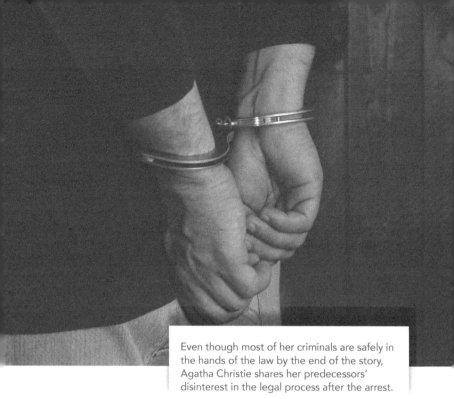

Even though most of her criminals are safely in the hands of the law by the end of the story, Agatha Christie shares her predecessors' disinterest in the legal process after the arrest.

- Marlowe feels that poetic justice, like the ideal of chivalry that he supposedly personifies, is a luxury he can't afford.

POETIC JUSTICE AS VIGILANTE JUSTICE

- Mickey Spillane's Mike Hammer novels eschew complexity and ambiguity altogether. In fact, the author and his avatar have an exceptionally simple and brutally satisfying approach to justice. For Spillane and Hammer, poetic justice and vigilante justice are one and the same.

- In *I, the Jury*, Mike Hammer has a deeply personal investment in the crime he's investigating. The murder of his war buddy Jack

Williams has hit Hammer hard, and he promises that he'll find and kill his friend's murderer in exactly the same manner that Jack was killed—with a bullet in the gut.

- By the end of the novel, thanks to a variety of extralegal acts of violence, Hammer finally achieves his goal and keeps his promise to his dead friend. The fact that the murderer Hammer kills is Dr. Charlotte Manning, the woman with whom he's fallen in love, makes his attachment to his version of poetic justice even more striking. Unlike Spade, Hammer has no qualms about imposing justice on the woman he loves and is even willing to do it himself. As she is dying, Manning asks him how he could do such a thing, and Hammer famously replies, "It was easy."

AN INSPIRATIONAL FORM

- A detective's ethical commitment to his or her work can result in a very inspirational form of poetic justice.

- For example, Chester Himes's *Cotton Comes to Harlem*—which features his series characters, black homicide cops Grave Digger Jones and Coffin Ed Johnson—is a typically over-the-top, action-packed, and absurd tale revolving around the theft of $87,000 from 87 poor Harlem families by a fraudulent Back to Africa movement. Grave Digger and Coffin Ed's priority is to recover the money.

- Although Grave Digger and Coffin Ed recover the money, it means letting a murderous racist escape. The families get their money back, and the villain is shocked when he realizes that these two detectives are letting him go because of their love for other black people. In this instance, two sworn officers of the law are willing to place poetic justice above legal justice.

1. How would you define poetic justice?

2. Why are so many examples of the genre attracted to poetic justice rather than justice in the accepted legal sense of the term?

SUGGESTED READING

Kertzer, *Poetic Justice and Legal Fictions.*

Masson and O'Connor, eds., *Representations of Justice.*

POETIC JUSTICE

W hat constitutes justice in mystery and suspense fiction? The most obvious answer is the apprehension of the criminal, and then that criminal's passage through the legal system until they are sentenced, and the sentence is carried out. That sounds fine in theory, but in practice, it turns out that the genre contains a range of other possibilities.

In fact, many mystery and suspense tales are simply uninterested in the legal system. In these instances, the story usually ends with the arrest or death of the guilty party. In other cases, the outcomes are inconsistent with the standards of the legal system, for example, criminals may escape or even be let off by the detective. Yet in the vast majority of these cases, we still feel that justice has been done.

Why? Because although the type of justice meted out in mystery and suspense fiction may not always match the technical, legally accepted definition of justice, it still falls under the heading of poetic justice. But what exactly is poetic justice, why is there so much of it in the genre, and why we find it satisfying? This lecture will be devoted to answering these questions.

Let's begin by taking a look at what Edgar Allan Poe's foundational mystery tales have to say about the subject of justice. In "The Murders in the Rue Morgue," Auguste Dupin successfully identifies the parties responsible for the death of Madame and Mademoiselle L'Espanaye, but neither of the parties are brought to justice. The orangutan is sold to a zoo, and the sailor whose carelessness led to the animal escaping and killing two women profits greatly from the sale.

In "The Mystery of Marie Rogêt," Dupin ends the tale by predicting confidently how the police might go about finding the perpetrator, and Poe confirms in a footnote that Dupin's prediction was correct. But we never see justice done. Instead, we have to trust Dupin and Poe when they tell us the murderer of Marie Rogêt was found!

And finally, in "The Purloined Letter," we come closest to the traditional understanding of justice. The stolen letter is recovered, and Dupin sets up a situation that will eventually lead to the Minister's destruction. But even here we never see that destruction. We simply have to imagine it happening at some unspecified point in the future.

Why are Poe's mystery tales so little concerned with justice? The simple answer is that Poe is not interested in justice. Instead, his subjects in these stories are analysis and Dupin, the character that personifies the power of analysis. So, from Poe's point of view, it's enough for us to see Dupin at work and for him to conclude each of his cases successfully. Justice in the legal sense of the word is beside the point.

Although the orangutan and its master may have been technically guilty of a crime, I doubt many readers would have enjoyed seeing them hauled off to jail at the end of "Rue Morgue." Similarly, even though we don't get to see a criminal arrested at the end of "Marie Rogêt," we've seen Dupin at work, and we derive immense satisfaction from that fact. Finally, because the competition between Dupin and the Minister D– is at the heart of "The Purloined Letter," we feel that justice has been done when the former beats the latter at his own game. In particular, we delight in the knowledge that the Minister will be destroyed by the very same letter that he's been using to influence and control others.

It's easy to see from Poe's stories, then, that the absence of legal justice doesn't take anything away from mystery and suspense fiction. Indeed, if anything, poetic justice can often be more satisfying than legal justice because it speaks to our sense of the way the world should be, rather than the way it is.

If we now turn to the work of those writers who followed Poe's trailblazing path, we'll see that they also have a mix of attitudes toward justice in the conventional sense, though sometimes for different reasons.

Sir Arthur Conan Doyle's Sherlock Holmes stories, for example, have a much higher percentage of outcomes involving the perpetrator being taken into police custody think of bank robber John Clay, for example, being led away in handcuffs at the end of "The Red-Headed League."

Part of the reason for the increased frequency of such an ending has to do, of course, with the fact that Doyle wrote many, many more stories than Poe. But I think it also reflects Doyle's and his society's belief that the detective worked hand in hand with the legal system, and was particularly valuable precisely because he was often able to apprehend those slippery criminals who escaped the clutches of the dim-witted police.

But even in stories like "The Red-Headed League," Doyle is apparently completely uninterested in what happens to the criminal after he's led away by the police. This is partly because the ins and outs of the legal system wouldn't become the focus of mystery and suspense fiction until later in the 20th century, and partly because, in Doyle's brand of mystery fiction, the story ends with the detective's victory.

With this emphasis on the detective's victory in mind, we can see a number of other possible endings in Doyle's tales, all of which are meant to be considered just, but none of which would match society's ordinary understanding of justice. "The Adventure of the Speckled Band," for example, ends with the murderer's death at the hands of the very instrument that he used to kill and attempt to kill others.

This fact leads Holmes to comment drily "Violence does, in truth, recoil upon the violent, and the schemer falls into the pit which he digs for another." We're clearly meant to appreciate the fact that the murderer being killed by his own murder weapon is the quintessence of poetic justice.

In other instances, however, even a conservative individual like Doyle is capable of coming up with a version of poetic justice that seems positively subversive of society's typical understanding of justice. In "The Adventure of the Blue Carbuncle," Holmes is attempting to recover the titular jewel, which has been stolen from the Countess of Morcar. Even though he solves the case and discovers the identity of the criminal, James Ryder, Holmes decides not to have Ryder arrested and instead lets him escape to the Continent.

Why would Holmes do such a thing? Partly because the story is set during the Christmas season and Holmes is feeling charitable toward Ryder. He regards Ryder as a petty thief rather than a criminal mastermind and feels that sending him to prison would only result in making him a hardened criminal.

More importantly from Holmes' point of view, however, Ryder's absence means that the case against John Horner, who has been falsely arrested and accused of the crime, will collapse. In other words, what we see here is an example of the detective allowing a technical injustice in order to prevent an even greater injustice from taking place. Or as Holmes puts it: "I suppose that I am commuting a felony, but it is just possible that I am saving a soul."

But let's not forget that at the end of "Blue Carbuncle," Holmes also remarks to Watson that "I am not retained by the police to supply their deficiencies" as a way of justifying his actions. This suggests the possibility that sometimes poetic justice exists to remedy the inadequacies and even corruption of the legal system. At the very least, it implies that part of the detective's job is to protect the powerless against the powerful.

An interesting example of this variety of poetic justice in Holmes can be found in "A Scandal in Bohemia." Bearing in mind the fact that Doyle is well-known for creating Holmes as an apparently infallible detective, he does something extraordinary in this story: he not only has Holmes lose, but also has him beaten by a woman!

Holmes is hired by the King of Bohemia to recover a compromising photograph of him and Irene Adler, an American opera singer with whom the king previously had an indiscreet liaison. Not only does Holmes fail to recover the photograph, but he's also outwitted by Adler, who escapes to Europe with the photograph.

Even though we may be shocked by Holmes' defeat, we take some comfort from the fact that Adler had clearly been wronged by the selfish and arrogant king, and so we're pleased to see Adler come out on top.

This aspect of the story is driven home by the closing episode, in which the king laments that Adler had not been his social equal so that he could have married her and made her his queen. Holmes' only response to this is to comment acidly, "From what I have seen of the lady she seems indeed to be on a very different level to your Majesty." The king, of course, doesn't get the point. But the reader sees that justice has been done in the form of Irene Adler being free of the king, who was unworthy of her.

Given the fact that so many of Agatha Christie's novels finish with a grand climax where the detective reveals the identity of the murderer, it should come as no surprise that much of her work contains a more conventional sense of justice than either Poe or Doyle. But even though most of her criminals are safely in the hands of the law by the end of the story, Christie shares her predecessors' disinterest in the legal process after the moment of arrest. Once again, the detective's supremacy over the criminal is the ultimate payoff and the typical evocation of justice in a Christie novel.

And yet, because Christie, probably more than anyone else in the mystery and suspense fiction genre, understood the importance of balancing formula and innovation, we can find some notable examples of more creative versions of poetic justice in her work.

For example, in *The Murder of Roger Ackroyd*, a novel that is justly famous or infamous, depending on your point of view for its disrespect toward generic convention, Hercule Poirot not only allows Dr. Sheppard to do the decent thing and take his own life rather than be arrested by the police, but he also gives Sheppard the time to finish his record of the case before killing himself.

This is a strikingly self-referential moment in Christie's work, where completing the record of the case so that we may have access to the truth about what happened takes precedence over justice in the narrow sense of the word. This outcome also indicates the way in which, more than once in Christie's oeuvre, the murderer is someone to be pitied as well as punished, which means we're unlikely to resent Poirot's considerate treatment of Sheppard.

Another interesting example of the "poetic justice" approach to murder in Christie's work can be found in *Sleeping Murder*, her final novel. Even though Miss Marple is convinced that a murder took place in the past that has gone unsolved and that the murderer is still alive, she initially recommends that the murder not be investigated.

Why? Partly because Marple realizes that an investigation will inevitably cast suspicion upon innocent people and cause them grief. More importantly, however, Marple believes that the dormant murderer will come back to life and strike again in order to protect himself, thus leading to more deaths. Miss Marple is proven right on both counts, and her preference to let sleeping dogs lie instead of following the letter of the law is a good example of the preference for poetic justice.

Even more striking, however, is the fact that Miss Marple changes her mind about investigating the crime at the heart of *Sleeping Murder* when she realizes that the victim's husband had tortured himself to death through guilt, believing he'd killed his wife, even though he was completely innocent. In other words, once Miss Marple understands that the negative consequences of the investigation are outweighed by the need to both solve the murder and find justice for the victim's husband, she goes ahead and solves the case. Sometimes legal justice is not enough; it needs to be supplemented by its more powerful cousin, poetic justice.

It's well-known that hard-boiled crime fiction was a revolution in the genre, and so we might expect to see big changes in how this variety of mystery fiction treats the concept of poetic justice. In some respect, change is exactly what we find, but there are also significant continuities.

In terms of what's different about hard-boiled justice, one thing that jumps out immediately is that many criminals wind up dead at the end of a hard-boiled narrative rather than under arrest. In the pioneering stories of Carroll John Daly, for example, featuring his archetypal private eye Race Williams, it often seems that the only acceptable form of closure is a room filled with dead bodies.

To take one example among many others, "I'll Tell the World," a story that was first published in Black Mask in 1925, tells the story of Race's investigation into a complex scheme organized by a lawyer, a doctor, and a United States senator. These three individuals conspire to institutionalize a man, supposedly because he's insane, but really because they want control over his money. At the climax of the story, having already committed his usual quota of violent acts, Race shoots and kills the doctor and the senator, but not before being shot three times and nearly dying himself.

Needless to say, Race survives the gunfight. Given the obvious affinities between Race Williams and the heroes of both Westerns and dime novels, the reader sets the story aside with the comforting sense that a frontier-style form of justice has been carried out. We might call the climax of a typical Race Williams story "Gunfight in Midtown Manhattan" at high noon if you will.

It's also worth noting the villains in Daly's story. They aren't low-life members of the underworld but instead respectable and even powerful, members of mainstream society. One reason for the prevalence of poetic justice in hard-boiled mysteries is that the official law enforcement and justice systems are frequently seen as either corrupt or inefficient. In other words, in a society where official justice is not to be trusted, poetic may be not only an alternative but also the best possible form of justice.

And yet, even if this is so, the official system can't simply be set aside and ignored as it so often is in Daly's stories, which is one sign of his attachment to melodrama rather than realism. We find evidence of the increased realism of the work of writers like Dashiell Hammett and Raymond Chandler from their realization of the limits of poetic justice.

For example, at the end of *The Maltese Falcon*, Sam Spade has to make one of the most difficult decisions he's ever made when he decides to turn femme fatale Brigid O'Shaughnessy over to the police. This is a decision that Spade knows will result, at the very least, in a long jail term for Brigid, and perhaps even her execution.

Why is this such a hard decision for Sam to make? Partly because he's in love with Brigid. But even though that may be the most important reason, it's just the tip of the iceberg. In the longest speech he makes in the entire novel, Sam tries to explain to Brigid why he's sending her over. The bottom line, in as much as there is one, is that Sam is a realist.

Once he realizes that Brigid murdered his partner Miles Archer, Sam can't save Brigid even if he wanted to and he does want to. Why? Not because he liked Miles, but because it's his duty as a private eye to see that his slain partner is avenged. In a more practical vein, if he were to let Brigid go, it would be bad for business because it would make him look soft, whereas so much of his reputation is based on his appearing to be a hard man with no feelings.

But Spade is also a realist in another sense. Remember that he's a private eye not as a hobby, or out of a sense of vocation, but as a professional. He's in business, and so he needs to be able to have a working relationship with the cops in San Francisco, even if he detests them, and there's ample evidence that he does! Just as he demands a fall guy from Casper Gutman so that he isn't left holding the bag, so Spade has to turn Brigid over to the police if he wants to continue working as a private eye.

Poetic justice might dictate that Sam finds a way to spare Brigid so that she doesn't share the same fate as her coconspirators Wilmer Cook, Joel Cairo, and Gutman, none of whom, we should note, survive long enough to be arrested—a fact that underlines my earlier point about death, rather than the legal system, being the ultimate form of justice in hard-boiled mysteries. However, poetic justice in the world of The Maltese Falcon is simply not an option.

And so Spade sends Brigid off to meet her fate with the following brutal words ringing in her ears: "I'm going to send you over. The chances are you'll get off with life. That means you'll be out again in 20 years. You're an angel. I'll wait for you… If they hang you, I'll always remember you."

We see another example of the private eye's recognition of the limits of justice in Raymond Chandler's The Big Sleep. By the end of the novel, Philip Marlowe has solved both mysteries presented to him by the Sternwood family. The first was the mystery he was actually hired by General Sternwood to solve—that is, who was blackmailing the General. That mystery was solved in the conventional sense that nearly everyone involved with the scheme was either killed or arrested. The second mystery, however, turns out very differently. This mystery, which involves the question of what happened to Rusty Regan, Vivian

Sternwood's husband, has an outcome that many readers will find much more unsatisfying because it's much more open-ended.

Even though Marlowe realizes that Regan was shot and killed by Carmen, Vivian's sister who also tried to kill Marlowe, and that Vivian helped to cover up her husband's murder, the novel ends with Carmen being sent to a sanatorium for treatment and with Vivian being unpunished beyond having to live with the consequences of her actions.

Why doesn't Marlowe do the just thing and have the Sternwood sisters arrested, given that he has ample evidence to do so? Because, as Marlowe has already demonstrated earlier in the novel when he refuses to share information about the case with members of law enforcement, his ultimate loyalty is to his client, General Sternwood. Faced with a choice between punishing the guilty and sparing the General from the knowledge of just how rotten the fruit of his family tree really is, Marlowe chooses to let the General die a death defined by blissful ignorance.

Is this justice? Opinions will vary from reader to reader, but we should note Marlowe's own verdict about what he has done: "Me, I was part of the nastiness now." We might feel that Marlowe is judging himself too harshly when he suggests that there's no essential difference between himself and the corruption embodied by the Sternwood family. But there's no arguing with the fact that Marlowe, like Spade, feels that poetic justice, just like the ideal of chivalry that he supposedly personifies, is a luxury he can't afford given the corrupt world in which he lives.

Given the complexity and ambiguity of the conclusion of *The Big Sleep* and the fact that these qualities might leave some readers feeling dissatisfied, it becomes much easier to understand the phenomenal popularity of Mickey Spillane's Mike Hammer novels. Eschewing complexity and ambiguity altogether, the author and his avatar have a brutally simple and, for millions of readers, brutally satisfying approach to justice. For Spillane and Hammer, poetic justice and vigilante justice are one and the same.

In *I, the Jury*, as is typical in Spillane's work, Mike Hammer has a deeply personal investment in the crime he's investigating. The murder of his war buddy Jack Williams has hit Hammer hard, and he promises that he'll find and kill his friend's murderer in exactly the same manner that Jack was killed—with a bullet in the gut.

Ironically, the main obstacles between Hammer and him achieving his goal, other than the criminals themselves, are Pat Chambers, Hammer's friend on the police force, and the legal system in general. Whenever Hammer discusses the case with Pat, he makes no bones about the fact that the two of them are engaged in a race to the finish line, and that he's determined to beat the police to the murderer.

Hammer recognizes that the police have levels of manpower and resources that far outstrip whatever he can muster, and he feels free to draw on those resources whenever it suits him to do so. But he also feels that he has distinct advantages over the police. As he explains to Pat, the police are bound by the law to treat suspects with a certain degree of restraint. Hammer is bound by no such law and so is perfectly free to knock out teeth, break arms, or do whatever's necessary to achieve his goals.

Hammer proceeds to put his words to Pat into practice, and he does so with great gusto. By the end of the novel, thanks to a variety of extra-legal acts of violence, he finally achieves his goal and keeps his promise to his dead friend. The fact that the murderer Hammer kills is Dr. Charlotte Manning, the woman with whom he's fallen in love, makes his attachment to his version of poetic justice even more striking. Unlike Spade, Hammer has no qualms about imposing justice on the woman he loves and is even willing to do it himself. When Manning asks him, quite reasonably, how he could do such a thing, Hammer famously replies, "It was easy."

Other than his desire to avenge his friend's death and his competition with the police, Hammer is also driven in *I, the Jury* by his fear of what will happen if the legal system gets hold of the killer first. In particular, Hammer's convinced that the killer or his slippery lawyer will somehow get him off the hook so that he'll go unpunished. In Spillane's work, the perceived inadequacies of the form of justice meted out by the legal system are used to justify brutal acts of vigilante violence.

However, I want to emphasize that being able to see the shortcomings of the official definition of justice doesn't always have to lead to this degraded form of poetic justice in mystery and suspense fiction. Depending on the nature of the detective's ethical commitment to their work, a more inspirational form of poetic justice can result.

For example, Chester Himes' Cotton Comes to Harlem, which features his series characters, black homicide cops Gravedigger Jones and Coffin Ed Johnson, is a typically over-the-top, action-packed, and absurd tale revolving around the theft of $87,000 from 87 poor Harlem families by a fraudulent Back to Africa movement. Gravedigger and Coffin Ed's priority is to recover the money and restore it to those who were robbed and to do so by any means necessary.

Even though it means letting a murderous white Southern racist escape back to the South, where he'll never be extradited to stand trial for his crimes, when they have a chance to achieve that goal, Gravedigger, and Coffin Ed don't hesitate. The families get their money back, and the villainous Colonel Calhoun has his mind permanently blown when he realizes that these two black detectives are letting him go because of their love for other black people.

In this instance, the fact that two sworn officers of the law are willing to place poetic justice above justice in the accepted sense of the word emphasizes just how powerful poetic justice can be and why examples of it can be found throughout the mystery and suspense fiction genre.

COURTROOM DRAMA

M ystery and suspense narratives featuring lawyers and the legal process are more popular than ever before. In this lecture, we'll look at the origin of the courtroom drama and the legal thriller, and we'll discuss why legal dramas have remained so popular for so long in a variety of different mediums.

EPHRAIM TUTT

- Fictional lawyer Ephraim Tutt was the creation of Arthur Cheney Train, a Harvard-educated lawyer. Train began his career as a writer in 1904, when he was the Assistant District Attorney for New York County. Fascinated by the human drama unfolding in the city's legal and prison system, Train wrote a mystery story entitled "The Maximilian Diamond" that involved the theft of the Mexican crown jewels.

- Train conceived of Ephraim Tutt, his most famous creation, in 1919, and he once described him in the following terms: "Spiritually, I suppose that Mr. Tutt is a combination of most of the qualities which I would like to have, coupled with a few that are common to all of us. One critic has disposed of him by saying that his popularity is due to the fact that he is a hodgepodge of Puck, Robin Hood, Abraham Lincoln and Uncle Sam. I am willing to let it go at that."

- Tutt uses his knowledge of the law to protect the average person. In a typical Tutt case, he becomes involved in a situation where an ordinary fellow is out of his depth because he's being victimized or scammed by an unscrupulous wealthy individual or corporation. Although Tutt himself has something of an aristocratic demeanor, his inclinations are decidedly populist, and the resolution of the narrative usually involves his winning a resounding victory for his client by means of perfectly legal but also ingenious trickery.

- Beginning with the publication of *Tutt and Mr. Tutt* in 1919, Train went on to write more than 100 stories featuring Ephraim Tutt. But Train's 1943 book entitled *Yankee Lawyer: The Autobiography of Ephraim Tutt* undoubtedly had the biggest impact.

- Even though Tutt was by this time a well-known fictional character, Train made it appear as if this were Tutt's real-life autobiography. Tutt's name, rather than Train's, appeared on both the title and the copyright page, and Train had Tutt appear and converse with historical figures, including Calvin Coolidge and Edith Wharton. Tutt's autobiography set off a firestorm of controversy because readers simply refused to believe that it was a work of fiction.

PERRY MASON

- Between them, Erle Stanley Gardner and his character Perry Mason took the genre of the courtroom drama to new heights. Like Arthur Cheney Train, Gardner was a lawyer by profession, but by all accounts, he found the practice of law rather boring. In his spare time, he began writing pulp fiction and published his first story in 1923.

- Perry Mason, a defense lawyer, is Gardner's most popular fictional creation. Like Ephraim Tutt, Mason speaks to the reader's desire to make sure that the legal system works ethically and successfully to protect ordinary people from exploitation. And, like Tutt, Mason is also something of a detective as well as a lawyer. He's attracted to difficult, if not impossible, cases and is often driven by intellectual curiosity rather than the desire for money. What readers see in Mason is someone who recognizes that there's sometimes a gap between law and justice. Perry Mason makes sure that no one falls into that gap, and that's what people love about him.

- Another reason for the phenomenal success of Perry Mason has to do with an aspect of Gardner's work that we also find in Arthur Cheney Train's Tutt stories—but that Gardner develops in much more detail. Gardner appreciates the fact that the courtroom can be turned into a stage, and he exploits the theatrical potential of the legal process as no one else did before him.

- The best evidence of this is Gardner's fondness for the cliff-hanger ending in a Perry Mason story. All the Perry Mason stories are highly formulaic by definition. Critic Russell Nye has identified the following unvarying elements in a Perry Mason story: the case is introduced, Mason investigates, Mason's client is accused of a crime, there's more investigation, the trial ensues, and finally there is the dramatic last-minute introduction of new evidence that

The British courtroom drama bears a much closer resemblance to cozy mysteries than it does to the hard-boiled atmosphere of American legal thrillers.

resolves the case. It's this final element in particular that became the hallmark of a Mason mystery, and it demonstrates that Perry Mason tales are as much works of suspense as they are of mystery.

INFLUENCE ON THE LEGAL PROFESSION

- Another reason Erle Stanley Gardner and Perry Mason are so important to the genre of courtroom drama is that they demonstrate how well these stories can be adapted to the medium of television. Perry Mason achieved even greater visibility, starting in 1957, thanks to the television series *Perry Mason*, which starred Raymond Burr in the title role. The original television series ran until 1966, and then Burr reprised the role in a series of made-for-TV movies between 1985 and his death in 1993.

- The influence of Perry Mason on both the courtroom drama and the representation of lawyers in American culture more generally cannot be overstated. Thanks to Mason, the reputation of the American legal system was rehabilitated. Although lawyers continue to have a somewhat ambivalent reputation in American culture, defenders can always point to Mason as an example of what the profession can and should be.

- In fact, the American Bar Association announced in 2015 that its publishing imprint would begin reissuing Gardner's Perry Mason books—a fitting tribute to this author's influence on the legal profession.

HORACE RUMPOLE

- In 1978, a series entitled *Rumpole of the Bailey* debuted on British television. The fictional barrister Horace Rumpole is an elderly and eccentric man who works as a criminal defense lawyer at the Old Bailey, England's Central Criminal Court. The series proved to be so popular that it was not only repeatedly renewed, but it also inspired a series of books that were based on the television scripts. Both the scripts and the books were written by John Mortimer, a lawyer and author who wrote in a range of different genres.

- The popularity of the Rumpole character is interesting for several reasons. Because of differences between the two legal systems, the Rumpole television show and books are very different from American courtroom dramas. What's more, although they often feature serious crimes, the Rumpole series focuses more on characterization and the eccentric habits of the lead character. The British courtroom drama bears a much closer resemblance to cozy mysteries than it does to the hard-boiled atmosphere of American legal thrillers.

SCOTT TUROW

- Author Scott Turow has put his background in both creative writing and law to very good use in a series of legal thrillers. Like Erle Stanley Gardner, Turow frequently portrays the legal system as corrupt and self-serving. Unlike Gardner, however, Turow doesn't put his trust in a single, maverick crusading lawyer in the Perry Mason mold to save the day. Turow believes that the system is too powerful and complex for any one person to triumph over it.

- Turow's novels are just as likely to portray lawyers as victims rather than as champions of the rights of others. In both Gardner's Perry Mason novels and in Turow's work, lawyers are the protagonists— but in a very different sense. Mason works for others, and the reader isn't particularly interested in Mason's background or history. For Turow, by contrast, the lawyer is the main character. In the earlier version of the legal thriller, the lawyer helped the innocent to escape the clutches of a corrupt legal system. In Turow's hands, the lawyer is more apt to be the one who needs help.

JOHN GRISHAM

- Just as Turow explores the notion of the lawyer as victim, novelist John Grisham takes this idea to its logical conclusion. In Grisham's first best-selling novel, *The Firm*, young and ambitious lawyer Mitchell McDeere joins a law firm in Memphis, Tennessee. Mitch's dream of becoming the youngest partner in the firm's history, however, is derailed when he finds out the firm is connected to organized crime and that any lawyer who realizes this is killed off.

  the American Bar Association announced in 2015 that its publishing imprint would begin reissuing Gardner's Perry Mason books — a fitting tribute to this author's influence on the legal profession.

- At this point, Mitch turns into a combination of both detective and lawyer as he works to accumulate enough evidence to turn over to the FBI—while staying alive in the process. The happy ending to this drama helped to ensure the success of both Grisham's novel and its subsequent film adaptation starring Tom Cruise. Grisham both solidifies the legal thriller's view of the legal system as corrupt, even murderously corrupt, and extends Turow's presentation of the lawyer as victim rather than crusading hero.

COURT TV

- The courtroom drama and the legal thriller have now liberated themselves from the context of mystery and suspense fiction, as it were, and now exist on their own terms. In the American context, two developments in particular helped this shift come about.

- The first was the launch of the Court TV cable television network on July 2, 1991. The programming on Court TV (renamed TruTV in 2008) was centered on live transmission of legal proceedings with commentary from legal experts, and it was a game changer for courtroom dramas and legal thrillers.

- Second, the trial of O.J. Simpson in 1994–1995, probably the most highly publicized trial in judicial history, allowed Court TV to come into its own. The decision to allow live trial transmission in the courtroom not only influenced the outcome of the trial itself but also changed the genre of the legal thriller forever.

- Consider the *Law & Order* television franchise. While the original series was launched in 1990, its popularity exploded thanks to the phenomena of Court TV and the Simpson trial. What sets *Law & Order* apart is the fact that the audience now views the legal process and the justice system largely from the perspective of the prosecution rather than the defense. The presumption of innocence, the notion of the justice system as corrupt, and the preponderance of wrongly accused individuals that dominated earlier examples of the genre have, for the most part, disappeared.

- Instead, the police and the prosecutors are now the heroes, the Thin Blue Line that protects us from hordes of violent predators. If the suspense in early legal thrillers and courtroom dramas was generated by the prospect of the innocent being falsely convicted, now it seems that what we fear is the prospect of the guilty getting away.

1. What factors led to the rise of mystery and suspense fiction texts that put the legal system at the center of their narratives?

2. How do examples of this subgenre exploit the dramatic possibilities of the legal process?

Suggested Reading

Bounds, *Perry Mason*.

White, *Justice Denoted*.

COURTROOM DRAMA

The legal process in general and the figure of the lawyer, in particular, are both so popular in mystery and suspense fiction today that it's easy to assume that this has always been the case. In fact, it took a long time for the genre to become interested in anything that happened after the apprehension of the criminal.

Why? You can blame the detective! As long as the genre was focused on the activities of the detective, whether classical or hard-boiled, then everyone else, including the police and members of the legal profession, were likely to remain in the background. The detective focused his or her efforts on discovering the identity of and/or catching the criminal. Once the narrative reached that point, the story was basically over, and anything that happened afterward was a mere detail.

Today, the situation is very different. Mystery and suspense narratives featuring lawyers are more popular than ever before. In this lecture, we'll look at the origin of the courtroom drama and the legal thriller, and we'll discuss why legal dramas have remained so popular for such a long period of time over a variety of different mediums.

If you asked most people who they associate with the term courtroom drama with, they'd probably say Perry Mason. There's no denying that Erle Stanley Gardner's famous creation had a huge influence on mystery and suspense fiction with a legal emphasis, but there's another figure I regard as equally influential but who goes practically unread today: Ephraim Tutt.

"Who?" you ask! Although very few people read the Tutt stories today, at one point they were enormously popular among American readers, and they blazed the trail for the appearance of lawyers in the genre later on.

Tutt was the creation of Arthur Cheney Train, a Harvard-educated lawyer born in 1875. Train began his career as a writer in 1904 when he was the Assistant District Attorney for New York County. Fascinated by the human drama that he saw around him every day in the city's legal and prison system, Train wrote a mystery story entitled "The Maximilian Diamond" that involved the theft of the Mexican crown jewels.

Train's story was published in Leslie's Monthly, and he soon became a regular contributor to several glossy rather than pulp magazines. Most of what he wrote during the early part of his career consisted of short stories inspired by aspects of the law, but Train also became known for writing nonfiction that attempted to shed light on the workings of the legal profession. And in all of his work, he used a straightforward and uncomplicated narrative style that won him many readers.

Train conceived of Ephraim Tutt, his most famous creation, in 1919, and he once described him in the following terms:

> Spiritually, I suppose that Mr. Tutt is a combination of most of the qualities which I would like to have, coupled with a few that are common to all of us. One critic has disposed of him by saying that his popularity is due to the fact that he is a hodgepodge of Puck, Robin Hood, Abraham Lincoln, and Uncle Sam. I am willing to let it go at that.

What exactly does this critic's description of Ephraim Tutt mean? The most important feature of Tutt that explains his popularity is that he uses his knowledge of the law to protect the average person. In a typical Tutt case, he becomes involved in a situation where an ordinary fellow is out of his depth because he's being victimized or scammed by an unscrupulous wealthy individual or corporation. Although Tutt himself has something of an aristocratic demeanor, his inclinations are decidedly populist, and the resolution of the narrative usually involves his winning a resounding victory for his client by means of perfectly legal but also ingenious trickery.

Here we should note the similarities between Tutt and the classical detective. Like Auguste Dupin and Sherlock Holmes, Tutt usually only takes cases that appeal to him because they're unusual and challenging. Moreover, like the philanthropic Holmes, he'll often represent people who can't afford to pay him, simply because he believes in justice so strongly that he can't bear to see it abused by the unscrupulous and greedy.

The fact that Tutt was such a huge hit with readers can be explained by a combination of several factors: his eccentric personality and appearance; the way he consistently stuck up for the underdog; the way Tutt stories were always based on a kernel of truth about the law, which gave them an air of realism; and the fact that the stories he appeared in usually concluded with a very unambiguous resolution in the form of a verdict that exonerated his client.

Beginning with the publication of "Tutt and Mr. Tutt" in 1919, Train went on to write over one hundred stories featuring Ephraim Tutt, which were reprinted in fourteen collections, but Train's 1943 book featuring Tutt, *Yankee Lawyer: The Autobiography of Ephraim Tutt*, undoubtedly had the biggest impact.

Even though Tutt was by this time a very well-known fictional character, Train went out of his way to make it appear as if this were Tutt's real-life autobiography. Tutt's name, rather than Train's, appeared on both the title and the copyright page, and Train had Tutt appear to converse with actual figures, including Calvin Coolidge and Edith Wharton. In fact, even Arthur Train himself appears in the book!

Tutt's autobiography set off a firestorm of controversy because readers simply refused to believe that it was a work of fiction. Even though

Train published a disclaimer, people wanted this fictional character to exist so badly that they ignored Train's protests and insisted that this kindly, erudite, and quietly heroic lawyer had to be real.

Before the world had ever heard of Perry Mason, Ephraim Tutt showed writers of mystery and suspense fiction just how popular lawyers and the legal process could be with readers. Moreover, Tutt's success was also proof that readers felt that the law was often abused at the price of justice and that ordinary people often needed someone to protect them not only from criminals but also from the law that was supposedly on the side of the innocent.

With these points in mind, let us now turn to the work of Erle Stanley Gardner and his character of Perry Mason. Between them, they took the genre of the courtroom drama to new heights. Like Train, Gardner was a lawyer by profession, but by all accounts, he found the practice of law rather boring. In his spare time, he began writing pulp fiction and published his first story in 1923.

Over the next few years, Gardner wrote an astonishing range and amount of fiction, and he set himself an unbelievably high word quota of 1.2 million words a year. His pulp series characters included Lester Leith, a parody of the gentleman thief tradition, and Ken Corning, a lawyer who is in many ways an archetype for his later creation of Perry Mason. It's also important to note that Gardner's later fictional creations include Doug Selby, a district attorney who Gardner presents as brave and very good at his job. So Gardner also wrote about the legal profession from the point of view of the prosecution rather than the defense.

Despite the fact that not all of Gardner's characters were defense lawyers, given the success of Arthur Cheney Train's Ephraim Tutt, we shouldn't be surprised that Perry Mason, a defense lawyer, is easily Gardner's most popular fictional creation. Like Tutt, Mason speaks to the reader's desire to make sure that the legal system works ethically and successfully to protect the little guy from being exploited.

Gardner worked as a full-time lawyer until the publication of the first novel featuring Perry Mason, *The Case of the Velvet Claws*, in 1933. After that, he devoted himself to writing full-time. The phenomenal success of his most famous character, who eventually appeared in more than eighty novels and short stories, was a big part of the reason why Gardner was able to dedicate himself to his work.

Mason's description of himself in Velvet Claws tells us a lot about the reasons for his popularity:

> You'll find that I'm a lawyer who has specialized in trial work, and in a lot of criminal work... I'm a specialist on getting people out of trouble. They come to me when they're in all sorts of trouble, and I work them out... If you look me up through some family lawyer or some corporation lawyer, he'll probably tell you that I'm a shyster. If you look me up through some chap in the District Attorney's office, he'll tell you that I'm a dangerous antagonist, but he doesn't know very much about me.

This quote indicates that Mason is a controversial character among some members of the legal profession because he has a reputation for fighting hard for his clients. Like Ephraim Tutt, Mason is also something of a detective as well as a lawyer. He's attracted to difficult, if not impossible, cases, and is often driven by intellectual curiosity rather than the desire for money. Indeed, in some cases, he even finances his investigations himself if the client can't pay.

Mason is motivated not only by the desire to win but also by the desire to see justice done. In *The Case of the Drowsy Mosquito*, Mason defends himself from the accusation that he sticks up for criminals by saying: "I have merely asked for the orderly administration of an impartial justice... Due legal process is my own safeguard against being convicted unjustly. To my mind, that's government. That's law and order."

Mason's defense might seem self-serving, but in fact, it is the key to the success of both this character and the novels and stories he appears in. If readers had felt that Mason was using his knowledge of the legal system to undermine it and let criminals get off scot-free, there's no doubt in my mind they would have rejected him very quickly. Instead, what readers see in Mason is someone who recognizes that there's sometimes a gap between law and justice. Mason makes sure that no one falls into that gap, and that's what people love about him.

But the other reason for the phenomenal success of Perry Mason has to do with an aspect of Gardner's work that we also find in Arthur Cheney Train's Tutt stories, but which Gardner develops in much more detail. In short, Gardner appreciates the fact that the courtroom can be turned into a stage, and he exploits the theatrical potential of the legal process like no one else before him.

The best evidence of this fact is Gardner's fondness for the cliffhanger ending in a Perry Mason story. All of the Mason stories are highly formulaic by definition. Critic Russell Nye has identified the following unvarying elements in a Perry Mason story: the case is introduced, Mason investigates, Mason's client is accused of a crime, there's more investigation, followed by the trial, and then the dramatic last-minute introduction of new evidence that resolves the case.

It's this final element in particular that became the hallmark of a Mason mystery, and it indicates that, among other things, Perry Mason tales are as much works of suspense as they are of mystery. Even though we know Mason will eventually win the case, exactly how and when that's going to happen is in doubt right up until the last minute, and the resolution of that suspense gives us much pleasure.

The other reason Erle Stanley Gardner and Perry Mason are so important to the genre of courtroom drama is that they demonstrate how well these stories can be adapted to the medium of television. Although a number of film adaptations of Perry Mason novels had appeared in the 1930s, this figure achieved even greater visibility starting in 1957 thanks to the television series *Perry Mason*, which starred Raymond Burr in the title role. The original television series ran until 1966, and then Burr reprised the role in a series of made-for-TV movies between 1985 and his death in 1993.

By accentuating the dramatic and theatrical aspects of the legal process, Gardner had already made the courtroom a highly visual space, even in print. The television series simply translated that theatricality into visual terms. Thanks to both *Perry Mason*, the series, and to Raymond Burr, who quickly became synonymous with Gardner's famous lawyer, the character of Perry Mason became an even more indelible part of American popular culture. Even as Gardner's novels, many of which provided the source material for episodes in the television series, started to go out of print, the syndication of the television show kept Mason in the public eye.

The influence of *Perry Mason* on both the courtroom drama and the representation of lawyers in American culture more generally cannot be overstated. Thanks to Mason, I would argue, the reputation of the American legal system was rehabilitated. Although lawyers continue to have a somewhat ambivalent reputation in American culture, defenders can always point to Mason as an example of what the profession can and should be. The American Bar Association announced in 2015 that its publishing imprint, Ankerwycke, would begin reissuing Gardner's Perry Mason books. What a fitting tribute to this author's influence on the legal profession!

What happened to the courtroom drama and legal thriller after the very high benchmark set by Erle Stanley Gardner? Part of the answer to that question involves jumping across the pond and visiting the United Kingdom for a moment.

In 1978 a series entitled *Rumpole of the Bailey* debuted on British television. The series starred the actor Leo McKern as Horace Rumpole, an elderly and eccentric lawyer who works as a criminal defense lawyer at the Old Bailey, England's central criminal court.

The series proved to be so popular that it was not only repeatedly renewed, but it also inspired a series of books that were based on the television scripts.

Both the scripts and the books were written by John Mortimer, a lawyer and author who wrote in a range of different genres. The popularity of the Rumpole character is interesting for a couple of reasons. First, the tone of the both the television show and the books is very different from American courtroom dramas, and that's because of differences between the two legal systems.

Perry Mason's cases were usually murder trials, and this was regarded not explicitly, but implicitly as necessary in order to make the outcome of the trial sufficiently high-stakes to hold the reader's and later the television viewer's interest. That's not the case with the Rumpole stories. Although they often feature serious crimes, much more attention is paid in both the television and novel versions of these stories to characterization, and especially to the eccentric habits of the lead character.

This means that the British version of the courtroom drama can often bear a much closer resemblance to so-called "cozy" mysteries than the hard-boiled atmosphere that usually characterizes American legal thrillers. This illustrates the way in which the courtroom drama can be quite a flexible genre, taking in and adapting itself to variations in legal standards and practices in a manner that makes it, potentially at least, quite a portable genre.

The other notable feature of John Mortimer's Rumpole stories is that they began on television and then migrated into books, rather than the other way around. This suggests the possibility that, after the success of the Perry Mason television series, other media were now in a position to lead the way in terms of producing courtroom dramas and legal thrillers. They no longer had to depend on mystery and suspense fiction writers to first produce source material for them to adapt.

In a moment, we'll discuss some more evidence to support this statement, but before doing so, we need to acknowledge that in the post–Perry Mason era, legal thrillers are still very much a force to be reckoned with in mystery and suspense fiction, as we can see in the work of two of the leading practitioners of the genre: Scott Turow and John Grisham.

Scott Turow has put his background in both creative writing and law to very good use in a series of novels that are all legal thrillers set in the fictional Midwestern setting of Kindle County. Turow is known for drawing upon the same pool of recurring characters in his novels, which not only gives his work elements of continuity but also serves as a canny marketing strategy that keeps readers coming back for more. This has proved to be a wonderfully successful strategy for Turow, who's sold over 30 million books over the course of his career.

There are a number of continuities between Turow's work and those who came before him in the genre. Like Gardner, Turow frequently portrays the legal system as corrupt and self-serving. Unlike Gardner, however, Turow doesn't put his trust in a single, maverick crusading lawyer in the Perry Mason mold to save the day. Why not? Because Turow believes that the system is too powerful and complex for any one person to triumph over it.

For this reason, his novels are just as likely to portray lawyers as victims rather than champions of the rights of others. In his first novel *Presumed Innocent,* for example, prosecutor Rusty Sabich is accused of the murder of his fellow prosecutor Carolyn Polhemus. Over the course of a long and labyrinthine plot, Sabich is eventually found innocent, but not before having to confront the fact that loyalty and affection mean very little when you're assumed to be guilty rather than being presumed innocent.

In both Gardner's Perry Mason novels and in Turow's work, lawyers are the protagonists, but in a very different sense. Mason works for others, and in that respect, the reader isn't particularly interested in

Mason's background or history. In fact, we learn very little about him. For Turow and his ilk, by contrast, the lawyer is our main character, and consequently, we learn everything we could possibly want to know about him so that we can sympathize with the difficult situation he's in.

This difference doesn't necessarily make a Turow novel any less formulaic than a Gardner novel, but it does mean that our attention is focused on a very different place. In the earlier version of the legal thriller, the lawyer helped the innocent to escape the clutches of a corrupt legal system. In Turow's hands, the lawyer him- or herself is more likely to be the one who needs help.

The careers of Scott Turow and John Grisham seem so similar that the only difference is one of scale: Grisham has published much more, and the 275 million copies of his work sold dwarfs Turow's sales figures. Their work shares many similarities: just as Turow explores the idea of the lawyer as victim, Grisham takes this idea to its logical conclusion in his first best-selling novel, *The Firm*.

In this novel, young and ambitious lawyer Mitchell McDeere joins a law firm in Memphis, Tennessee, mostly because of their very generous salary and benefits offer. Mitch's dream of becoming the youngest partner in the firm's history, however, is derailed when he finds out the firm is connected to organized crime and that any lawyer who realizes this is killed off.

At this point, Mitch turns into a combination of both detective and lawyer as he works to accumulate enough evidence to turn over to the FBI so that they can prosecute his bosses while also figuring out how to stay alive in the process. The happy ending to this drama helped to ensure the success of both Grisham's novel and its subsequent film adaptation starring Tom Cruise. In the process, Grisham both solidifies the legal thriller's view of the legal system as corrupt, even murderously corrupt, while also extending Turow's presentation of the lawyer as the victim rather than the crusading hero.

At this point, it would have been easy for Grisham to keep reproducing the same formula and thus guarantee further success, but to his credit he has used the genre to explore a range of social issues, including vigilantism and racism in *A Time to Kill* and political corruption and environmentalism in *The Pelican Brief.*

Even more unusual for a mystery and suspense fiction writer, in 2010 Grisham began publishing the *Theodore Boone* series, legal thrillers for children that aim to both entertain children and instruct them about certain aspects of the legal profession. This most recent work from Grisham suggests that legal thrillers can be taken in a variety of different directions if the author is willing to think outside the box.

In closing, I'd like to return to a comment I made earlier about John Mortimer's Rumpole of the Bailey, which is that Rumpole began first as a television series and only later became a series of books. I think there's evidence to suggest that the courtroom drama and the legal thriller have now liberated themselves from the context of mystery and suspense fiction, as it were, and now exist on their own terms.

In the American context, two developments, in particular, helped this shift come about. The first was the launch of the Court TV cable television network on July 2, 1991. The programming on Court TV—which was renamed TruTV in 2008—was centered on live transmission of legal proceedings with commentary from legal experts and was a game-changer for courtroom dramas and legal thrillers.

Why? Because it allowed the American public to become better informed about the American legal process than ever before, and to appreciate the theatrical dimensions of the justice system more vividly than ever before.

Both of these trends were intensified tremendously by the second development that gave the legal profession a much higher profile on American television, and that's the trial of O.J. Simpson, which ran from November 9, 1994, to October 3, 1995. Probably the most highly publicized trial in judicial history, the Simpson case allowed Court TV to come into its own, and the decision to allow cameras in the courtroom during the trial not only influenced the outcome of the trial itself but also changed the genre of the legal thriller forever.

In my opinion, the best evidence of this influence can be found in a television show that actually began before either Court TV or the Simpson trial, but whose popularity exploded thanks, in part, to these phenomena. I'm referring to the *Law & Order* television franchise and its various spin-offs. The original series was launched by Dick Wolf in 1990 and has since expanded across a variety of media, including TV, films, video games, and adaptations of the series formula in a number of other countries.

What sets the various iterations of Law & Order apart from the other materials we've discussed in this lecture is the fact, by and large, the audience now views the legal process and the justice system largely from the perspective of the prosecution rather than the defense. The presumption of innocence, the notion of the justice system as corrupt, and the preponderance of wrongly-accused individuals that dominated earlier examples of the genre are now all pretty much gone.

Instead, the police and the prosecutors are now the heroes, the thin blue line that protects us from hordes of viciously violent superpredators who always seems to be on the verge of escaping just punishment. If the suspense in early legal thrillers and courtroom dramas was generated by the prospect of the innocent being falsely convicted, now it seems what we fear is the prospect of the guilty getting away.

What led to this seismic shift? That's a question with no easy answer. But I would point to the persistent perception among the American public that violent crime is rising whereas it's falling and that they're likely to be victims of violent crime whereas the odds are very much in their favor. In other words, today's courtroom dramas and legal thrillers are both symptoms of and contributors to the overrepresentation of violent crime in our media and popular culture.

It's this overrepresentation that potentially has a variety of damaging consequences for the ways in which we think about crime and victimization. And yet, there's some reason for cautious optimism. Documentaries such as *Making a Murderer* and the podcast *Serial* are both examples of contemporary legal thrillers that are still wrestling with and confronting the imperfections of our justice system. As long as that search for justice continues, the influence of Ephraim Tutt and Perry Mason will persist.

GAY AND LESBIAN MYSTERY AND SUSPENSE

I n many ways, the history of mystery and suspense fiction can be summed up in a single word: diversification. The process of increased diversity is not a result of a deliberate or conscious policy or an impulse of political correctness. Rather, it is a consequence of the fact that the genre has always been finely attuned to changes in the culture and has taken the opportunity to reflect and comment on those changes. Gay and lesbian mystery and suspense fiction demonstrates the flexibility and innovativeness of the genre as a whole. This lecture will examine the reasons for its popularity, focusing in particular on how these narratives both draw on and selectively reinterpret traditional elements.

CRITICAL APPROACHES

- Critics have explored various approaches to reconstructing the origins of gay and lesbian mystery and suspense fiction.

- Some have chosen to go back to canonical authors in the genre and present what they would describe as "queer" readings of this work. For example, some critics have reexamined the frequency of intense male friendships in Raymond Chandler's work and have interpreted that as evidence of a repressed strain of homosexual desire that runs throughout such novels as *The Big Sleep* and *Farewell, My Lovely.*

- Other have chosen a different approach and have returned to the work of writers in the genre that were rumored to have been gay or lesbian, such as Ngaio Marsh and Patricia Highsmith. In Highsmith's case, this approach focuses on the fact that her second published novel, 1952's *The Price of Salt*, was a lesbian romance with a happy ending that was extremely unusual for its time.

- In this lecture, we focus only on self-identified gay and lesbian writers who publish novels featuring self-identified gay and lesbian characters. There are two reasons for this—one pragmatic and one more abstract.
  - › The pragmatic reason is that foregrounding self-identification makes it easier to trace the history and evolution of this subgenre.

  - › The more-abstract reason is that self-identification emphasizes the assertiveness of both these authors and their works. Rather than sneaking gay and lesbian themes and characters into the genre, instead they assert the right of their work and its subject matter to be a part of mystery and suspense fiction.

JOSEPH HANSEN
- Joseph Hansen is generally regarded as the father of the gay mystery novel. Hansen's breakthrough came in 1970, when Joan Kahn, the mystery editor at Harper & Row, agreed to publish his novel *Fadeout*, the first book to feature private eye Dave Brandstetter, Hansen's series protagonist.

- Hansen described the goal of *Fadeout*: "to write a truly orthodox mystery novel this time and make the detective—more or less in the tough-guy mold of the detectives of Ross Macdonald, Raymond Chandler, and Dashiell Hammett—a homosexual; because it was, as far as public opinion is concerned, the least likely sort of profession that could be given to a homosexual."

- In *Fadeout*, Hansen challenges stereotypes about gay men in a subgenre, the hard-boiled private-eye novel, that is synonymous with a very particular and stylized version of tough straight masculinity.

- In the Brandstetter novels, Hansen attempts to provide a complex and nuanced picture of gay life while at the same time force mystery and suspense fiction to revise itself in order to accommodate his vision. As Hansen noted, "I wanted to correct as many misapprehensions ordinary mortals have about homosexuals and the way they live as I could in the space of fifty thousand words."

- The richness of Hansen's work can be attributed partly to the fact that he had the opportunity to write a series of novels. The development of series characters facilitates reader identification. This is particularly important with regard to gay and lesbian mystery characters because some readers may have difficulty in relating to these men and women. Having these characters develop over the course of a series of novels makes it easier for readers to bond with them.

MICHAEL NAVA

- Michael Nava, whom many consider to be the finest contemporary writer of gay and lesbian mystery and suspense fiction, has been profoundly influenced by his model and mentor, Joseph Hansen. Nava said of Hansen, "He used the mystery to actually explore what it means to be gay. In the classic American mystery, the private investigator is an outsider who's generally viewed [as] fairly disreputable by the people who hire him. So if you are in fact an outsider because you're gay or a woman or African-American, it's a very interesting vehicle to explore the whole issue of being on the fringe."

- There are a number of similarities between the work of Hansen and that of Nava, as we might expect, but there are also some interesting differences. Nava was born in 1954 in Stockton,

California, and grew up in a poor Mexican neighborhood in Sacramento. After graduating from Stanford Law School in 1980, he began working as an attorney and simultaneously started on his first novel.

- Later, Nava would recall the origins of that novel. It was his job "to interview arrestees after they were booked to determine whether they should be released on their own recognizance or held overnight until a judge could set bail." While conducting these interviews, Nava started jotting down notes about the activities in the jail, and these notes became the germ for *The Little Death*, which was published in 1986.

- In *The Little Death*, which Nava has described as "a sort of Raymond Chandler with a gay Philip Marlowe," we meet Henry Rios, a burned-out public defender in his early 30s who would go on to become Nava's series character. Over the course of seven novels, Nava develops Rios into a fascinatingly complex character whose cases cover many different issues, not unlike Hansen's Dave Brandstetter. Unlike Brandstetter, however, Rios is considerably more troubled and vulnerable and less hard-boiled and tough. As such, the typical Nava novel tends to be more emotionally fraught than Hansen's work.

- As the Rios series evolves, Nava starts to focus more attention on Rios's Chicano identity in order to explore the way in which this character is dealing with a double form of marginalization. As a result, Nava's novels are arguably more complex than those of Hansen in terms of their consideration of race and ethnicity.

LESBIAN MYSTERY AND SUSPENSE FICTION
- According to the critic Lori L. Lake, "Unlike male authors who, in the early 1960s, began creating gay detectives and exploring homosexual themes, publication for lesbian mystery writers didn't get going in earnest until the mid-80s."

- One reason is that lesbian mystery and suspense fiction, perhaps more than any other variety of the genre, is peculiarly dependent on the existence of small publishers who are willing to publish work that mainstream publishing houses would consider too marginal to garner a significant audience. Once these small presses, such as Naiad Press and Seal Press, began to spring up in the 1970s, the stage was set for the emergence of lesbian mystery fiction.

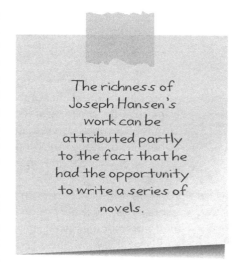

The richness of Joseph Hansen's work can be attributed partly to the fact that he had the opportunity to write a series of novels.

KATHERINE V. FORREST

- The breakthrough author in lesbian mystery and suspense fiction is undoubtedly Katherine V. Forrest, born in Windsor, Ontario in 1939. Forrest's landmark novel was *Amateur City*, published in 1984, which introduced Forrest's series character, ex-Marine and LAPD homicide detective Kate Delafield. Forrest innovates the police procedural by putting a lesbian cop at the center of her narratives.

- Forrest wanted the novel to have a high degree of realism with regard to how it treated actual developments in law enforcement organizations in the real world—a decision that can also be read as an implicit engagement with the realism of the police procedural genre. What's more, throughout the series in which she appears, Kate Delafield remains closeted. This has been one of the most controversial aspects of the series, for at least two reasons.

> First, Delafield is often criticized by other characters in the novels for not coming out, especially as she achieves greater and greater seniority in the police force.

> Second, as the series moved through the 1980s, 1990s, and finally into the 21st century, many of Forrest's readers became more and more frustrated with the fact that Delafield remained in the closet. These readers felt that Delafield's decision made her out of step with the times and ran the risk of making the series as a whole quite conservative.

■ What we're seeing here is an example of the way in which gay and lesbian mystery writers often have to steer a course between what their communities want and feel is appropriate and affirmative and what the writers want to do with their creations. It's another fascinating instance of the way in which innovations in the genre can be both welcomed and somewhat controversial.

THE GREATEST MYSTERY OF ALL

■ Barbara Wilson is the author of two series of mysteries that both feature amateur detectives. Wilson's first series character, the printer Pam Nilsen, is not only an amateur detective, she's probably the most amateurish detective ever. Wilson radically democratizes the idea of what it means to be a detective, especially in her 1984 novel *Murder in the Collective*, the first novel in which Nilsen appears.

■ In *Murder in the Collective*, which revolves around a murder that takes place in a printing collective in Seattle, Nilsen investigates the crime alongside a lesbian woman named Hadley. As the investigation proceeds, Pam learns two things simultaneously: the identity of the killer and the truth about her own sexual orientation, as she realizes that she's in love with Hadley. Just as the novel emphasizes that anyone has the ability to be a detective (all you need is a desire to find out the truth), so the trajectory of Nilsen's character suggests that any woman can be a lesbian.

- In this way, Wilson not only makes a thought-provoking point about sexual orientation but also suggests, like the other writers we've studied in this lecture, why mystery and suspense fiction appeals to so many gay and lesbian writers. Over the course of its long and diverse history, the genre has been concerned with a number of mysteries, including the mystery of identity—who people are and how they became that way.

- In gay and lesbian mysteries, therefore, we often find that the investigation into a crime is accompanied by a parallel investigation into what some regard as the greatest mystery of all—the human condition.

QUESTIONS TO CONSIDER
1. Why is mystery and suspense fiction so well-suited to exploring issues surrounding gay and lesbian identity?

2. How do examples of this subgenre revise the assumptions about masculinity and femininity that dominate other types of mystery and suspense fiction?

SUGGESTED READING
Betz, *Lesbian Detective Fiction*.

Markowitz, *The Gay Detective Novel*.

GAY AND LESBIAN MYSTERY AND SUSPENSE

I n many ways, the history of mystery and suspense fiction can be summed up in a single word: diversification. The genre has repeatedly diversified itself not as a result of a deliberate or conscious policy or from political correctness but rather as a consequence of the fact that mystery and suspense narratives have always been finally attuned to changes taking place in the culture around them. Time and time again, the genre has demonstrated its ability to reflect and comment upon those changes.

For example, as gender roles began to change in the early decades of the 20th century and women started to move closer and closer to the center of public life, so the roles they played in the genre started to change. Rather than being merely victims, vulnerable maidens, or housewives, figures like the femme fatale opened up doors that would eventually lead to the emergence of female detectives, who became protagonists of mystery and suspense narratives in their own right.

In the same spirit, thanks to the civil rights era and other related social movements, the dismissive and racist characterization of African-Americans and other ethnic and racial minorities in mystery and suspense narratives became increasingly outdated and unacceptable. And so once again, the genre both reflected and contributed to ongoing discussions in the societies it was a part of by introducing more complex and three-dimensional examples of characters from all races and ethnicities, as we witnessed with the rise of black mystery fiction, Latino mystery fiction, Native American mystery fiction, and so on.

The appearance of gay and lesbian characters in the genre took a little longer to happen. But given the diverse history of mystery and suspense fiction, we have no reason to be surprised that it finally did take place. Moreover, when gay and lesbian mysteries began to appear, they soon became extremely popular.

This lecture will examine the reasons for this popularity, focusing in particular on how these narratives both draw upon and selectively reinterpret elements of the tradition from which they emerge. In this respect, gay and lesbian mystery and suspense fiction is a perfect example of the flexibility and innovativeness of the genre as a whole.

As we've seen in other lectures in this series, reconstructing the origins of a subgenre in mystery and suspense fiction can be quite difficult, and gay and lesbian mystery fiction is no exception to this rule. Critics have explored various approaches to this problem. Some have chosen to go back to canonical authors in the genre and read their work against the grain, as it were, in order to develop what they would describe as queer readings of this work.

For example, some critics have reexamined the frequency of intense male friendships in Raymond Chandler's work and have interpreted that frequency as evidence of a repressed strain of homosexual desire that runs throughout novels such as *The Big Sleep* and *Farewell, My Lovely*.

Other have chosen a different approach, and have returned to the work of writers in the genre that were rumored to have been gay or lesbian such as Ngaio Marsh and Patricia Highsmith. In Highsmith's case, this approach focuses on the fact that her second published novel, 1952's *The Price of Salt*, was a lesbian romance with a happy ending that was extremely unusual for its time for this type of novel. Revealingly, Highsmith published the novel under the pseudonym Claire Morgan because she didn't want to be pigeonholed as a lesbian writer.

In this lecture, my approach is somewhat different. I'm going to focus only on self-identified gay and lesbian writers who publish novels featuring self-identified gay and lesbian characters. I'm making this choice for two reasons, one pragmatic, and one more abstract. The pragmatic reason is that foregrounding self-identification makes it easier to trace the history and evolution of this subgenre.

The more abstract reason is that self-identification emphasizes the assertiveness of both these authors and the work they write. Rather than sneaking gay and lesbian themes and characters into the genre, instead, they assert the right of their work and its subject matter to be a part of mystery and suspense fiction. It seems to me that this assertiveness is an integral part of the subgenre's significance for the genre as a whole.

Apart from emphasizing self-identification, I'm also going to focus on novel series, rather than stand-alone texts. Why? Because, as we've seen in a number of other lectures in this course, the development of series characters facilitates reader identification with those characters, because they get to know them over a long period of time.

This is particularly important with regard to gay and lesbian mystery characters because some readers of mystery and suspense fiction may have difficulty in relating to these characters. Having these characters develop over the course of a series of novels is one thing that makes it easier for readers to bond with characters.

With these points in mind, let's now turn to gay mystery and suspense fiction and see what we find in terms of its origins. Gay pulp fiction of the 1960s introduced some of the first gay characters into mystery novels. The problem, however, is that these novels tended to be parodies and as such paid just as much attention to humor as they did to developing a mystery in a satisfying manner. In 1966, for example, Victor J. Banis, using the pseudonym Don Holliday, published *The Man from C.A.M.P.*, a hilarious send-up of macho spy thrillers. But it works much better as a parody than a mystery.

It's really not until the groundbreaking work of Joseph Hansen appeared that the gay mystery proper can be said to have begun, and so we need to examine his work in some detail. Generally regarded as the father of the gay mystery novel, Hansen was born in 1923 in Aberdeen, South Dakota, and took a circuitous route to becoming a writer.

During the 1940s, Hansen worked a variety of jobs. Although he already identified as homosexual—in fact, he avoided military service in World War II by declaring his homosexuality—in 1943 he married a lesbian woman named Jane Bancroft, and their daughter was born in 1944. Even though he found more secure employment at a film-processing plant in Hollywood, Hansen still seemed no nearer to achieving his goal of becoming a writer.

The turning point came in the early 1960s when Hansen met Don Slater, a gay activist who edited a magazine called One and who published a number of Hansen's short stories. This exposure gave Hansen the contacts he needed to publish a series of erotic gay-themed pulp novels. This wasn't the kind of writing Hansen necessarily wanted to do, but it did give him the opportunity to write *Known Homosexual*, published in 1968 and Hansen's first attempt at a mystery novel.

Hansen's real breakthrough, however, had to wait until 1970, when Joan Kahn, the mystery editor at Harper & Row, who had previously published many well-known mystery authors, including Tony Hillerman, agreed to publish the novel *Fadeout*, the first book to feature insurance investigator and later private eye Dave Brandstetter, who would go on to becomes Hansen's series protagonist.

Hansen once described the goal of Fadeout:

> To write a truly orthodox mystery novel this time and make the detective—more or less in the tough-guy mold of the detectives of Ross Macdonald , Raymond Chandler, and

Dashiell Hammett—a homosexual; because it was, as far as public opinion is concerned, the least likely sort of profession that could be given to a homosexual.

As such, Hansen also commented, "The whole novel is a headstand."

What does Hansen mean? A brief summary of Fadeout's plot will shed light on this question. When Fox Olson is found murdered, Doug Sawyer, his lover, is suspected of killing him. Brandstetter's investigation, however, reveals that Olson's brother-in-law killed Olson in cold blood for the insurance money. In other words, in Fadeout, the heterosexual characters commit adultery, blackmail, bribery, embezzlement, and murder, while the gay lovers appear as decent, kind, and faithful.

Hansen clearly works hard not only to challenge stereotypes about gay men but also does so in a subgenre, the hard-boiled private eye novel, that is synonymous with a very particular and stylized version of tough straight masculinity. In this respect, Fadeout is typical of the Brandstetter novels as a whole, which attempt to provide a complex and nuanced picture of gay life while at the same time forcing mystery and suspense fiction to revise itself in order to accommodate his vision. As Hansen once put it, "I wanted to correct as many misapprehensions, ordinary mortals have about homosexuals, and the way they live as I could in the space of fifty thousand words."

Even though Fadeout initially sold rather poorly and even though Hansen hadn't planned to write another novel featuring Dave Brandstetter, the positive critical reaction to his work changed his mind, and he eventually went on to feature Brandstetter in twelve novels and two short stories.

According to the critic Karl L. Stenger,

Commentators such as Robert A. Baker and David Geherin have stressed the unity of the Brandstetter series and have suggested that the mysteries should be read as one continuing novel since in their totality they provide a multifaceted picture of the gay existence in post-Stonewall America. Brandstetter's character develops and matures over a span of twenty years and is shaped by the societal and cultural changes of the 1970s and 1980s.

This multifaceted picture includes non-sympathetic portrayals of gay characters. Indeed, Hansen has sometimes been criticized by those within the gay community for not providing enough positive representations of gay men. Despite this criticism, Hansen has been unflinching in providing gay characters who are promiscuous, effeminate, or closeted, fanatic gay activists, hustlers, and even murderers.

The richness of Hansen's work can be attributed partly to the fact that he had the opportunity to write a series of novels. I commented earlier on the importance of the series in gay and lesbian mystery and suspense fiction for the way it allows readers to gradually identify with a particular character. Hansen's Brandstetter novels are a perfect example of this phenomenon.

Over the course of the series, Hansen had the opportunity to address not only issues relevant to gay men but also issues relevant to society as a whole, including religious fanaticism, the porn industry, the dumping of toxic waste, right-wing paramilitary groups, AIDS, drugs, and organized crime. Gay mystery and suspense fiction really came into its own with the work of Joseph Hansen.

Michael Nava, who many consider to be the best contemporary gay mystery writer, has been profoundly influenced by his model and mentor Joseph Hansen. As Nava once said of Hansen,

> He used the mystery to actually explore what it means to be gay. In the classic American mystery, the private investigator is an outsider who's generally viewed [as] fairly disreputable

by the people who hire him. So if you are in fact an outsider because you're gay or a woman or African-American, it's a very interesting vehicle to explore the whole issue of being on the fringe.

There are a number of similarities between the work of Hansen and that of Nava, as we might expect, but there are also some interesting differences. Nava was born in 1954 in Stockton, California, and grew up in a poor Mexican neighborhood in Sacramento. After graduating from Stanford Law School in 1980, he began working as an attorney and simultaneously started on his first novel.

Later, Nava would recall the origins of that novel. It was his job "to interview arrestees after they were booked to determine whether they should be released on their own recognizance or held overnight until a judge could set bail." While conducting these interviews, Nava started jotting down notes about the activities in the jail, and these notes became the germ for *The Little Death*, which was published in 1986.

In this novel, which Nava has described as a sort of Raymond Chandler with a gay Philip Marlowe, we meet Henry Rios, a burned-out public defender in his early 30s who would go on to become Nava's series character. The plot revolves around Rios' relationship with Hugh Paris, a troubled young gay man from a wealthy and influential family. Although Rios first meets Paris in a professional context, the two later become lovers. When Paris is later found dead, apparently from an accidental drug overdose, Rios is determined to get to the bottom of the mystery.

Over the course of seven novels, Nava develops Rios into a fascinatingly complex series character whose cases cover many different issues, not unlike Hansen's Dave Brandstetter. Unlike Brandstetter, however, Rios is often considerably more troubled and vulnerable and less hardboiled and tough. As such, the typical Nava novel tends to be more emotionally fraught than Hansen's work.

As the Rios series evolves, Nava starts to pay more and more attention to the complexities and contradictions of Rios' Chicano identity, in order to explore the way in which this character is dealing with a double form of marginalization. As a result, Nava's novels are arguably more complex than those of Hansen in terms of their consideration of race and ethnicity.

There's a final difference between Hansen and Nava that's actually quite unusual in the context of not only gay and lesbian mystery fiction in particular but also the genre as a whole. Nava has apparently had enough, at least for the time being, of writing mysteries! As he explained to his friend and fellow mystery writer Katherine V. Forrest in 2001, "Over time the constraints imposed by the mystery form have been harder and harder to transcend without ignoring them altogether." Nava added that the mystery form "increasingly gets in the way of the stories I really want to tell."

Nava should be given credit for his honesty here. If mystery and suspense fiction once provided him with an ideal outlet for the stories he wanted to tell, that's no reason to assume that the genre will continue to serve that purpose forever.

In a moment, we'll look at the work of Nava's friend Katherine V. Forrest in more detail, but first I want to sketch out the origins of lesbian mystery fiction, in the same way, I did for gay mystery fiction earlier in this lecture. According to the critic Lori L. Lake, "Unlike male authors who, in the early 1960s, began creating gay detectives and exploring homosexual themes, publication for lesbian mystery writers didn't get going in earnest until the mid-80s."

There are various reasons for this difference, but the one I'd like to highlight has to do with the fact that lesbian mystery and suspense fiction, perhaps more than any other variety of the genre, is peculiarly dependent upon the existence of small publishers who are willing to take a gamble and publish work that mainstream publishing houses would consider too marginal to garner a significant audience. Once these small presses, such as Naiad Press and Seal Press, began to spring up in the 1970s, the stage was set for the emergence of lesbian mystery fiction.

The breakthrough author in this subgenre is undoubtedly Katherine V. Forrest. Born in Windsor, Ontario in 1939, Forrest is probably one of the most well-known writers of lesbian fiction working today. She gained a lot of attention with her first novel, *Curious Wine*, published in 1983, which contained quite explicit descriptions of lesbian sexuality and sold over three hundred thousand copies.

From the perspective of mystery and suspense fiction, however, the landmark novel of Forrest's career was *Amateur City*, published in 1984, which introduced Forrest's series character, ex-Marine, and LAPD homicide detective Kate Delafield to the world. Just as Joseph Hansen rewrote the traditional private eye novel with *Fadeout*, and Michael Nava deals with aspects of the legal thriller in his Henry Rios novels, so Forrest innovates the police procedural by putting a lesbian cop at the center of her narratives.

Forrest created a tremendously influential character almost by accident. As she once explained in an interview:

> I'd intended to write a conventional mystery, but when I decided that the detective involved with the police investigation would be a woman, Kate Delafield walked onto the stage and immediately became central because of the fascinating set of complexities she presented: a closeted lesbian in a high-profile, high-pressure profession. She emerged out of her times—1984, when the stories began, when women were emerging into some of the higher echelons of police work, and all police officers were driven into the closet by the intense homophobia of their paramilitary organizations.

Forrest makes some very interesting and important observations here that are helpful in explaining the significance of her work. First, it's clear she wanted the novel to have a high degree of realism with regard to how it treated actual developments taking place in law enforcement organizations in the real world, a fact that I think can also be read as an implicit engagement with the realism of the police procedural genre. Second, throughout the series in which she appears, Kate Delafield remains closeted. This has been one of the most controversial aspects of the series, for at least two reasons.

First, Delafield is often criticized by other characters in the novels who know she's lesbian for not coming out, especially as she becomes a more and more senior police officer. Second, many of Forrest's readers, as the series moved through the 1980s, 1990s, and finally into the 21st century with the publication of *Hancock Park* in 2004 and *High Desert* in 2013, in which Delafield has retired from the LAPD, became more and more frustrated with the fact that Delafield remained in the closet. These readers felt that Delafield's decision made her out of step with the times and ran the risk of making the series as a whole quite conservative.

Delafield's decision to hide her sexual orientation is certainly a major difference between her and both Dave Brandstetter and Henry Rios. It's also a sharp contrast with Forrest's own assertiveness about her identity as a lesbian. So why has Forrest been so insistent on this point?

When asked about this issue in a 2005 interview, Forrest first tried to turn this issue aside by saying that the decision to remain in the closet has been Delafield's and not hers. But Forrest then went on to say that "from the get-go I knew I was writing about a character who presented the very best case possible for being in the closet, and that I wanted to explore that best possible case."

Kate's homophobic paramilitary organization remains so to this very day despite significant, court-mandated progress in its tolerance of its gay and lesbian officers. In an organization where her peer group wears guns, where life and death decisions affecting its officers are made according to mutual loyalties, her choice to remain closeted as the series opened was hardly arbitrary. But her refusal to confront the very real and devastating costs of this choice at every opportunity she's given to confront them is for me the underlying dramatic theme threaded throughout the series."

Two points emerge from this quote. First, Delafield remaining in the closet can be defended on the grounds of realism. So again we're dealing with the fact that this character appears in police procedurals rather than private eye novels. And second, as the series has progressed, Delafield's decision has become, for better or worse, one of the defining traits of her character and one of the major themes of the novels in which she appears.

In the same 2005 interview with Bett Norris, Forrest elaborates on this latter point.

> The series has had a twenty-year trajectory and is reflective of those times and some of the great issues affecting our community over that period. It's dealt in a primary way with gay bashing, with numerous manifestations of abuse of power, and more than anything else, the closet, which affects far more people in these novels than just Kate, and is my abiding passion as a writer. The closet kills. It kills us emotionally, spiritually and physically. The eight Kate Delafield books are the most eloquent testimony possible from this particular writer of that fact.

Once again, what we're seeing here is an example of the way in which gay and lesbian mystery writers often have to steer a course between what their communities want and feel is appropriate and affirmative, and what the writers want to do with their creations. It's another fascinating instance of the way in which innovations in the genre can be both welcomed and somewhat controversial.

My final example of this diverse subgenre draws upon the work of Barbara Wilson. Born in 1950 in Long Beach, Wilson is the author of two series of mysteries that both feature amateur detectives, one a printer, and the other a translator. The latter character, Cassandra Reilly, first appears in the 1990 novel *Gaudi Afternoon*. Note the title. It's a double pun, referring both to Dorothy L. Sayers' 1935 novel *Gaudy Night* and to the Catalan architect Antoni Gaudí—the novel is set in Barcelona.

But it's Wilson's first series character, the printer Pam Nilsen that I want to focus on, not only because she's an amateur detective but also because she's probably the most amateur detective in this whole course. I don't mean that as a criticism but instead as an observation of the extent to which Wilson radically democratizes the idea of what it means to be a detective, especially in her 1984 novel *Murder in the Collective*, the first novel in which Nilsen appears.

In this novel, which revolves around a murder that takes place in a printing collective in Seattle, Pam investigates the crime alongside a lesbian woman named Hadley. As the investigation proceeds, Pam learns two things simultaneously: the identity of the killer and the truth about her own sexual orientation, as she realizes that she's in love with Hadley. Just as the novel emphasizes that anyone has the ability to be a detective all you need is a desire to find out the truth, so the trajectory of Pam's character suggests that any woman can be a lesbian.

In this way, Wilson not only makes a thought-provoking point about sexual orientation but also suggests, like the other writers we've looked at in this lecture, why mystery and suspense fiction appeals to so many gay and lesbian writers. Over the course of its long and diverse history, the genre has been concerned with a number of mysteries, including the mystery of identity—who people are, and how they became that way. In gay and lesbian mysteries, therefore, we often find that the investigation into a crime is accompanied by a parallel investigation into what some regard as the greatest mystery of all—human subjectivity.

ADAPTING THE MULTIMEDIA MYSTERY

Mystery and suspense fiction has had a profound effect on popular culture, as evidenced by the numerous adaptations of the genre to other mediums. In this lecture, by studying the genre's adaptations, we'll understand which elements are considered sacrosanct and which are expendable or changeable. In considering adaptations, there are two schools of thought. One stresses fidelity and asserts that the ultimate goal is to translate the original into another medium so seamlessly that the audience is hardly aware of any differences. Another school of thought argues that adaptations have no responsibility to be faithful to their source material; instead, adaptations should be free to be creative re-appropriations of their sources.

A FAITHFUL FILM SERIES

- Let's consider three different versions of one of the most popular characters in the history of mystery and suspense fiction: Sherlock Holmes. Beginning in 1939 with *The Hound of the Baskervilles* and ending with *Dressed to Kill* in 1946, 14 film adaptations of Sherlock Holmes were released that starred Basil Rathbone as Holmes and Nigel Bruce as Dr. Watson.

- This film series is regarded with great fondness and a considerable degree of nostalgia as being one of the most faithful adaptations of Sherlock Holmes ever committed to film. The secret is in the casting. Rathbone and Bruce were considered the perfect exemplars of the characters of Holmes and Watson.

A RESPECTFUL REIMAGINING

- While the characters in mystery and suspense fiction are regarded as the essential part of any adaptation, the circumstances surrounding the characters are, by comparison, adaptable.

- A good test of this proposition is to examine a very different adaptation of Holmes, the television series featuring Benedict Cumberbatch as Holmes and Martin Freeman as Dr. Watson that debuted in 2010 under the title *Sherlock*. In this case, the differences between the original and the adaptation couldn't be more pronounced. Not only is *Sherlock* set in the 21st century, but also many details in the episodes have been transformed.

- The episodes clearly take their inspiration from the original Holmes stories, however. The first episode of the series, "A Study in Pink," is loosely based on Doyle's 1887 novel, *A Study in Scarlet*. But as the series creator Steven Moffat commented, "There are many elements of the story, and the broad shape of it, but we mess around with it a lot."

- For example, both versions of the story contain the same clue, the word "Rache" written at the scene of the crime. In Conan Doyle's novel, Holmes scoffs at the idea that the victim was trying to write "Rachel" and instead points out that *Rache* is the German word for "revenge." In the television episode, on the other hand, Holmes dismisses the "revenge" explanation and instead suggests that the victim was trying to write "Rachel."

- Millions of viewers love this updated version of Holmes, even though it isn't faithful to the original. Part of the reason is the casting. Both Cumberbatch and Freeman are brilliant in their roles because they resemble what Conan Doyle's characters might have become in the 21st century. Ultimately, though, the success of *Sherlock* comes down to the spirit in which the changes are made. The series is infused with a tremendous sense of affection for the original characters. The originals are treated with respect as a source of inspiration, while at the same time, they are updated to reflect contemporary circumstances.

HOLMES AS ACTION HERO

- Not all adaptations are created equal. In 2009, British director Guy Ritchie released the film *Sherlock Holmes*, starring Robert Downey, Jr., as Holmes and Jude Law as Dr. Watson. Although the film has a period Victorian setting that gives it a surface resemblance to the original, many believe it is the least faithful version of Holmes of the three we're considering.

- One of the biggest problems with Ritchie's version of Holmes is that he turns him into an action hero. Granted, as we've seen in other lectures in this series, there was always a flavor of the adventure tale in Conan Doyle's work, which is one of the reasons why the word "adventure" appears in the titles of so many Holmes stories. But it was only a flavor, and in Ritchie's movie, it becomes the substance—with ratiocination, analysis, and indeed any form of higher-order thinking apparently thrown out of the window.

COMICS

- The relationship between the medium of comics and the mystery and suspense fiction genre goes back a long way. For example, in October 1931, the *Detroit Mirror* introduced a new comic-book character by the name of Dick Tracy. Chester Gould would go on to write and draw Dick Tracy's adventures for an astonishing 46 years. Dick Tracy's origins are clearly indebted to the figure of the hard-boiled private eye as he appeared in *Black Mask*.

- In 1940, long before he dreamed up hard-boiled private eye Mike Hammer, Mickey Spillane worked as a writer and assistant editor for a comic book company in New York City called Funnies, Inc. Whereas it took the other writers a week to produce a Captain Marvel story, Spillane could reportedly turn one out in a day. In fact, he originally conceived of the story that would become his first novel, *I, the Jury*, as a comic book.

■ According to critic J. Kenneth Van Dover, Spillane's time in the world of comics had a permanent impact on his writing: "His novels transpose into literary form several aspects of the art of the comic book. Spillane's characters are designed for immediate recognition. Their outlines are simple; their colors are primary. His men are muscular; his women voluptuous. His landscapes—usually cityscapes—are generalized and are often rendered with ominous angles and dark shadows. Spillane's plots are far more complicated than those employed by the comics, but they progress in much the same manner."

FILM NOIR

■ No lecture on adaptations of mystery and suspense fiction would be complete without noting the contributions of film noir. Critics have termed noir a genre, a style, a mood, a series, a cycle, a period, or any combination of the above. As one study puts it, with a fine sense of understatement, "There is no consensus on the matter."

■ In recent years, as adaptations of noir texts have continued to multiply, the situation has become even more complicated, thanks to the development of what film scholar James Naremore calls the "noir mediascape," which he describes as "a loosely related collection of perversely mysterious

In 1940, long before he dreamed up hard-boiled private eye Mike Hammer, Mickey Spillane worked as a writer and assistant editor for a comic book company in New York City called Funnies, Inc.

motifs or scenarios that circulate through all the information technologies."

- Crime novelist George Pelecanos has made a thought-provoking observation: "First of all, most producers don't even understand what noir is. Sure, they know the signs: Venetian blind shadows, cigarette smoke, etc. But they don't understand the core psychological aspects, the undercurrents of claustrophobia and anxiety which drive noir."

- In other words, according to Pelecanos, more than anything, noir is mood. If you're in the presence of a narrative that is pessimistic about everything, then you're in the presence of a noir narrative. That atmosphere, that mood, can encompass any number of characters and settings.

Crime-related television shows mirror the diversity and complexity of mystery and suspense fiction as a whole.

CRIME ON TV

■ As we survey the contemporary mediascape of crime shows on TV, two elements stand out: their variety and their hybridity. In that sense, crime-related television shows mirror the diversity and complexity of mystery and suspense fiction as a whole.

■ Consider the following examples. *Law & Order*, which debuted in 1990 and eventually ran for 20 seasons, combines the courtroom drama with the police procedural. *CSI*, which began in 2000 and ran for 15 seasons, blends the forensic thriller with the police procedural. *Criminal Minds*, which premiered in 2005 and is still going strong, brings together the psychological thriller with the police procedural.

■ What these shows demonstrate is the importance of hybridity. By bringing together and blending aspects of mystery and suspense narratives that may have previously remained discrete, these shows and their numerous spin-off series have hit on a winning formula.

■ But their hybrid elements are only part of the story. If we also consider the popularity and influence of shows such as *The Sopranos*, *Dexter*, *Boardwalk Empire*, and *The Wire*, it's clear that there's also great demand for narratives with criminal, rather than law enforcement protagonists. Crime is not only a source of fear but of fascination.

FAN FICTION

■ Fans of mystery and suspense fiction have always had a strongly participatory relationship with the genre. An early example of this phenomenon occurred when Sir Arthur Conan Doyle attempted to kill off his famous creation, Sherlock Holmes, in "The Final Problem" in 1893. Conan Doyle didn't anticipate the passionate public reaction to Holmes's death. He received thousands of letters begging him to bring Holmes back; "Let's Keep Holmes Alive!" clubs were founded in American cities;

and Conan Doyle was offered incredible sums of money to write more Holmes stories.

- By far the most significant type of fan participation in mystery and suspense fiction today, however, comes in the form of fan fiction. In fan fiction, lovers of mystery and suspense fiction write the adaptations themselves.

- Fan fiction is not only varied in terms of the range of texts and characters it reworks but also in terms of its attitudes toward that material. Some of it is homage; some of it is parody. While the literary quality of this fan fiction varies, what all the stories have in common is that they come out of a deep engagement with mystery and suspense fiction. In this respect, they are the most heartfelt, if not always the most skilled adaptations around.

- It's also worth noting that some fan fiction comes with a warning sign for adult content. This is where we draw a distinction between fan fiction and slash fiction. Slash fiction refers to a specific type of fan fiction that focuses on interpersonal, frequently sexual, relationships between members of the same sex.

- As Elinor Gray has commented in the website Sherlockian.net, "Fan fiction is subversive in ways that only free media can be." Slash fiction is an excellent example of her point. Like the other adaptations we've discussed in this lecture, slash fiction takes what it regards as the core features of its source material and then adapts those features to suit its purposes. In the process, some aspects of mystery and suspense fiction get left behind and some get picked up and transmuted, but the genre as a whole continues to do what it's always done: evolve, innovate, and entertain.

QUESTIONS TO CONSIDER
1. What's the difference between faithful and creative adaptations of mystery and suspense fiction?

2. Can you discern any patterns in what elements of the genre tend to survive in adaptations and which elements tend to be discarded?

SUGGESTED READING

Perry and Sederholm, eds., *Adapting Poe.*

Reynolds and Trembley, eds., *It's a Print!*

ADAPTING THE MULTIMEDIA MYSTERY

O ne of the most exciting and also challenging aspects of doing this course has been figuring out how to fit a very large amount of information into very short lectures. I always try to include enough information to give you a good sense of the range of any particular type or aspect of mystery and suspense fiction. But I'm always aware of how much I have to leave out. Nowhere is this more true than in this lecture, which will look at adaptations of written mystery and suspense fiction narratives in a variety of other media.

Even though addressing such a wide variety and huge amount of material in a single lecture is a daunting prospect, it has to be done. Why? Because no study of mystery and suspense fiction would be complete without talking about the influence of the genre in popular culture more generally. Moreover, such adaptations and variations both reflect and contribute to the success of the genre.

Obviously, these adaptations take a huge variety of forms, from versions of foundational characters, such as Sherlock Holmes, Hercule Poirot, and Miss Marple, to the long afterlife of Edgar Allan Poe, to film noir, to contemporary television crime shows, and much more.

We'll see that both variations and continuities in these adaptations give us insight into which elements of mystery and suspense fiction are considered sacrosanct and which are considered expendable or changeable. This gives us a good sense of what's considered essential to the genre's success. And finally, adaptations also give fans of mystery and suspense fiction an opportunity to give back to the genre they love by both reproducing and changing the aspects of the genre that excite them most.

Let's begin by looking at two ways of thinking about adaptations that influence how people react to adaptations of mystery and suspense fiction in particular. On the one hand, there's a school of thought that stresses fidelity. This point of view judges adaptations according to how faithful, or unfaithful, they are in relation to the source material. Presumably, the ultimate goal of the faithful adaptation is to translate the original into another medium so successfully that the audience is hardly aware of any differences.

A different school of thought argues that adaptations have no responsibility to be faithful to their source material at all. Instead, adaptations should be free to be creative reappropriations of their sources, choosing selectively what to keep and what to discard.

Everyone feels differently about the debate that revolves around faithfulness versus creative adaptation, and we may even move from one side of the debate to the other depending on who or what is being adapted. However, there's no denying the fact that we can feel very strongly about this issue, and there can be a lot at stake when one of our favorite characters or books gets adapted into another medium.

Let me demonstrate what I mean by looking at three different versions of one of the most popular characters in the history of mystery and suspense fiction: Sherlock Holmes. Beginning in 1939 with *The Hound of the Baskervilles* and ending with *Dressed to Kill* in 1946, 14 film adaptations of Sherlock Holmes were released that starred Basil Rathbone as Holmes and Nigel Bruce as Dr. Watson. The first two films were set in the Victorian era, but later films in the series sometimes updated the characters so that Holmes and Watson investigate the Nazis—for instance, in the 1943 film Sherlock Holmes in Washington.

Given this type of historical anomaly, one might expect this film series to be criticized for being unfaithful, but in fact, it's generally regarded with great fondness and a considerable degree of nostalgia as being one of the most faithful adaptations of Sherlock Holmes ever committed to film. Why is this?

The secret, I think, is the casting. Rathbone and Bruce were regarded as so perfectly exemplifying the characters of Holmes and Watson that the vast majority of viewers tolerated them being placed in different circumstances. This indicates that the characters in mystery and suspense fiction are regarded as being the essential part of any adaptation. The circumstances surrounding the characters are, by comparison, malleable.

A good test of this proposition is to look at a very different adaptation of Holmes, a television series featuring Benedict Cumberbatch as Holmes and Martin Freeman as Watson that debuted in 2010 under the title *Sherlock*. In this case, the differences between the original and the adaptation couldn't be more pronounced. Not only is Sherlock set in the 21st century, but also most of the episodes, although they take their inspiration from the original Holmes stories, feel free to change and eliminate details as they see fit.

The first episode of the series, "A Study in Pink" is loosely based on Doyle's 1887 novel, *A Study in Scarlet*. But as the series creator, Steven Moffat commented: "There are many elements of the story and the broad shape of it, but we mess around with it a lot." For instance, both versions of the story contain the same clue, the word "Rache" written at the scene of the crime.

In Doyle's novel, Holmes scoffs at the idea that the victim was trying to write "Rachel" and instead points out that Rache is the German word for "revenge." In the television episode, on the other hand, Holmes dismisses the "revenge" explanation and instead suggests that the victim was trying to write "Rachel"!

Although I was initially skeptical when I heard about this updated version of Holmes, when I sat down and watched it, I found that I, like millions of other viewers, absolutely loved it, even though it wasn't faithful to the original. How did the makers of the show get away with it? Once again, I think casting is a big part of the answer. Both Cumberbatch and Freeman are brilliant in their respective roles, not so much because they resemble Doyle's original characters, but more because they resemble what Doyle's characters might have become in the 21st century.

In a similar vein, some of the other changes the series makes to the original make perfect sense, such as the extensive use that Holmes makes of the Internet and the way in which Watson writes about the cases they investigate in the form of a blog. In many cases, the characters behave and do the same things they did in the original version, but now realistically updated to conform to a contemporary setting.

More than either of these factors, however, I think the success of *Sherlock* ultimately comes down to the spirit in which these changes are made. By this, I mean that the series is infused with a tremendous sense of affection for the original characters, an affection that dictates the changes that are made and how they are made. The originals are never mocked for being old-fashioned or out of place. Instead, they're treated with respect as a source of inspiration, while at the same time being updated to reflect contemporary circumstances.

But not all updates are created equal. In 2009, British director Guy Ritchie released the film *Sherlock Holmes*, starring Robert Downey, Jr., as Holmes and Jude Law as Watson. Although the film has a period Victorian setting that gives it a surface resemblance to the original, in my view it is by far the least faithful version of Holmes of the three we're considering, and that's why I absolutely hated it!

OK, I'll be honest, I also hated it because I hate Robert Downey, Jr. Don't ask me why I just do! In fact, whenever I discuss Conan Doyle's

Sherlock Holmes in class, I write Robert Downey, Jr. on the board and then I cross it out as a reminder to my students never to mention that name in the same breath as Sherlock Holmes!

But the biggest problem with Ritchie's version of Holmes is that he turns him into an action hero. Granted, as we've seen in other lectures in this series, there was always a flavor of the adventure tale in Conan Doyle's work, which is one of the reasons why the word adventure appears in the titles of so many Holmes stories. But it was only a flavor, and in Ritchie's movie, it becomes the substance, with ratiocination, analysis, and indeed any form of higher-order thinking apparently thrown out of the window.

Let me finish this rant by quoting one reviewer of the film, who sums up my feelings perfectly: "The makers of this film are mainly interested in action; that, they believe, is all that gets young audiences into cinemas today. They may be right, but they have ridden roughshod over one of literature's greatest creations in the process."

As I said earlier, people get very passionate about the subject of adaptations of mystery and suspense fiction, and I'm no exception to that rule. Let's try and cool things down for the remainder of this lecture by moving on to examine some other examples of the influence of the genre in popular culture.

I want to begin with comics because it gives us an opportunity to remind ourselves that the relationship between this medium and mystery and suspense fiction goes back a long way. For example, in October 1931, the Detroit Mirror introduced a new comic book character by the name of Dick Tracy.

The invention of Chester Gould, who would go on to write and draw Dick Tracy's adventures for an astonishing 46 years, the character underwent a lot of changes during that period. Dick Tracy's origins, however, are clearly indebted to the figure of the hard-boiled private eye as he appeared in *Black Mask*, and we can see that he also responds to the crime wave associated with Prohibition and the rise of the gangster by the fact that he frequently battles mob bosses.

In an attempt to compete with and capitalize upon the success of Dick Tracy, in 1934 a company named King Features persuaded the master of the private eye story, Dashiell Hammett, to collaborate with artist Alex Raymond, who was responsible for the Flash Gordon comics, to produce a comic strip.

The result was called *Secret Agent X-9*, and unfortunately, it was a bit of a mess, precisely because the company and Hammett disagreed about which features of the private eye archetype to adapt and which to leave out. Whereas Hammett wanted the hero to be a private eye in the Sam Spade mode, King Features wanted a secret government agent. As you can imagine, neither side got what they wanted and so Hammett left the project as soon as his contract expired.

Mickey Spillane had a somewhat happier relationship with the comic book medium. In 1940, long before he dreamed up hard-boiled private eye Mike Hammer, Spillane worked for a comic book company in New York City called Funnies, Inc. as a writer and assistant editor. Whereas it took the other writers a week to produce a Captain Marvel story, Spillane could reportedly turn one out in a day. In fact, he originally conceived of the story that would become his first novel, *I, the Jury*, as a comic book featuring a character named Mike Danger, but he was unable to sell the idea because of a slump in the comic book market at the time.

Despite the fact that Spillane eventually found lasting fame by writing novels rather than comic books, according to critic J. Kenneth Van Dover, Spillane's time in the world of comics had a permanent impact on his writing:

> His novels transpose into literary form several aspects of the art of the comic book. Spillane's characters are designed for immediate recognition. Their outlines are simple; their colors

are primary. His men are muscular; his women voluptuous. His landscapes—usually cityscapes—are generalized and are often rendered with ominous angles and dark shadows. Spillane's plots are far more complicated than those employed by the comics, but they progress in much the same manner.

Since the hard-boiled era, of course, the comics medium has continued to grow and evolve by leaps and bounds, and today one can find hundreds of comics and graphic novels that draw on mystery and suspense fiction themes. Some of these are adaptations of actual crime fiction texts, such as series of graphic novels written and illustrated by Darwyn Cooke that adapt the novels featuring a career criminal named Parker that were written by Richard Stark a pseudonym for Donald E. Westlake beginning in the 1960s.

Others, such as the brilliant series Criminal, written by Ed Brubaker and illustrated by Sean Phillips, is clearly inspired by the defining elements of hard-boiled crime fiction but also looks to update those conventions. The genre's been booming for so long that today you can find crime-themed comic books and graphic novels to suit every conceivable taste including, arguably, those with no taste at all!

I know that we've already talked about film adaptations a little bit in this lecture, but I want to return to the subject of film briefly because no lecture on adaptations of mystery and suspense fiction would be complete without saying at least a few words about film noir. I must confess that part of me is hesitant to raise this subject because I once literally had to separate two people who disagreed so vehemently about whether or not Orson Welles' 1958 film *Touch of Evil* was a film noir or not that they came to blows!

So, at the risk of starting a fight, let me ask: what is film noir? I think we can all agree that many examples of film noir adapt mystery fiction texts, but beyond that, things get confusing quickly. Why is this? Partly because film noir has always been a fairly loose and baggy category. As far back as 1955, in their book *A Panorama of American Film Noir*, the original and therefore seminal extended treatment of the subject, Raymond Borde and Étienne Chaumeton say that "We'd be oversimplifying things in calling film noir oneiric, strange, erotic, ambivalent, and cruel…" In other words, film noir is even more complicated than that definition suggests!

Subsequent critics would go on to define noir even more broadly, some calling it a genre, others a style, or a mood, a series, a cycle, a period, or any combination of the above. As one study puts it, with a fine sense of understatement, "There is no consensus on the matter."

In recent years, as adaptations of noir texts have continued to multiply, the situation has become even more complicated, thanks to the development of what film scholar James Naremore, in a fine book called *More Than Night: Film Noir in Its Contexts*, calls the noir mediascape, which he describes as follows: "A loosely related collection of perversely mysterious motifs or scenarios that circulate through all the information technologies."

Given all this confusion about noir in general and film noir, in particular, it's tempting to make things simpler by constructing a canon of noir adaptation, accompanied by a strict list of dates and criteria that will enable us to say "This one is in and this one is out!" I want to resist this temptation, not least because it tends to lead to fights over Orson Welles-like the one I mentioned earlier.

But I do want to share with you a very thought-provoking observation crime novelist George Pelecanos made when he was asked whether he thought contemporary noir was in danger of becoming a parody. Here's what he said:

> First of all, most producers don't even understand what noir is. Sure, they know the signs: Venetian blind shadows, cigarette smoke, etc. But they don't understand the core

psychological aspects, the undercurrents of claustrophobia and anxiety which drive noir.

Earlier, we saw that sometimes it's characters that define an adaptation, while on other occasions it's setting. What I take from Pelecanos' comments is that, with noir, adaptations are defined by a mood more than anything. If you're in the presence of a narrative that has a downbeat, paranoid, and hopeless view of the world, if you're in the presence of a narrative that is pessimistic about everything, but particularly about whether people can ever understand or be happy with each other, then you're in the presence of a noir narrative. That atmosphere, that mood, can encompass any number of characters and settings, and perhaps we should be celebrating that diversity rather than arguing about when film noir began and when it ended.

The fact that George Pelecanos, apart from being a very fine crime novelist, also worked as a writer on David Simon's award-winning TV drama *The Wire* allows me to now transition into a brief discussion of television adaptations. In earlier lectures, I've mentioned *Dragnet*, which, by the way, was itself an adaptation of an earlier radio show with the same name. Ever since it burst onto American television screens in December 1951, crime-related programming has been a staple feature of the televisual medium.

If we survey the contemporary mediascape of crime shows on TV, two things stand out: their variety and their hybridity. In that basic but nonetheless important sense, crime-related TV mirrors the diversity and complexity of mystery and suspense fiction as a whole.

Consider the following examples: *Law & Order*, which debuted in 1990 and eventually ran for 20 seasons, combines the courtroom drama with the police procedural. *CSI*, which began in 2000 and ran for 15 seasons, blends the forensic thriller with the police procedural, while *Criminal Minds*, which premiered in 2005 and is still going strong, brings together the psychological thriller with the police procedural.

Apart from confirming the triumph of varieties of the police procedural in contemporary crime television, what these shows also demonstrate is the importance of hybridity. By bringing together and blending aspects of mystery and suspense narratives that may have previously have been discrete, these shows, and their numerous spinoff series, have hit on a winning formula.

But hybridity is only part of the story. If we also consider the popularity and influence of shows like *The Sopranos*, *Dexter*, *Boardwalk Empire*, and *The Wire*, it's clear to see that there's also a great demand for narratives with criminal, rather than law enforcement protagonists. Some have argued that the boom in law-enforcement-related TV shows is a product of the public's fear of crime, but if that's so, then that fear is also clearly accompanied by an ongoing fascination with criminality.

The variety of crime-related television programming is not only a good business decision, it's also a reflection of the incredible diversity of the genre that this programming draws upon. Long before television even existed, mystery and suspense fiction was already hard at work generating an incredible number of subgenres and niche audiences for later media to adapt and update for their own ends.

In the final part of this lecture, I want to address a very particular kind of adaptation that flies under most people's radars—namely, the contributions of mystery and suspense fiction fans themselves to adapting the narratives that they love.

Fans of mystery and suspense fiction have always had a strongly participatory relationship with the genre. A great early example of this phenomenon occurred when Sir Arthur Conan Doyle attempted to kill off his famous creation, Sherlock Holmes, in "The Final Problem" in 1893. Doyle couldn't have anticipated the public reaction to Holmes' death. He received thousands of letters begging him to bring Holmes back, many "Let's Keep Holmes Alive!" clubs were founded in American cities, and Doyle was offered incredible sums of money to write more Holmes stories, such as an offer of $5,000 from America, and a fee of £100 pounds for every 1,000 words from the British magazine the Strand.

Doyle eventually succumbed to the pressure, and *The Hound of the Baskervilles* began to appear in serialized form in 1901. Even then, Doyle gave himself an out, in that this new Holmes novel was set at a time before "The Final Problem" as Watson carefully explains in Hound, and so, technically speaking, this new novel was not the return of Holmes. The public, however, obviously began to suspect that Holmes was coming back to life, and when he did, in October 1903, in a story entitled "The Adventure of the Empty House," the anticipation was so intense that huge lines formed outside the offices of the Strand Magazine. Strangely enough, Doyle received his knighthood in 1902, becoming Sir Arthur Conan Doyle, and people couldn't decide whether the award was for his propaganda work for the Boer War in South Africa, or for bringing Holmes back to life!

Today, there are thousands of Sherlock Holmes societies all over the world where fans gather to read and discuss their favorite stories. In fact, I am a proud if somewhat nerdy member of the Buffalo branch, which is called "An Irish Secret Society at Buffalo" after a reference to the city of Buffalo in the Holmes story "His Last Bow."

By far the most significant type of fan participation in mystery and suspense fiction today, however, comes in the form of fan fiction. If you were to visit the website fanfiction.net, for example, you would find literally thousands of stories about a wide range of genres, characters, and TV shows. Let me give you a few examples. "Brown-Eyed Girl" by LJC is based on Dashiell Hammett's *The Maltese Falcon* and reimagines the character of Effie Perine. Loverofanime713's "Bond Meets Elmo" takes Ian Fleming's hero to *Sesame Street* where, to quote the story description, "It doesn't go well." Finally, "Here Be Dragons" by spartanster007 is a story based on Ellis Peters' *Brother Cadfael*.

As I hope this small selection of titles indicates, fan fiction is not only various in terms of the range of texts and characters it reworks, but also in terms of its attitudes toward that material. Some of it is homage, some of it is parody, and some of it is, quite frankly, difficult or even impossible to classify! As you can imagine, the literary quality of this fan fiction varies, too, but what all the stories have in common is that they come out of a deep engagement with mystery and suspense fiction. In this respect, in my view, they are the most heartfelt if not always the most skilled adaptations around.

It's also worth noting that some fan fiction comes with a warning. Why? For what is rather ominously described as adult content. This is where we need to draw a distinction between fan fiction in general and slash fiction, which refers to a specific type of fan fiction that focuses on interpersonal, frequently sexual, relationships between members of the same sex.

As Elinor Gray has commented in a column on the website Sherlockian.net, "Fan fiction is subversive in ways that only free media can be." Slash fiction is an excellent example of her point. Once again, Sherlock Holmes and John Watson tend to attract a lot of attention from writers of slash fiction and although the results may not be to everyone's taste, especially those who insist on fidelity in their adaptations, you could hardly find a better example of many of the points I've been making in this lecture.

Like the other adaptations we've discussed, slash fiction takes what it regards as the core features of its source material and then adapts those features to suit its purposes. In the process, some aspects of mystery and suspense fiction get left behind, some get picked up and transmuted, but the genre as a whole continues to do what it's always done: evolve, innovate, and entertain.

MYSTERIOUS EXPERIMENTS

S ome recent forms of mystery and suspense fiction experiment radically with the genre's conventions. Experimental examples of the genre are often very open-ended, leaving the reader puzzled and uncertain at the story's conclusion. What's more, some experimental texts take their hybrid nature to the extreme, combining the conventional elements of the genre with those of other genres, including science fiction, fantasy, thrillers, and literary fiction. Nevertheless, as we'll see in this lecture, even the most experimental examples of mystery and suspense fiction remain in dialogue with and are structured and influenced by the formulas of the genre.

JORGE LUIS BORGES

- Celebrated writer Jorge Luis Borges has been a principal influence on writers of experimental mystery and suspense fiction. Consider the significance of the labyrinth in Borges's works. Sometimes these labyrinths are physical; sometimes they are metaphysical. But regardless of the form they take, they symbolize the complexity of the world and the intellectual folly of believing that one can interpret and understand that world by imposing patterns on it or by using logic.

- With that image of intellectual folly in mind, we can understand why Borges was attracted to the idea of using a detective in his work. A great admirer of the work of Edgar Allan Poe, Borges would have been familiar with Poe's tales of ratiocination, the activity of analysis, and the character of C. Auguste Dupin. The classic detective's confidence about his ability to explain, order, and make sense of the world around him constitutes an irresistible target for Borges—because this is precisely the kind of certainty that he wants to critique and undermine.

■ In his short story "Death and the Compass," Borges writes his own experimental and subversive version of the detective story. When a rabbi is murdered, Erik Lönnrot, the story's detective, is assigned to investigate the case. Based on a mysterious message found at the scene of the crime, Lönnrot is convinced the rabbi's death is part of a series of murders that follow an elaborate pattern based on the Kabbala, an esoteric Jewish tradition. Based on his theory, Lönnrot stakes out a particular location, only to find out that he's the one who has walked into a trap.

■ The rabbi was in fact killed by accident; however, the mysterious message at the crime scene was planted to trick the detective into believing in the existence of an elaborate scheme. Once Lönnrot had accepted the appearance of that scheme as reality and acted accordingly, he was doomed.

■ According to Borges, the detective's mistake was to believe that the world was a comprehensible place that can be ordered and predictable. In fact, the world is chaotic, labyrinthine, and meaningless, and the detective pays with his life.

ALAIN ROBBE-GRILLET
■ French writer Alain Robbe-Grillet, like other French intellectuals of his generation who had been deeply influenced by the country's experiences in World War II, began to cast philosophical doubt on the concepts of meaning and identity. According to Robbe-Grillet, traditional forms of humanism were bankrupt because they assumed a depth to the world that simply didn't exist. He and other writers with similar views put their ideas into practice in works that became known as the *nouveau roman*, or "new novel."

- Robbe-Grillet was attracted to the concept of writing his own version of the detective novel precisely because the traditional form of that novel exemplified that "depthful" world in which meaning and identity are clear. Just as Borges was looking to subvert the icon of the detective, Robbe-Grillet was looking to subvert a genre that he believed epitomized the folly of clarity and certainty.

French writer Alain Robbe-Grillet, like other French intellectuals of his generation who had been deeply influenced by the country's experiences in World War II, began to cast philosophical doubt on the concepts of meaning and identity.

- Robbe-Grillet has claimed that his novel *Les Gommes*, which was translated into English as *The Erasers*, is faithful to the mystery genre. And in a limited sense, it is: There is a murder, a detective, an investigation, red herrings, suspense, and a resolution at the end.

- But in another sense, Robbe-Grillet is being deliberately disingenuous because in *The Erasers*, none of these typical elements relates to each other in the conventional way. Most strikingly, Wallas, the detective figure, turns out to be the murderer.

- Just as Wallas feels trapped in a situation that is under someone else's control, so the reader feels trapped inside Robbe-Grillet's ingenious fictional creation. Instead of enjoying a comforting sense of completion and resolution, the reader feels frustrated and unsure.

RECONSIDER THE RELATIONSHIP TO REALITY

- Robbe-Grillet's aim in *The Erasers* and Borges's purpose in "Death and the Compass" is not simply to annoy and frustrate the reader, however. In fact, there's a curious and unexpected kinship between writers of conventional mysteries and writers of experimental mystery narratives. Both use the same set of generic conventions to educate their readers and make them think, but their pedagogic purposes are very different.

- As we've seen in previous lectures, the aim of writers of traditional mystery and suspense fiction is to reassure their readers that, despite the fact that the world has been temporarily disrupted by a violent crime, that world can be restored to order and made comprehensible again by the work of the detective.

- Borges and Robbe-Grillet have a very different aim. They don't want to reassure us; they want to unsettle us, force us to ask questions, and encourage us to have a more active and critical attitude. They want us to reconsider our relationship with reality.

THE NEW YORK TRILOGY

- American writer Paul Auster has described his detective novels this way: "Mystery novels always give answers; my work is about asking questions." Auster's novels, known as *The New York Trilogy*, play with and revise mystery and suspense fiction quite radically.

- The first novel in the trilogy, *City of Glass*, begins when Daniel Quinn, a writer of conventional detective fiction, gets a phone call from someone looking for Paul Auster "of the Auster Detective Agency." Quinn hangs up, but when the person calls back later, Quinn pretends to be Paul Auster. Peter and Virginia Stillman hire Quinn, or "Auster," to protect them from Peter's father. Still pretending to be a detective, Quinn obsessively follows the father on his walks around the city and records the father's activities in a red notebook. At the end of the novel, Quinn disappears, and we discover that another writer has used Quinn's red notebook to tell the story that is *City of Glass*.

■ Given the experimental nature of *City of Glass*, Auster initially had problems finding a publisher for the novel. What's more, the novel inspired widely conflicting reactions from critics—with some hailing it as a work of genius and others dismissing it as an esoteric and pointless experiment.

■ The other two novels in the trilogy also inspired conflicting reactions. *Ghosts*, published in 1986, also features a man hired to follow another man. On the surface, the story is quite straightforward. As Auster explains at the start of the novel, "The case seems simple enough. White wants Blue to follow a man named Black." Needless to say, things get complicated very quickly, and it becomes increasingly difficult to tell the characters apart.

■ Also published in 1986, the final novel in the trilogy, *The Locked Room*, takes up some of the subject matter and themes of the first two novels, such as a mysterious disappearance, an attempt to get inside the mind of another, and doubling. Indeed, toward the end of the novel, Auster himself draws attention to the similarities between the three novels in the trilogy when his narrator observes that the "three stories are finally the same story but each one represents a different stage in my awareness of what it is about. I don't claim to have solved any problems."

THE HEIGHT OF REALISM?

■ *The New York Trilogy* has attracted more critical attention than any of Auster's other works. As Auster himself has noted, the criticism starts to overwhelm the novels themselves: "Who cares about finding the right label for my books? ... To read these critics, my novels somehow become aesthetic tracts—when in

fact they're stories about flesh and blood people. Contradictions abound: there's no one line of thought I'm pushing."

- Keeping Auster's words in mind, consider *The New York Trilogy* from the point of view of our knowledge of mystery and suspense fiction. Auster makes extensive use of various conventions from the genre, including the detective, an investigation, disappearances, and questions of identity. In an ordinary mystery narrative, these conventions would eventually lead to some kind of resolution.

- This is not so in Auster's work. Auster takes a genre that's synonymous with providing answers and a sense of resolution and uses that very same genre to instead ask questions without providing any answers. This emphasizes the fact that in the real world, just as in *The New York Trilogy*, we often have to content ourselves with not knowing. From this perspective, we have to consider a startling possibility: Perhaps examples of experimental mystery and suspense fiction are among the most realistic examples of the genre.

A WORLD THAT MAKES SENSE

- William Friedkin's 1980 film *Cruising* destabilizes the figure of the detective and turns it into something very different from its archetypal version.

- The story begins with a series of murders of gay men in Manhattan. Al Pacino stars as police detective Steve Burns, who, because he resembles the victims, is sent undercover into the city's gay subculture to find the killer. Initially very uncomfortable with this assignment, as the investigation proceeds, Burns begins to change. Not only does he feel more and more comfortable in this subculture, but he also begins to side with gay men against the police.

- By the end of the film, the murders have apparently been solved, but this is by no means a satisfactory or persuasive resolution. First, we're not sure that the police have caught the right man. And second, we suspect that Burns himself may have become the killer.

- By the time we get to *Cruising*, it's clear that we have traveled a very long way from our starting points in this course: Edgar Allan Poe, "The Murders in the Rue Morgue," and C. Auguste Dupin. Instead of answers, we have questions. Instead of analysis, we have violence that begets more violence. And instead of a detective who is firmly in control, we have a detective who might well be losing control.

- Although experimental examples of mystery and suspense fiction may be well respected as aesthetic objects, they aren't popular with wide audiences. In the final analysis, it seems that we can tolerate only so much experimentation and frustration. Perhaps the ultimate secret to great mystery and suspense fiction is that, in one way or another, it satisfies a deep-seated desire we all have for the world around us to make sense.

QUESTIONS TO CONSIDER
1. Why are so many experimental writers drawn to the genre of mystery and suspense fiction?

2. How can experimental examples of the genre potentially change the way we read conventional mystery and suspense fiction narratives?

SUGGESTED READING
Merivale and Sweeney, eds., *Detecting Texts*.

Most and Stowe, eds., *The Poetics of Murder*.

Mysterious Experiments

The success of mystery and suspense fiction has always depended on its ability to combine tradition and innovation, but some recent forms of the genre experiment with its conventions more explicitly and more radically.

In some narratives, the detective is no longer a figure in control, or someone on the side of good who has all the answers. Instead, in such narratives, the detective is thoroughly compromised, confused, and corrupt.

Even though many examples of the genre are known for finishing with a strong sense of resolution in which the mystery is cleared up and the criminal apprehended, experimental examples of the genre are often very open-ended, suggesting our inability to ever arrive at a secure or satisfactory answer to a mystery. This open-endedness is reflected in the fact that, in these texts, it's acceptable for the reader to be left puzzled and uncertain at the story's conclusion.

Some examples of traditional mystery and suspense fiction have always been hybrid, such as the Sherlock Holmes stories, many of which are as much adventure tales as they are puzzle mysteries. More recent experimental texts, however, often take this hybridity to another level by combining the accepted elements of the genre with those of other genres, including science fiction, fantasy, the thriller, and literary fiction.

Nevertheless, we'll also see in this lecture that despite this hybridity, even the most experimental examples of mystery and suspense fiction are still in dialogue with and both structured and influenced by the formulaic traits that have been our focus throughout this series of lectures.

And curiously, these experimental texts also tend to have another thing in common: none of them sell anywhere near as much as other types of mysteries. In trying to figure out why, we'll consider the possibility that despite everything, we want a resolution. We need the world to make sense even though or especially when we know it often makes no sense at all.

Considering that we'll be looking at texts in this lecture that don't seem to obey the rules of logic, it's ironic that there's a very logical place to begin our discussion: the work of the famed Argentinean writer Jorge Luis Borges. As we saw in another lecture in this course, a 1980 novel by Italian writer Umberto Eco entitled *The Name of the Rose*, which is a fine example of experimental mystery fiction in its own right contains a tribute to Borges in the form of the blind librarian Jorge of Burgos. Why is Borges considered to be such an influential figure by other writers who experiment with mystery and suspense fiction?

The beginning of an answer to this question is to stress the importance of the symbol of the labyrinth in many of Borges's works. Sometimes these labyrinths are physical; sometimes they are metaphysical. But regardless of the form they take, they frequently symbolize the same thing in Borges's work: the complexity of the world and the folly of believing that one can interpret and understand that world by imposing any kind of pattern or logic onto it.

With that image of intellectual folly or even hubris, in mind, we can begin to see why Borges might have been attracted to the idea of using a detective in his work. A great fan and student of the work of Edgar Allan Poe, Borges would definitely have been familiar with Poe's tales of ratiocination, the activity of analysis, and the character of Auguste Dupin.

The classical detective's confidence about his ability to explain, order, and make sense of the world around him constitutes an irresistible target for Borges because this is precisely the kind of certainty that he wants to critique and undermine. How does he do it? In his short story, "Death and the Compass," published in 1942 and translated into English in 1954, Borges writes his own experimental and subversive version of the detective story.

When a rabbi by the name of Marcel Yarmolinsky is murdered, Erik Lönnrot, the story's detective, is assigned to investigate the case. Based upon a mysterious message found at the scene of the crime, Lönnrot quickly convinces himself that the rabbi's death is part of a planned series of murders, a series that follows an elaborate pattern based on the Kabbalah that the erudite Lönnrot believes he has figured out.

Based on his theory, Lönnrot stakes out a particular location in order to trap the killer, only to find out that he's the one who has walked into a trap. Lönnrot is captured by Red Scharlach, whose brother Lönnrot had previously arrested. We learn that Scharlach, having sworn to avenge his brother, was able to trap Lönnrot by creating the appearance of a pattern to the murders.

The rabbi was in fact killed by accident. But seeing an opportunity to get back at Lönnrot, Scharlach planted the mysterious message at the crime scene to trick the detective into believing in the existence of an elaborate scheme. Once Lönnrot had accepted the appearance of that scheme as reality and acted accordingly, he was doomed. The story ends with Scharlach killing Lönnrot.

What was Lönnrot's mistake? Or to put the same question in a different way: according to Borges, what was the detective's mistake? To believe that the world was a comprehensible place that can be ordered and predictable. For forgetting the truth, which is that the world is chaotic, labyrinthine, and meaningless, the detective pays with his life. A harsh punishment for such a minor mistake, we might think, but doubtless, a very effective way for Borges to undermine the confidence and certainty we usually associate with the figure of the detective.

If the detective in Borges's story is undone by the sin of pride, the detective who appears in the equally experimental work of French writer Alain Robbe-Grillet appears to be guilty through no fault of his own. The origins of Robbe-Grillet's contribution to mystery narratives lies in the mid-1950s when, like a number of other French intellectuals of his generation who had been deeply influenced by the country's experiences in World War II, he began to cast philosophical doubt on the concepts of meaning and identity.

According to Robbe-Grillet, traditional forms of humanism were bankrupt because they assumed a depth to personality, nature, and the world as a whole that simply didn't exist. In other words, where others saw depth and a firm foundation upon which to build and make assumptions about reality, Robbe-Grillet saw only instability, indeterminacy, and relativity. He and other writers with similar views, such as Nathalie Sarraute, Robert Pinget, and Marguerite Duras, began to put their ideas into practice in works that collectively became known as examples of the *nouveau roman*, or new novel.

According to the critic John Fletcher:

> Robbe-Grillet himself is in favor of a literature that is all on the surface, postulating nothing about what may or may not lie behind phenomena; of a novel that presents characters with little or no previous history, and without conventional names to identify them; of a treatment of time which renders faithfully the achronological leaps of the imagination and the temporal distortions of memory and emotion; and of narrative which is not afraid of being inconsistent and reflecting a reality that has its own recurring bafflements.

Given the existence of the *nouveau roman* and its defining ideas, why would a writer like Robbe-Grillet be attracted to the concept of writing his own version of the detective novel? Precisely because the traditional form of that novel, from Robbe-Grillet's point of view, exemplifies that depthful world in which meaning and identity are clear, or at least can be made clear. Just as Borges was looking to subvert the icon of the detective, Robbe-Grillet was looking to subvert a genre that, he believed, epitomized the folly of believing in a world that contained certainty. How did he go about doing this?

The answer to this question can be found in Robbe-Grillet's 1953 novel *Les Gommes*, which was translated into English in 1964 with the title *The Erasers*. Robbe-Grillet has claimed that his novel is faithful to the mystery genre. And in a limited sense, he's right: there is a murder, a detective, an investigation, red herrings, a strong feeling of suspense as the narrative unfolds, and by the end of the novel the crime has been solved.

But in another sense, Robbe-Grillet is being deliberately disingenuous, because, in *The Erasers*, none of these typical elements relate to each other in the way they usually do in an ordinary mystery novel. Most strikingly, Wallas, the detective figure, turns out to be the murderer, not through any fault of his own, but because he has been manipulated into this situation. By whom? For what purpose? Robbe-Grillet drops some hints but gives the reader no definitive answers to these questions.

Just as Wallas feels trapped in a situation that is under someone else's control, so the reader feels trapped inside Robbe-Grillet's ingenious fictional creation. Instead of the comforting and enjoyable sense of completion and resolution that we usually feel at the end of a typical puzzle mystery, Robbe-Grillet deliberately leaves us feeling frustrated and unsure. The places, people, and events in *The Erasers* appear to make sense, but, upon closer inspection, they make no sense at all.

The perfect example of the dilemma into which Robbe-Grillet places the reader is the object the novel is titled after. Soon after arriving in the unnamed provincial town in which *The Erasers* is set, Wallas buys an eraser from a stationery shop. Partly because of some confusing and incomplete information that Robbe-Grillet gives us about it, the eraser acts as a symbol, or to be more precise, as a clue. In this sense, it cries out to be interpreted, understood, and used in such a manner that it will help us solve the mystery. But Robbe-Grillet makes it impossible for the reader to use the eraser in this way because he doesn't give us enough information about it. This object is the perfect example of the way in which Robbe-Grillet waves the typical features of mystery and suspense fiction in our face while simultaneously emptying them of meaning.

But why do this? Is Robbe-Grillet's aim in *The Erasers* and Borges' purpose in "Death and the Compass" simply to annoy and frustrate us? Not at all. In fact, there's a curious and unexpected kinship between writers of conventional mysteries and those who write experimental mystery narratives. Both use the same set of generic conventions to educate their readers and make them think, but their pedagogic purposes are very different.

As we've seen in other lectures in this series when we looked at the puzzle mysteries of writers like Edgar Allan Poe, Agatha Christie, and Ellery Queen, part of the aim of these writers is to reassure their readers that, despite the fact that the world has been temporarily disrupted by a violent crime, that world can be restored to order and made comprehensible again by the work of the detective.

Borges and Robbe-Grillet have a very different aim: they don't want to reassure us, they want to unsettle us, to force us to ask questions about those things we think we know, to have a more active and critical attitude to the world around us and the people in it. We may not always like being forced into reconsidering our relationship with reality, but potentially it's a valuable experience.

We can see this same questioning attitude in the work of American writer Paul Auster. And once again, Auster uses the conventions of mystery and suspense fiction to ask the questions he wants his readers to contemplate. Auster's engagement with and admiration for the detective novel form began to appear early in his career.

One of his first novels, *Squeeze Play*, written in 1978 and published under the name "Paul Benjamin" in 1982, is a more or less conventional detective story with a baseball theme. Even here, though, Auster is beginning to play with the conventions of the genre, as he later explained in his 1997 memoir *Hand to Mouth*:

> One of the conventional plot gimmicks of these stories was the apparent suicide that turns out to have been a murder... I thought: why not reverse the trick and stand it on its head? Why not have a story in which an apparent murder turns out to be a suicide?

Auster's next detective novels, however, would experiment with the genre's conventions in a much more radical manner. And the clue to how he does so comes in a statement Auster once made in an interview with Larry McCaffery and Sinda Gregory: "Mystery novels always give answers; my work is about asking questions." The novels known as *The New York Trilogy* ask questions rather than providing answers, and in the process, they play with and revise mystery and suspense fiction quite substantially.

The first novel in the trilogy, *City of Glass*, begins when Daniel Quinn, a writer of conventional detective fiction, gets a phone call from someone looking for Paul Auster of the Auster Detective Agency. Quinn hangs up, but when the person calls back later, Quinn pretends to be Paul Auster. Peter and Virginia Stillman hire Quinn, or Auster, to protect them from Peter's father, who is also called Peter and who has just been released from prison, where he had been serving a sentence for locking his son in a room for nine years as an experiment in language acquisition.

Far from attempting to harm his son, however, the father spends his time roaming Manhattan collecting random items, again as a language experiment. This time, the father is attempting to generate or discover "a language that will, at last, say what we have to say." Still pretending to be a detective, Quinn obsessively follows the father on his walks around the city and records all of the father's activities in a red notebook. Quinn even seeks out the real Paul Auster to get his advice about the case, but when he finds him, he discovers that Auster is a writer and not a detective. At the end of the novel Quinn disappears and we discover that another writer, who is a friend of Auster's, has used Quinn's red notebook to tell the story that is *City of Glass*.

Given the experimental nature of *City of Glass*, Auster initially had problems finding a publisher for the novel. But Sun & Moon Press, a small company in Los Angeles known for publishing innovative fiction, brought the novel out in 1985. It inspired widely divergent reactions from critics, with some hailing it as a work of genius, while others dismissed it as an esoteric and pointless experiment.

The other two novels in the trilogy also inspired divergent reactions. *Ghosts*, published in 1986, also features a man hired to follow another man. But this novel is set in 1947, rather than present-day Manhattan. On the surface, the story is quite straightforward. As Auster explains at the start of the novel, "The case seems simple enough. White wants Blue to follow a man named Black and to keep an eye on him for as long as necessary." Needless to say, things get much more complicated very quickly, as it becomes increasingly difficult to tell the characters apart from each other.

Also published in 1986 and the final novel in the trilogy, *The Locked Room* takes up some of the subject matter and themes of the first two novels, such as a mysterious disappearance, an attempt to get inside the mind of another, and doubling. Indeed, toward the end of the novel, Auster himself draws attention to the similarities between the three novels in the trilogy when he has his narrator observe that the "three stories are finally the same story, but each one represents a different stage in my awareness of what it's about. I don't claim to have solved any problems."

I'm sure you'll agree that this last sentence is ominous for anyone trying to understand Auster's *The New York Trilogy*. But let's ask the question anyway: what is Auster trying to do in these novels? Lots of people have tried to answer the question, and indeed *The New York Trilogy* has attracted more critical attention than any of Auster's other works.

The problem here isn't just that, by trying to explain these novels we feel we're falling into Auster's trap, but also, as Auster himself has pointed out, the criticism starts to overwhelm the novels themselves:

> Who cares about finding the right label for my books? To read these critics, my novels somehow become aesthetic tracts— when in fact, they're stories about flesh and blood people. Contradictions abound: there's no one line of thought I'm pushing.

Keeping Auster's words in mind, let's take a look at *The New York Trilogy* from the point of view of our knowledge of mystery and suspense fiction and see what we find. As I mentioned earlier, throughout the trilogy, Auster makes extensive use of various conventions from the genre, including the detective, an investigation, disappearances, and questions of identity. In an ordinary mystery narrative, however, these conventions would eventually lead to some kind of resolution.

I'm not saying that every example of mystery and suspense fiction always has a firm and unambiguous sense of resolution. Indeed, as we've seen in a number of other lectures in this course, even the most conventional mystery narratives can have a degree of open-endedness when it comes to their conclusions. Think, for example, of the fact that we still don't know for sure who the murderer is at the end of Edgar Allan Poe's "The Mystery of Marie Rogêt" and you'll see what I mean.

But at least conventional mystery narratives make some gesture toward resolution, rather than leaving things completely up in the air. Not so Auster. As we saw earlier, Auster has described his mystery novels as focusing more on asking questions than providing answers, and by the time we get to the final volume of The New York Trilogy, we can see what he means. But again, we're compelled to ask why. What's the point?

In my opinion, Auster sees value in taking a genre that's synonymous with providing answers to questions to give readers at least a temporary sense of resolution and using that very same genre to instead ask questions without providing any answers. Why? Because it emphasizes the fact that we live in a world that's often stubbornly incomprehensible or senseless, a world in which we do not, in fact, experience the satisfaction of an answer.

In the real world, just as in The New York Trilogy, we often have to content ourselves with not knowing. From this perspective, we have to consider a startling possibility: perhaps examples of experimental mystery and suspense fiction are among the most realistic examples of the genre we've encountered in this course. Only this type of narrative, it seems, respects the complexity and yes, incomprehensibility, of the world we actually live in.

In other lectures in this course, we've often looked at examples of mystery and suspense narratives from other media, rather than focusing exclusively on print. With this in mind, I'd like to conclude this lecture by discussing a film that—although most people wouldn't think of it in this way—destabilizes the figure of the detective and turns it into something very different from the archetypal version of this figure that we first saw in the work of Edgar Allan Poe.

When William Friedkin's 1980 film *Cruising* was released, it did poorly at the box office, partly because it had been dogged by controversy from the beginning thanks to its representations of gay men and partly because it was dismissed as nothing more than a cheap exploitation flick. While it is certainly sensationalistic and does contain stereotypical images of homosexuals, it is also a fascinating examination of the evolution of its detective protagonist over the course of the film.

The story begins with a series of murders of gay men that have been taking place in Manhattan. Al Pacino stars as police detective Steve Burns who, because he resembles the victims, is sent undercover into the city's gay subculture to see if he can find the killer. Initially very uncomfortable with this assignment, as the investigation proceeds, Burns begins to change. Not only does he feel more and more comfortable in this subculture, he also begins to side with gay men against the police when an incident of police brutality connected to the investigation takes place.

By the end of the film, the murders have apparently been solved, but this is by no means a satisfactory or persuasive resolution, for at least two reasons. First, we're not sure that the police have caught the right man. And second, we suspect that Burns himself may either have become a killer and/or is questioning his own sexual orientation.

In the film's brilliant final shot, Burns is staring at himself in a mirror while shaving off the beard he grew while undercover. In the background, we can hear his girlfriend walking toward him, and we know she's wearing the distinctive clothes that Burns wore during the investigation. On the surface, Burns is now back to normal and has put the investigation behind him.

But has he? What's going through his mind? The film refuses to answer these questions, and so we're struck by the difference between the detective Burns was at the start of the film—detached, professional, and objective—with the person he's become. Unlike Poe's Dupin, who began and ended each of his investigations as exactly the same person, Burns has clearly been changed profoundly by what he's gone through.

By the time we get to a film like *Cruising*, it's clear that we have traveled a very long way from our starting points in this course: Edgar Allan Poe, "The Murders in the Rue Morgue," and Auguste Dupin. Instead of answers we have questions. Instead of analysis, we have violence that only seems to beget more violence. And instead of a detective who is firmly in control, we have a detective who might well be losing control.

We also have a narrative that, like most of the other narratives we've looked at in this lecture, didn't sell particularly well. Although experimental examples of mystery and suspense fiction may be well-respected as aesthetic objects, they aren't popular with wide audiences. Why is this?

Over the course of these lectures, we've encountered a fantastically wide variety of mystery and suspense narratives, including many that play with the conventions of the genre and sometimes frustrate our desire to see mysteries resolved. In the final analysis, however, it seems that we can only tolerate so much experimentation and frustration.

Perhaps the ultimate secret to great mystery and suspense fiction is that, in one way or another, it satisfies a deep-seated desire we all have for the world around us to make sense. As the 21st century continues to unfold in all of its complexity and contradiction, it seems that in the future, mystery and suspense fiction, the genre we all love, is destined to become more important than ever.

BIBLIOGRAPHY

Abbott, Megan E. *The Street Was Mine: White Masculinity in Hardboiled Fiction and Film Noir.* New York: Palgrave Macmillan, 2002. This book focuses on the figure of the tough guy, a solitary white man moving through urban space, in the works of Raymond Chandler and James M. Cain and their popular film noir adaptations. Abbott argues that the tough guy embodies the promise of white masculinity amidst the turmoil of the Depression through the beginnings of the Cold War.

Asong, Linus. *Detective Fiction and the African Scene: From the Whodunit? to the Whydunit?* Oxford: African Books Collective, 2012. A study of how some of the central tropes of detective fiction have been used by major African writers, including Doris Lessing, Ousmane Sembène, and Ngũgĩ wa Thiong'o. Asong argues that these writers have domesticated the detective fiction genre for their own purposes and in the process have increased the popularity of the genre in Africa.

Åström, B., K. Gregersdotter, and T. Horeck, eds. *Rape in Stieg Larsson's Millennium Trilogy and Beyond: Contemporary Scandinavian and Anglophone Crime Fiction.* New York: Palgrave, 2012. Focusing on the sexualized violence of Stieg Larsson's best-selling Millennium trilogy—including the novels, Swedish film adaptations, and Hollywood blockbusters—this collection of essays puts Larsson's work into dialogue with Scandinavian and Anglophone crime novels by writers including Jo Nesbø, Håkan Nesser, Mo Hayder, and Val McDermid.

Bailey, Frankie Y. *African American Mystery Writers: A Historical and Thematic Study.* Jefferson, NC: McFarland, 2008. This book analyzes works by modern African American mystery writers, focusing on sleuths, the social locations of crime, victims and offenders, the notion of justice, and readers and reading. Bailey also discusses the issue of African American mystery writers' access to the marketplace.

Bargainnier, Earl F. *The Gentle Art of Murder: The Detective Fiction of Agatha Christie.* Bowling Green, OH: Bowling Green University Popular Press, 1980. This examination of Agatha Christie's literary techniques was one of the first extensive analyses of her accomplishment as a writer. The author focuses on Christie's intimate knowledge of genre conventions and her astounding ability to keep generating variations on those conventions for more than 50 years.

Bedore, Pamela. *Dime Novels and the Roots of American Detective Fiction.* New York: Palgrave, 2013. This book explores the influence of the understudied genre of the dime novel on subsequent types of mystery and suspense fiction. In particular, Bedore argues that tensions between subversive and conservative impulses—theorized as contamination and containment—explain detective fiction's ongoing popular appeal.

Betz, Phyllis M. *Lesbian Detective Fiction: Woman as Author, Subject and Reader.* Jefferson, NC: McFarland, 2006. This book examines how lesbian detective and mystery fiction represents lesbian characters and experiences, concentrating on how the lesbian characters' public and private lives intersect. Betz also discusses the lesbian detective's confrontation with two crucial elements of the investigator's role: the use of violence and the exercise of authority.

Biressi, Anita. *Crime, Fear and the Law in True Crime Stories.* London and New York: Palgrave Macmillan, 2001. Biressi examines the origins and development of true crime and its evolution into a range of contemporary forms, including true-crime books and magazines, law-and-order television, and popular journalism. The book examines how true crime explores current concerns about law and order, crime and punishment, and vulnerability.

Bounds, J. Dennis. *Perry Mason: The Authorship and Reproduction of a Popular Hero.* Westport, CT: Greenwood Press, 1996. This study explores the characters and situations of the narratives featuring lawyer and detective Perry Mason over time and in different media.

Bounds identifies a series of stylistic devices and motivations that govern these narratives, and the book contains an exhaustive list of the various manifestations of Perry Mason in novels, films, television, radio, comic strips, and other media.

Braham, Persephone. *Crimes against the State, Crimes against Persons: Detective Fiction in Cuba and Mexico*. Minneapolis: University of Minnesota Press, 2004. This book demonstrates how the detective genre is an effective way of examining and critiquing the social and political histories of post-1968 Mexico and Castro-era Cuba. Braham shows how the Cuban *novela negra* examines the revolution by chronicling life under a decaying regime and how the Mexican *neopoliciaco* reveals the oppressive politics of modern Latin America.

Breu, Christopher. *Hard-Boiled Masculinities*. Minneapolis: University of Minnesota Press, 2005. This book examines and critiques the ideal of hard-boiled masculinity found in magazines such as *Black Mask*. Breu shows how and why hard-boiled masculinity emerged during a time of increased urbanization and discusses changes in this ideal by examining the work of Ernest Hemingway, Dashiell Hammett, Chester Himes, and William Faulkner, among others.

Browne, Ray B. *Murder on the Reservation: American Indian Crime Fiction*. Bowling Green, OH: Bowling Green University Popular Press, 2004. This study surveys the work of several of the best known writers of crime fiction involving American Indian characters and argues that this genre has played a powerful democratizing role in American society. Browne shows that some American Indian mystery fiction is intended to right the wrongs the authors feel have been suffered by American Indians. The author demonstrates how writers use American Indian lore and locales as exotic elements and locations to create entertaining and commercially successful stories.

Browne, Ray B., and Lawrence A. Kreiser Jr., eds. *The Detective as Historian: History and Art in Historical Crime Fiction*. Newcastle, UK: Cambridge Scholars, 2009. In this collection of essays, the authors argue that historical crime fiction has a double purpose: to entertain and to teach. What's more, writers in the subgenre of historical crime fiction can fill in human motivations and drives where no records exist and in doing so can both aid professional historians and entertain readers.

Cameron, Ann. *Sidekicks in American Literature*. Lewiston, NY: Edwin Mellen Press, 2002. This book examines a range of American novels to illustrate how sidekicks have evolved from direct imitations of Sancho Panza into mentors, rustic scouts, or even demonic characters bent on harming their masters or mistresses. The sidekick raises issues related to the education of the hero, initiation into adulthood, and the role of the trickster, masquerade, and deception in the formation of character.

Cawelti, John G. *Adventure, Mystery, and Romance: Formula Stories as Art and Popular Culture*. Chicago: University of Chicago Press, 1976. This groundbreaking book provides the first general theory of the analysis of popular literary formulas. Cawelti discusses such diverse works as Mario Puzo's *The Godfather*, Dorothy Sayers's *The Nine Tailors*, and Owen Wister's *The Virginian*; describes the important artistic characteristics of popular formula stories; and examines the differences between popular literature and high or serious literature.

————. *Mystery, Violence, and Popular Culture: Essays*. Bowling Green, OH: Bowling Green University Popular Press, 2004. This book discusses the relationship between American popular culture and violence. In analyzing the work of such famous pop-culture icons as Alfred Hitchcock, the Beatles, and Andy Warhol, and looking at a range of texts, from *Psycho* to *Catch 22*, Cawelti argues that examples from popular movies, television, literature, and music capture the evolving psychological, sociological, and political state of a nation.

Collins, Max Allan, and James L. Traylor. *One Lonely Knight: Mickey Spillane's Mike Hammer*. Bowling Green, OH: Bowling Green University Popular Press, 1984. This book provides a complete survey of the controversial and phenomenally popular work of Mickey

Spillane. Collins and Traylor examine why Spillane's work was loathed by most critics and loved by millions of readers, and the authors connect Spillane's work to hard-boiled crime fiction as a whole.

Cook, Michael. *Narratives of Enclosure in Detective Fiction: The Locked Room Mystery.* New York: Palgrave, 2011. This book discusses one of the most iconic forms of detective fiction: the locked-room mystery. Cook examines the influence of this type of story on the genre as a whole and looks at a wide range of examples from Edgar Allan Poe to writers of the present day.

Delamater, Jerome, and Ruth Prigozy, eds. *Theory and Practice of Classic Detective Fiction.* Westport, CT: Greenwood Publishing Group, 1997. This collection of essays explores classic detective fiction from both the theoretical and practical perspective. The essays interrogate the way the genre reflects social and cultural attitudes, describe how the genre contributes to a reader's ability to adapt to the challenges of daily life, and demonstrate how the genre provides alternate takes on the role of the detective as an investigator and arbiter of truth.

Denning, Michael. *Mechanic Accents: Dime Novels and Working-Class Culture in America.* New York: Verso, 1998. This influential book studies the relationship between American popular fiction and working-class culture and provides a comprehensive overview of an important subgenre of mystery fiction. Combining Marxist literary theory with American labor history, Denning explores the cultural and political impact of working people beginning to read dime novels in the 19th century.

Dove, George N. *The Police Procedural.* Bowling Green, OH: Bowling Green University Popular Press, 1982. In one of the first comprehensive surveys of the police procedural subgenre of mystery fiction, Dove examines the origins and reasons for the popularity of the procedural. Unlike narratives featuring amateur detectives or hard-boiled private eyes, Dove explains, police procedurals are populated by law enforcement professionals and often focus on the mundane and routine details of police procedure.

Emerson, Kathy Lynn. *How to Write Killer Historical Mysteries: The Art and Adventure of Sleuthing through the Past*. Gardena, CA: SCB Distributors, 2008. This book is a how-to guide for those who want to write historical mystery fiction. Emerson focuses on how to bring past periods and characters to life rather than simply writing standard mystery fiction in historical costume.

Emsley, Clive, and Haia Shpayer-Makov, eds. *Police Detectives in History, 1750–1950*. London: Ashgate, 2006. This book focuses on themes central to the history of detection, such as the unstable distinction between criminals and detectives and the professionalization of detective work, in order to provide the first detailed examination of detectives as an occupational group. Essays discuss the complex relationship between official and private law enforcers and the dynamic interaction between the fictional and the real-life image of the detective.

Forshaw, Barry. *Death in a Cold Climate: A Guide to Scandinavian Crime Fiction*. London: Palgrave Macmillan, 2012. This book presents an analysis and celebration of Scandinavian crime fiction, from Maj Sjöwall and Per Wahlöö's Martin Beck series through Henning Mankell's Wallander series to Stieg Larsson's critique of Swedish social democracy in the publishing phenomenon *The Girl with the Dragon Tattoo*.

———. *Euro Noir: The Pocket Essential Guide to European Crime Fiction, Film & TV*. Harpenden, UK: Oldcastle Books, 2014. This book presents a concise and readable road map of the territory of European crime fiction. Authors covered include Andrea Camilleri and Leonardo Sciascia from Italy, Georges Simenon from Belgium, and Fred Vargas from France; the book also describes writers, films, and television shows from Spain, Portugal, Greece, Holland, and other European countries.

Forter, Greg. *Murdering Masculinities: Fantasies of Gender and Violence in the American Crime Novel*. New York: NYU Press, 2000. This study argues that the crime novel does not provide a consolidated and stable notion of masculinity. Forter examines five novels— Dashiell Hammett's *The Glass Key*, James M. Cain's *Serenade*, William Faulkner's *Sanctuary*, Jim Thompson's *Pop. 1280*, and Chester Himes's *Blind Man with a Pistol*—and reveals what he describes as a "generic unconscious" that sheds light on the complexities and contradictions of how crime fiction portrays masculinity and violence.

Geherin, David. *The Dragon Tattoo and Its Long Tail: The New Wave of European Crime Fiction in America*. Jefferson, NC: McFarland, 2012. This book uses the enormous popularity of Stieg Larsson's Millennium trilogy as an opportunity to explore other contemporary European examples of crime fiction, including authors from Sweden (Stieg Larsson and Henning Mankell), Norway (Karin Fossum and Jo Nesbø), Iceland (Arnaldur Indridason), Italy (Andrea Camilleri), France (Fred Vargas), Scotland (Denise Mina and Philip Kerr), and Ireland (Ken Bruen). Geherin argues that these writers are reshaping the landscape of the modern crime novel.

———. *Small Towns in Recent American Crime Fiction*. Jefferson, NC: McFarland, 2014. According to this study, small towns have long been a commonplace setting in cozy mysteries, but in recent years, writers of realistic crime fiction have discovered fresh possibilities in small-town settings. Geherin argues that because crimes in small communities hit closer to home, the human element can better be emphasized. This book focuses on the work of 10 contemporary authors whose work uses small-town settings, including Rocksburg, Pennsylvania (K. C. Constantine); Heartsdale, Georgia (Karin Slaughter); Millers Kill, New York (Julia Spencer-Fleming); Durant, Wyoming (Craig Johnson); and a number of national parks (Nevada Barr).

———. *Sons of Sam Spade: The Private-eye Novel in the 70s*. New York: Frederick Ungar, 1980. This book examines the state of the private-eye genre in the 1970s and compares it to the figure of the classic private eye developed in the work of Dashiell Hammett, Raymond Chandler, and Ross Macdonald. Geherin concludes that the work of Robert B. Parker, Roger L. Simon, and Andrew Bergman contains contemporary private-eye figures that are somewhat younger, even more cynical, and much more political than their 1940s counterparts.

Green, Joseph, and Jim Finch. *Sleuths, Sidekicks and Stooges: An Annotated Bibliography of Detectives, Their Assistants and Their Rivals in Crime, Mystery and Adventure Fiction, 1795–1995.* London: Scolar Press, 1997. This volume is a comprehensive reference work on British and American crime, mystery, and adventure fiction containing 7,000 entries, listed alphabetically by detective, providing information about sleuths, their sidekicks, and their rivals. A broad definition of detective is used, encompassing Batman, Sherlock Holmes, James Bond, Nero Wolfe, and Hercule Poirot.

Gregoriou, Christiana. *Deviance in Contemporary Crime Fiction.* New York: Palgrave, 2007. This book explores the linguistic, social, and generic aspects of deviance that contemporary crime fiction manipulates. Gregoriou conducts case studies into crime series by James Patterson, Michael Connelly, and Patricia Cornwell and investigates the way in which these novelists challenge crime fiction's generic conventions.

Halttunen, Karen. *Murder Most Foul: The Killer and the American Gothic Imagination.* Cambridge, MA: Harvard University Press, 1998. This book explores the changing view of murder—from early New England sermons read at the public execution of murderers, through the 19th century, when secular and sensational accounts replaced the sacred treatment of the crime, to today's true-crime literature and tabloid reports.

Haycraft, Howard. *Murder for Pleasure: The Life and Times of the Detective Story.* New York: Carroll & Graf, 1984. This collection of essays traces the history of the detective story in America and England, looks at how mysteries are written, and provides a comprehensive guide to detective characters and their creators.

Haycraft, Howard, ed. *The Art of the Mystery Story*. New York: Carroll & Graf, 1974. A classic and indispensable collection of essays about mystery fiction that includes such gems as Ronald Knox's "Detective Story Decalogue," the Detection Club Oath, Raymond Chandler's "The Simple Art of Murder," Edmund Wilson's "Who Cares Who Killed Roger Ackroyd?", G. K. Chesterton's "A Defense of Detective Stories," John Dickson Carr's "Locked-Room Lecture" from his novel *Three Coffins*, and Anthony Boucher on "The Ethics of the Mystery Novel."

Hedgecock, Jennifer. *The Femme Fatale in Victorian Literature: The Danger and the Sexual Threat*. Amherst, NY: Cambria Press, 2008. This book argues that the figure of the femme fatale in Victorian literature represents the real-life struggles of the middle-class Victorian woman who overcomes major adversities such as poverty, abusive husbands, abandonment, single parenthood, limited job opportunities, and Victorian society's harsh treatment of women. Hedgecock demonstrates that the femme fatale was an empowering position for women during the later part of the 19th century because it subverted patriarchal constructions of domesticity used to suppress women.

Hoffman, Megan. *Gender and Representation in British "Golden Age" Crime Fiction*. London: Palgrave, 2016. This book analyzes how British women's golden age crime narratives negotiate the conflicting social and cultural forces that influenced depictions of gender in popular culture between the 1920s and the 1940s. The book explores a wide variety of texts produced by writers such as Agatha Christie, Dorothy L. Sayers, Margery Allingham, Christianna Brand, Ngaio Marsh, Gladys Mitchell, Josephine Tey, and Patricia Wentworth. Hoffman demonstrates that seemingly conservative resolutions are often attempts to provide a solution to the conflicts raised in the work of these writers.

Irons, Glenwood, ed. *Feminism in Women's Detective Fiction*. Toronto: University of Toronto Press, 1995. The essays in this collection address a wide range of issues important to the depiction of the female sleuth in British and American detective fiction. Some of the essay writers see the female sleuth as a significant force in popular fiction, while others challenge the notion that the woman detective is a positive model for feminists.

Irwin, John T. *The Mystery to a Solution: Poe, Borges, and the Analytic Detective Story*. Baltimore: Johns Hopkins University Press, 1996. Combining history, literary history, and practical and speculative criticism, this book examines areas of study that are part of the detective genre: the history of mathematics, classical mythology, anthropology, chess, automata, the mind–body problem, and many others. Throughout his analysis, Irwin demonstrates how detective fiction uncovers mysteries, accumulates evidence, and traces clues before providing a solution.

Jaber, Maysaa Husam. *Criminal Femmes Fatales in American Hardboiled Crime Fiction*. New York: Palgrave, 2016. This book is the first major study of femmes fatales in hard-boiled crime fiction. Discussing the work of Dashiell Hammett, Raymond Chandler, James M. Cain, David Goodis, and Mickey Spillane, Jaber demonstrates that the femme fatale opens up powerful spaces for imagining female agency in direct opposition to the constraining forces of patriarchy and misogyny.

Kertzer, Jonathan. *Poetic Justice and Legal Fictions*. Cambridge: Cambridge University Press, 2010. This book examines a wide variety of texts, including Shakespeare's plays, Gilbert and Sullivan's operas, and modernist poetics, and argues that laws and values illuminate and challenge the jurisdiction of justice and the law. Kertzer examines how justice is articulated by its command of, or submission to, time, nature, singularity, truth, transcendence, and sacrifice—marking the distance between the promise of justice to satisfy our needs and its failure to do so.

Klein, Kathleen Gregory, ed. *Diversity and Detective Fiction*. Bowling Green, OH: Bowling Green University Popular Press, 1999. This collection of essays explores how detective fiction can be used to investigate the politics of difference. The essays combine a focus on teaching cultural diversity in the classroom and illustrating diversity through fiction to the general reader. Issues addressed include definitions of diversity; what constitutes ethnicity or race; how race, gender, and ethnicity are culturally constructed; and the role of identity politics.

Knight, Stephen. *The Mysteries of the Cities: Urban Crime Fiction in the Nineteenth Century*. Jefferson, NC: McFarland, 2011. Urban mysteries were a popular crime genre in the 19th century but are now understudied and underappreciated. This book examines the origins of the genre, focusing on its treatment of the rise of enormous, anonymous cities, beginning in France in 1842 and then spreading rapidly across the continent and to America and Australia. Writers discussed include Eugene Sue, George Reynolds, George Lippard, Ned Buntline, and Donald Cameron.

Macdonald, Gina, Andrew Macdonald, and MaryAnn Sheridan. *Shaman or Sherlock?: The Native American Detective*. Westport, CT: Greenwood Press, 2002. This book explores representations of justice, crime, and the investigation of crime created by both Native American authors and others. Although mystery fiction began as a manifestation of Enlightenment rationality and scientific methodology, Native American detective stories often move into the realm of the spiritual and intuitive. The book also includes an analysis of how geographical and tribal differences, degrees of assimilation, and the evolution of age-old cultural patterns all shape the Native American detective story.

Maida, Patricia D. *Mother of Detective Fiction: The Life and Works of Anna Katharine Green*. Bowling Green, OH: Bowling Green University Popular Press, 1989. This book is the first full-length critical analysis of the life and work of Anna Katherine Green, a significant and successful writer of detective fiction in the 19th century whose work influenced many later writers in the genre. Issues discussed include how Green's work provides a critical viewpoint of the situation of women in her era.

Mandel, Ernest. *Delightful Murder: A Social History of the Crime Story.* London: Pluto Press, 1984. This book analyzes crime narratives from a Marxist perspective, arguing that detective fiction is a quintessentially bourgeois genre that encodes capitalist values and prioritizes the restoration of order above all. Mandel discusses a wide range of texts from Europe, the United Kingdom, and the United States.

Markowitz, Judith A. *The Gay Detective Novel: Lesbian and Gay Main Characters and Themes in Mystery Fiction.* Jefferson, NC: McFarland, 2004. This book discusses how and why gay and lesbian detective fiction has become one of the fastest-growing segments of the genre—both by incorporating gay and lesbian cultural elements and also by offering crossover appeal. In her examination of mystery series and historically significant standalone novels published since the early 1960s, Markowitz argues that gay and lesbian authors provide new, more accurate images of lesbians and gay men than generally found in mainstream literature and popular media.

Masson, Antoine, and Kevin O'Connor, eds. *Representations of Justice.* New York: Peter Lang, 2007. This collection of essays examines how the public understanding of law is influenced by representations of justice in popular culture. Movies, caricatures, portrayal of trials by the media, and crime fiction all shape the image of justice. Writers of the essays argue that the representation of justice in society is noteworthy not only for citizens who want to understand popular culture but also for lawyers who want to understand their clients' expectations.

Merivale, Patricia, and Susan Elizabeth Sweeney, eds. *Detecting Texts: The Metaphysical Detective Story from Poe to Postmodernism.* Philadelphia: University of Pennsylvania Press, 1999. This essay collection focuses on the "metaphysical detective story," in which the detective hero's inability to interpret the mystery casts doubt on the reader's attempt to make sense of the text and the world. Although readers of detective fiction usually expect to learn the mystery's solution, the metaphysical detective story, which includes work by Edgar Allan Poe, Jorge Luis Borges, Alain Robbe-Grillet, and Paul Auster, ends with a question rather than an answer. The detective not only fails to solve the crime, but he or she also confronts mysteries of interpretation and identity.

Miller, D. A. *The Novel and the Police*. Berkeley: University of California Press, 1988. In this unusual, original, and influential book, rather than focus on the police in fiction, Miller examines fiction and policing— or the ways in which narrative serves a conservative function in the preservation of the state. Focusing on a series of Victorian novels, Miller demonstrates that these novels "police" their fictional worlds by means of strategies of surveillance and incarceration.

Moretti, Franco. *Signs Taken for Wonders: On the Sociology of Literary Forms*. London and New York: Verso, 2005. Moretti draws on structuralist, sociological, and psychoanalytic modes of analysis in order to read Shakespearean tragedy and *Dracula*, Sherlock Holmes and *Ulysses*, and *Frankenstein* and *The Waste Land* as literary systems that are tokens of wider cultural and political realities. In doing so, the author both explores the relationships between high and mass culture and also considers the relevance of tragic, Romantic, and Darwinian views of the world.

Most, Glenn W., and William W. Stowe, eds. *The Poetics of Murder: Detective Fiction and Literary Theory*. New York: Harcourt Brace Jovanovich, 1983. This indispensable and groundbreaking collection of essays provides a compendium of critical and theoretical approaches to detective fiction. The introduction provides an illuminating discussion of why the genre has attracted such a wide range of critics, while the essays explore the reasons for the popularity of murder mysteries and discuss the literary techniques and social aspects of detective novels.

Munt, Sally R. *Murder by the Book?: Feminism and the Crime Novel.* London and New York: Routledge, 1994. This book explores the genre of the feminist crime novel in Britain and the United States. Munt discusses why the form has proved so attractive as a vehicle for oppositional politics; whether the pleasures of detective fiction can be truly transgressive; and when the lesbian detective appeared as the new superhero for today. In doing so, Munt also poses some critical questions about the relationships between fiction and activism, politics and representation, and the writer and the reader.

Murley, Jean. *The Rise of True Crime: 20th-century Murder and American Popular Culture.* Westport, CT: Praeger, 2008. This book provides a comprehensive overview of the history of modern true crime, beginning with *True Detective* magazine in the 1950s, the blockbuster serial killer narratives of the 1970s and 1980s, and ending with the diverse and complex genre of today. Murley focuses on the pedagogical aspects of true crime, demonstrating how it has succeeded in turning its readers into "experts" on a wide range of crime-related issues.

Nestingen, Andrew. *Crime and Fantasy in Scandinavia: Fiction, Film, and Social Change.* Seattle: University of Washington Press, 2008. This book analyzes the changing nature of civil society in Scandinavia through the lens of popular culture. Nestingen develops his argument through the examination of genres where the central theme is individual transgression of societal norms: crime films and novels, melodramas, and fantasy fiction. Among the writers and filmmakers discussed are Henning Mankell, Aki Kaurismäki, Lukas Moodysson, and Lars von Trier.

Nickerson, Catherine Ross. *The Web of Iniquity: Early Detective Fiction by American Women.* Durham, NC: Duke University Press, 1998. This book focuses on detective fiction written by American women between the Civil War and World War II. Nickerson demonstrates how writers such as Metta Fuller Victor, Anna Katherine Green, and Mary Roberts Rinehart blended Gothic elements into domestic fiction to create a unique and all-but-ignored subgenre that she labels "domestic detective fiction." Nickerson concludes that this subgenre allowed women writers to participate in postbellum culture and to critique other aspects of a rapidly changing society.

Nicol, Bran, Eugene McNulty, and Patricia Pulham, eds. *Crime Culture: Figuring Criminality in Fiction and Film*. London and New York: Bloomsbury, 2010. The essays in this collection analyze a range of literature and film: neglected examples of film noir and true crime, crime fiction by female African American writers, reality TV, recent films such as *Elephant*, *Collateral*, and *The Departed*, and contemporary fiction by J. G. Ballard, Kazuo Ishiguro, and Margaret Atwood. The essay authors discuss such subjects as the mythology of the hit man, technology and the image, and the cultural impact of senseless murders and reveal why crime is a powerful way of making sense of the broader concerns shaping modern culture and society.

Palmer, Jerry. *Thrillers: Genesis and Structure of a Popular Genre*. New York: St. Martin's Press, 1979. This groundbreaking book explores the origins, literary characteristics, and sociohistorical roots of the thriller to reveal the factors underlying the development and increasing popularity of the genre.

Panek, Leroy Lad. *The American Police Novel: A History*. Jefferson, NC: McFarland, 2003. This book traces the emergence of the police officer as hero and the police novel as a popular genre, covering the cameo appearances of police in detective novels of the 1930s and 1940s through the serial killer and forensic novels of the 1990s. Writers discussed include Julian Hawthorne, S. S. van Dine, Ellery Queen, Erle Stanley Gardner, Ed McBain, Chester Himes, MacKinley Kantor, Hillary Waugh, Dorothy Uhnak, Joseph Wambaugh, and W.E.B. Griffin.

Perry, Dennis R., and Carl H. Sederholm, eds. *Adapting Poe: Re-Imaginings in Popular Culture*. New York: Palgrave Macmillan, 2012. This collection of essays explores the way Edgar Allan Poe has been adapted over the last hundred years in film, comic art, music, and literary criticism and explains the reasons for Poe's continuing iconic status.

Plain, Gill. *Twentieth Century Crime Fiction: Gender, Sexuality and the Body*. Edinburgh: Edinburgh University Press, 2001. This book uses a combination of feminist and psychoanalytic theory to analyze the roles that gender and sexuality play in the work of a wide range of writers, including Agatha Christie, Raymond Chandler, Joseph Hansen, Dick Francis, and Sara Paretsky. Plain pays particular attention to how crime fiction's treatment of these themes has changed over time.

Reynolds, William, and Elizabeth Trembley, eds. *It's a Print!: Detective Fiction from Page to Screen*. Bowling Green, OH: Bowling Green University Popular Press, 1994. This collection of essays studies the various ways in which television and cinema have adapted the raw materials of detective fiction to their own ends. The essays collectively debate tensions between faithful and creative adaptations and demonstrate what can be lost and gained in the process of adaptation.

Rodriguez, Ralph E. *Brown Gumshoes: Detective Fiction and the Search for Chicana/o Identity*. Austin: University of Texas Press, 2005. This is the first comprehensive study of Chicano detective fiction. Rodriguez examines the recent contributions to the genre by writers such as Rudolfo Anaya, Lucha Corpi, Rolando Hinojosa, Michael Nava, and Manuel Ramos and discusses how their work deals with the following subjects: feminism, homosexuality, family, masculinity, mysticism, nationalism, and U.S.–Mexico border relations. This study concludes by arguing that the detective novel, with its traditional focus on questions of knowledge and identity, is the perfect medium with which to examine these issues.

Roth, Marty. *Foul & Fair Play: Reading Genre in Classic Detective Fiction*. Athens, GA: University of Georgia Press, 1995. This book examines classic detective fiction as a genre—that is, a wide variety of texts by different authors that are variations on a common set of conventions. Roth covers the period from the prehistory of detective fiction in the works of Edgar Allan Poe, Charles Dickens, Wilkie Collins, Robert Louis Stevenson, and H. G. Wells and then concludes with the 1960s, which marked the end of the classic period. The detective fiction genre, as Roth defines it, includes analytic detective fiction, hard-boiled detective fiction, and the spy thriller.

Rzepka, Charles J., and Lee Horsley, eds. *A Companion to Crime Fiction*. New York and Oxford, 2010. This collection of 47 newly commissioned essays follows the development of crime fiction from its origins in the 18th century through to its present-day popularity. The book features critical essays on significant authors and filmmakers— from Arthur Conan Doyle and Dashiell Hammett to Alfred Hitchcock and Martin Scorsese—and explores the ways in which they have shaped and influenced the field.

Schmid, David. *Natural Born Celebrities: Serial Killers in American Culture*. Chicago: University of Chicago Press, 2005. This book provides an historical account of how serial killers became celebrated and how that fame has been used in popular media and in the corridors of the FBI. Schmid constructs a new understanding of serial killers by emphasizing both the social dimensions of their crimes and their susceptibility to multiple interpretations and uses.

Schmid, David, ed. *Violence in American Popular Culture*. Santa Barbara, CA: Prager, 2015. Few topics are discussed more broadly today than violence in American popular culture. Unfortunately, such discussion is often unsupported by fact and lacking in historical context. This two-volume work aims to remedy that through a series of concise, detailed essays that explore why violence has always been a fundamental part of American popular culture, the ways in which it has appeared, and how the nature and expression of interest in it have changed over time.

Shiloh, Ilana. *The Double, the Labyrinth and the Locked Room: Metaphors of Paradox in Crime Fiction and Film*. New York: Peter Lang, 2011. Even though mystery and suspense fiction usually celebrates the triumph of reason over the chaos of violence and crime, in this study, the author demonstrates that the genre has always been associated with three paradoxical motifs: the double, the labyrinth, and the locked room. Consequently, these paradoxes destabilize the genre's apparently secure reliance upon binaries such as reason versus madness and chaos versus order.

Shpayer-Makov, Haia. *The Ascent of the Detective: Police Sleuths in Victorian and Edwardian England*. Oxford: Oxford University Press, 2011. This book explores the diverse world of English police detectives during the formative period of their profession, from 1842 until World War I, with special emphasis on the famed detective branch established at Scotland Yard. Shpayer-Makov investigates the complex and symbiotic exchange between detectives and journalists and analyzes the detective's image as it unfolded in the press, literature, and their own memoirs.

Silver, Mark. *Purloined Letters: Cultural Borrowing and Japanese Crime Literature, 1868–1937*. Honolulu: University of Hawaii Press, 2008. This book tells the story of Japan's adoption of the detective story at a time when the nation was remaking itself in the image of the Western powers. Silver discusses a fascinating range of primary texts beginning with Tokugawa courtroom narratives and early Meiji biographies of female criminals, which dominated popular crime writing in Japan before the detective story's arrival. He then traces the mid-Meiji absorption of French, British, and American detective novels into Japanese literary culture.

Simpson, Philip L. *Psycho Paths: Tracking the Serial Killer through Contemporary American Film and Fiction*. Carbondale, IL: Southern Illinois University Press, 2000. This book provides an overview of the serial-killer genre in the media most responsible for its popularity: literature and cinema of the 1980s and 1990s. Simpson argues that the fictional serial killer is the latest manifestation of the multiple murderers and homicidal maniacs that haunt American literature— particularly visual media such as cinema and television. Simpson theorizes that the serial-killer genre results from a combination of earlier depictions of multiple murderers, Gothic storytelling conventions, and threatening folkloric figures reworked into a contemporary mythology of violence.

Smith, Erin. *Hard-Boiled: Working Class Readers and Pulp Magazines.* Philadelphia: Temple University Press, 2010. This book focuses on a distinctively American detective fiction that emerged from the pages of pulp magazines in the 1920s. Drawing on pulp-magazine advertising, the memoirs of writers and publishers, Depression-era studies of adult reading habits, and social and labor history, Smith offers an innovative account of how these popular stories were generated and read. She shows that although the work of pulp-fiction authors like Dashiell Hammett, Raymond Chandler, and Erle Stanley Gardner have become classics of popular culture, the hard-boiled genre was dominated by hack writers paid by the word, not self-styled artists.

Soitos, Stephen F. *The Blues Detective: A Study of African American Detective Fiction.* Amherst, MA: University of Massachusetts Press, 1996. This book argues for the existence of a tradition of African American detective fiction. Such writers as Pauline Hopkins, J. E. Bruce, Rudolph Fisher, Chester Himes, Ishmael Reed, and Clarence Major created a new genre that responded to the social and political concerns of the African American community. Soitos frames his analysis in terms of four tropes: altered detective personas, double-consciousness detection, African American vernaculars, and hoodoo. He argues that African American writers created sleuths who were in fact "blues detectives," engaged not only in solving crimes, but also in exploring the mysteries of African American life and culture.

Sotelo, Susan Baker. *Chicano Detective Fiction: A Critical Study of Five Novelists.* Jefferson, NC: McFarland, 2005. Sotelo examines how and why Chicano writers have embraced the detective novel, successfully diversifying and refining a traditional Anglo American and British genre. Focusing on the work of Rolando Hinojosa, Rudolfo

Anaya, Lucha Corpi, Michael Nava, and Manuel Ramos, Sotelo demonstrates how each writer departs from contemporary detective genre formulas, rendering a particular regional or cultural variation of what it means to be Chicano.

Stewart, R. F. *And Always a Detective: Chapters on the History of Detective Fiction.* Newton Abbot, UK: David & Charles, 1980. An examination of the defining tropes of the detective fiction genre, paying particular attention to the figure of the detective.

Thomas, Ronald R. *Detective Fiction and the Rise of Forensic Science.* Cambridge: Cambridge University Press, 2003. This book discusses the relationship between the development of forensic science in the 19th century and the invention of the literary genre of detective fiction in Britain and America. Thomas examines the criminal body as a site of interpretation and enforcement in a wide range of fictional examples, from Poe, Dickens, and Hawthorne, through Twain and Conan Doyle, to Hammett, Chandler, and Christie. Thomas is especially concerned with the authority the literary detective acquires through the devices—fingerprinting, photography, lie detectors—with which the detective discovers the truth and establishes his or her expertise.

Tucher, Andie. *Froth and Scum: Truth, Beauty, Goodness, and the Ax Murder in America's First Mass Medium.* Chapel Hill, NC: University of North Carolina Press, 1994. This book focuses on two notorious antebellum New York murder cases—a prostitute slashed in an elegant brothel and a tradesman bludgeoned by the brother of inventor Samuel Colt—and analyzes the resulting journalistic scrambles over the meanings of truth, objectivity, and the duty of the press that reverberate to this day. Tucher complicates the notion that objective reporting will discover a single, definitive truth. As they do now, news stories of the time aroused strong feelings about the possibility of justice, the privileges of power, and the nature of evil.

Walton, John. *The Legendary Detective: The Private Eye in Fact and Fiction*. Chicago: University of Chicago Press, 2015. This book offers a history of the American private detective in reality and myth, from the earliest detective agencies to the hard-boiled heights of the 1930s and 1940s. Drawing on previously untapped archival accounts of actual detective work, Walton traces both the growth of major private detective agencies like Pinkerton and the unglamorous work of small-time operatives. Walton demonstrates how writers like Dashiell Hammett and editors of pulp magazines like *Black Mask* embellished on actual experiences and fashioned an image of the private eye as a compelling, even admirable, necessary evil, doing society's dirty work while adhering to a self-imposed moral code.

Walton, Priscilla L., and Manina Jones. *Detective Agency: Women Rewriting the Hard-Boiled Tradition*. Berkeley, CA: University of California Press, 1999. This is the first book-length study of an important subgenre of crime fiction—narratives written by women and featuring a professional woman investigator—that has proliferated since the 1970s. Addressing the ways that Sara Paretsky, Sue Grafton, Marcia Muller, and others rework the conventions of the hard-boiled genre made popular by writers such as Dashiell Hammett, Raymond Chandler, and Mickey Spillane, the authors demonstrate how the male hard-boiled tradition has been challenged and transformed.

Wark, Wesley K., ed. *Spy Fiction, Spy Films and Real Intelligence*. New York: Routledge, 2013. This collection of essays explores the history of spy fiction and spy films and investigates the significance of their concepts and imagery. The volume discusses a wide range of authors, including John Buchan and Graham Greene, and offers new insights into the development and symbolism of British spy fiction.

White, Terry. *Justice Denoted: The Legal Thriller in American, British, and Continental Courtroom Literature*. Westport, CT: Greenwood Publishing Group, 2003. This book is the most comprehensive scholarly compilation of legal suspense fiction available. Primarily a bibliography of novels, it also annotates plays, scripts for film and television, novelizations, and short-story collections about lawyers and the law. An eclectic reference source that goes beyond a compilation of books about lawyers as protagonists, this compendium also includes suspense thrillers, science fiction, and philosophical novels—if justice is thematically important to the work.

Willett, Ralph. *The Naked City: Urban Crime Fiction in the USA.* Manchester, UK: Manchester University Press, 1996. The mean streets of San Francisco, New York, Los Angeles, and Chicago have dominated American crime fiction from Raymond Chandler and Dashiell Hammett to Sara Paretsky and Ed McBain. Willett analyzes the reasons why the city appeals to many writers of crime fiction; he also explores the city's varied setting, which allows writers to address a diversity of issues.

Image Credits

Page 7: © katalinks/Shutterstock.

Page 29: © welcomia/Shutterstock.

Page 47: © Photographee.eu/Shutterstock.

Page 71: © Photographee.eu/Shutterstock.

Page 88: © franz12/Shutterstock.

Page 108: © Kumpol Chuansakul/Shutterstock.

Page 131: © ESB Professional/Shutterstock.

Page 170: © Everett Collection/Shutterstock.

Page 192: © Michal Ludwiczak/Shutterstock.

Page 210: © Stokkete/Shutterstock.

Page 228: © Library of Congress, Prints and Photographs Division,
LC-USZ62-98325.

Page 232: © Richard Peterson/Shutterstock.

Page 250: © Elnur/Shutterstock.

Page 273: © Merydolla/Shutterstock.

Page 290: © Everett Collection/Shutterstock.

Page 332: © Andrey_Popov/Shutterstock.

Page 353: © Corepics VOF/Shutterstock.

NOTES

NOTES